Learn How to Play Electric

KEYBOARD OR PIANO

In a week!

Martin Woodward

Copyright © 2011 & 2017 by Martin Woodward

All rights reserved. This book or any portion thereof may not be reproduced or used in any manner whatsoever without the express written permission of the publisher except for the use of brief quotations in a book review or scholarly journal.

1st Edition 2011

2nd Edition 2017

ISBN: 978-0-244-32947-1

Enquiries: http://learn-keyboard.co.uk

Acknowledgements

To all the fantastic musicians who I've had the privilege of working with back in the 1960s / 70s including: Pip Williams (guitarist / record producer); Tex Marsh (drummer); Roger Flavell (bassist); Kevan Fogarty (guitarist); Ralph Denyer (singer / songwriter); Phil Childs (bassist); Jim Smith (drums); George Lee (saxophonist); Ron Thomas (bassist); Emile Ford (UK No. 1 singer / songwriter).

To my early mentors: Alan Simonds (guitarist / vocalist); big bruv Steve (guitarist) and Mr. Henley (my inspirational music teacher at Warlingham School 1960 - 65).

And to Myriad Software: http://www.myriad-online.com for the Melody Assistant music notation software which was used for the production of this book. - Thanks!

Contents

Introduction 7
    The Right Practice 7
    Motivation 7
    Talent / Gift 8
    Get the Best from this Book 8
    Using the in Book Links 9

Choosing Your First Keyboard 10

Your First Exercises 20
    Correct Hand and Seating Positioning 20
    Fingering 21
    Here We Go 21

The Notes of the Keyboard 27

Music Notation 29
    The Grand Staff 31
    How the Notes Relate to the Keyboard 34
    Sharps & Flats 36

Timing 38
    Time Signatures and Bars 38
    Note Values 40
    Rests 41
    Lead in Notes 41
    Dotted Notes 42
    Triplets 42
    Tied Notes 43
    Grace Notes 43
    Using a Metronome 44

5 Finger Exercises in Brief 45

Intervals 47
    Intervals from C 47

Copyright © Martin Woodward 2011 & 2017

Keys, Key Signatures & Transposition 50
- *Relative Minors* 52

Your First Scales 54
- *A Pre Scale Exercise* 54
- *The Major Scale* 56
- *Minor Scales* 57
- *The Whole Tone Scale* 59
- *The Chromatic Scale* 60
- *Pentatonic and Blues Scales* 61

Scale Modes Explanation 63
- *Modes of the Pentatonic Scales* 66

Chord Construction 69
- *A Few Important points about 7th Chords* 70
- *Suspended 2nd and 4th Chords* 72
- *Diminished 7th Chords* 72
- *Augmented Chords* 73
- *Inversions* 74
- *Chord Substitution* 75
- *Chord Substitutions as against Chord Alternatives* 76
- *Extensions Beyond the 7ths* 77

Chord Fingering 79
- *Left Hand Chord Fingering* 83

Chord Sequences 85

Arpeggios & Broken Chords in Brief 89

Important Musical Terms 91

Putting it all Together 99

Your First Tunes 102
- *A Simple Arpeggio Composition* 120

Playing from a Fake Book 127

Part 2 131

5 Finger Exercises 132

Scale Exercises (in full) 138

Pentatonic & Blues Scales in the most used keys **166**
Diatonic Chords **175**
Chords in Keyboard View **185**
Extended Chords **198**
Arpeggio Exercises **211**
 Broken Chords in the most used keys *224*
Thank You **227**
 Download Link *227*
 What Next? *227*
 Further Reading *227*
 Free Software *228*

Introduction

Ok, first let me make it clear that by *'learn in a week'* I'm not suggesting that you're going to be a virtuoso at the end of this period - especially if you an absolute beginner - it's simply not realistic! However, I assure you that the methods included herein will show you the fastest and easiest way to learn finger dexterity and *genuine* music notation. And furthermore, are geared towards all styles of music and applicable to both piano and electronic keyboard.

The key points to learning quickly and effectively are as follows:

- The right type of regular practice, spaced according to your ability;
- A high level of motivation;
- Being assured that it has nothing to do with age, talent or being gifted even to a professional level.

Let's look at the above in a little more detail.

The Right Practice

To be effective your practice should be short (initially) but regular. Three 20-minute sessions a day is ideal to begin with, which could be and should be extended as you gain more ability and finger strength. Having no practice for several days and then trying to make up for what you've missed by having a blitz, simply won't work, in fact this would more likely be a backward step. If you can't manage three sessions, then one 20 / 30-minute session per day is the absolute minimum to begin with, any less and you'd be basically wasting your time.

With the right practice, good progress will occur but it's normal for this to be in fits and jerks - good days and bad days - so don't get disappointed when it appears to be going wrong. In order to experience the peaks, you must also have the troughs! Keep doing it *every day* and it will happen!

Included herein are some superb 5 finger exercises, plus all the scales and arpeggios that you need to know. In order to be successful these *must* be practiced, but they can be fun as shown later.

Motivation

There's absolutely no doubt about it that your willingness to practice regularly is in a direct ratio to your degree of motivation. Clearly if you're not motivated you'll not bother. If you look at all really successful players, the one thing that they have in common is a high level of motivation - the greater the motivation - the greater the success! Jazz pianist Jamie Cullum has a keyboard in every room of his house - even the kitchen - so that he can *'have a twiddle'* any time he feels like it - even when he's boiling his eggs!

Before I turned professional I practiced about 4 hours a day every day. Having said this, you can attain a reasonable skill and have much fulfilment with as little as 20 / 30 minutes practice a day. The choice is yours - you're in charge of your life - *as long as your wife approves!*

Talent / Gift

Successful keyboard playing has nothing to do with age, talent or being gifted. Most of the so called *'talented / gifted'* musicians were simply born into the right environment where they were encouraged and taught from a very early age. So sure, maybe they were privileged - but not gifted. And this is the same with everything from being a *'gifted'* artist to a *'gifted'* motor mechanic! - Think about it! Do you think Mozart would have achieved what he did if his parents were Eskimos?

And look at Michael Jackson, perhaps you think he was born talented, yet it's widely known that he was *groomed* virtually from birth to be what he turned into at the expense of any form of normal childhood. And clearly this is the fate of many child *'prodigies'* - they're simply *forced* to accomplish what their parents couldn't!

Anyone who is motivated and practices as instructed can be a superb player in a direct proportion to the amount of effort put in. But don't get hung up on wanting to be *'better'* than someone else. Music is not a competition, it's *creative.* Just compete with *yourself* and you will achieve the greatest fulfilment.

Get the Best from this Book

Writing a book which is suitable for every different device is nigh on impossible especially when using music graphics; certainly, the ePub and Mobi versions are not ideal for these although I believe that I have succeeded to a great degree and probably better than most. But obviously I want you to get the very best from this book so with this in mind I recommend that you download the pdf version which can be found towards the end of the book - to get there quickly just click here - there's another link to whiz straight back! This can be printed out (for your own use) as and when required.

There are audio links throughout the book which can be accessed two ways:

- by using the free external link at: http://learn-keyboard.co.uk/keyboard_links.html which gives access to all the links in the order in which they appear in each chapter; or
- by using the links throughout the book which will work best in the pdf version.

Even if you have the printed version, you may still wish to download the included pdf version in order to gain easy access to the links as they appear in the book.

Using the *in-Book* Links

Quite probably you may only need to listen to some of the audio links, but several are included for your convenience.

To access the links easily, if you are viewing this on a laptop or PC first of all go to your browser and click the restore down button in order to reduce the view size to something like the image below to the right (by dragging the bottom and sides).

Restore Down Button

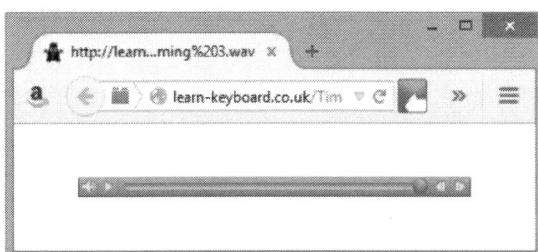

Then click on the link which should then appear in front of the document enabling you to move it out of the way of anything that you may wish to see at the same time.

If you are viewing this on an Android tablet as soon as you click on the link you will lose the book view until you push the *'Back'* button (shown below).

If you want to you can have a trial run now by clicking on the following graphic which actually is 'Pop Goes the Weasel'!

Note that the links may not work if you are viewing this in a Google or Amazon sample. Please go to http://learn-keyboard.co.uk/learn_in_a_week.html for a free *working* pdf sample.

Note also that each link will open a new page in your browser, so you will eventually need to cancel them (or just close the browser).

In addition to the external links, there are also numerous internal links to help you navigate to certain reference points in the book and return, including the arrows either side of the chapter headings. Clicking the green right-hand one will take you instantly to the next chapter and the red left-hand arrow to the beginning of the last chapter. There are also links to and from the coinciding chapters in Parts 1 & 2.

← Choosing Your First Keyboard →

If you haven't already bought a keyboard or if you are perhaps thinking of changing, you may find the following information useful.

Firstly, just in case you're wondering, there is no such thing as a *'left handed'* keyboard and if you ever come across one, it will have been created by an idiot just for a laugh! It makes no difference whether you are right or left handed for playing the keyboard as both are equally important (more or less). On all keyboards of every type, the high-pitched notes are to the right and generally played with the right hand and the low notes are to the left and generally played with the left hand.

There are many different types of keyboards - all have black and white keys and to the uninitiated all look the same. But they can be vastly different and which one will be right for you will be determined by:

- Your present needs;
- Available space;
- Your ultimate needs; and of course
- Your budget.

Prices can vary from as little as £50 to many thousands of pounds. The chances of buying one that is absolutely right for your initial and ultimate needs is about nil, but you can at least try!

Keyboards basically fall into the following categories:

a) Synthesizers (hi tech);

b) Workstations (hi tech);

c) Electronic digital pianos (hi tech / low tech);

d) Arranger keyboards (hi tech / low tech);

e) Organs (hi tech / low tech);

f) Controller keyboards with modules (hi tech);

g) A *mixed combination* of any of the above;

h) Acoustic pianos (low tech).

And of course, all of the above could be purchased either new or second-hand.

Now, you may have noticed that I've put in brackets *'hi tech'* - *'low tech'* or both. This is because there are two types of retail music shops - hi tech and low tech and it's very rare that you'll find the two combined in one shop. And by *'low tech'*, please don't think that I mean cheap or low quality or low price - quite the contrary - it's just a different market.

The typical low-tech shops are aimed at the home users and will sell:

- Pianos (acoustic and electronic);
- Organs for home use (low tech);
- Arranger keyboards (low tech);
- Sheet music;
- Possibly a small selection of guitars etc.

The typical hi-tech shops are primarily aimed at professional working musicians and will sell:

- Portable electronic stage pianos;
- Synths and workstations;
- Modules and controller keyboards;
- Hi tech (and expensive) arranger keyboards;
- Guitars (large selection);
- Amplifiers;
- Drum kits etc.

Ok, so let's look at what all these keyboards do.

Synths and Workstations

As both of these are hi tech and primarily used for music production / recording, I'm going to write these off as being unsuitable for your needs right now. After having gained some experience at playing perhaps one of these may suit your needs later - but these are not a good choice for a beginner, unless they also include the functions that you will need, which actually more and more now do - just to confuse things!

Nord Stage 3 Synth / Piano / Organ (73 keys) - very Hi Tech

Electronic Pianos

These are available as either low tech home pianos in glossy cabinets (and usually very expensive) to hi tech portable stage pianos and everything in between.

Most electronic pianos have graduated hammer action keys which simulate the feel and action of a real acoustic piano - this can be good or bad depending on your preferences. Most also have a full 88 key (7 octave plus) keyboard.

Clavia Nord Stage Piano 3 (88 keys)

The low-tech home pianos tend to have their own amplification and speakers built in, whereas hi tech stage pianos tend not to. All can be used with headphones.

Now, **most importantly** *some* in both categories have *'auto accompaniment'* features (which we'll deal with later) whereas some will be just simply pianos - now doubt with other sounds as well.

If it is your intention to play classical or jazz seriously, I would suggest that an electronic digital piano with a good hammer action keybed could be a good choice for you. But if you are an absolute beginner then consider one that also has auto accompaniment which in **no way** prevents the instrument from being used as a normal complete piano. A few years ago, I had a Korg SP500 which I used with and without the auto accompaniment for home and professional use. Now I have the Casio PX-560 (below) which is also an arranger / workstation and synth.

Casio Privia PX 560 Stage Piano / Arranger - with auto accompaniment

Casio, Korg, Roland, Yamaha, Nord, Kawaii and Kurzweil all do a good range of *hi-tech / low-tech* portables, some with and some without auto accompaniment, and some with or without internal amplification. All have their strong and weak points, but all are worth considering.

Acoustic Pianos

I would never discourage anyone from getting one of these if this is what they want, but the clear disadvantages are:

- They need periodic tuning;
- They are space greedy;
- They can be very expensive;
- They're not suitable for gigging;
- You will drive your family and neighbours nuts when you practice as these of course don't work too good with headphones.

On the plus side, when the world eventually runs out of electricity, everyone will want one!

But unless you are an absolute *'purist'*, you could never tell the difference between an acoustic and a good quality digital piano unless you pulled the plug out!

Organs

Again, these come in both *hi* and *low* tech, and both tend to be very expensive. The low-tech varieties tend to come with auto accompaniment as well as just about every gadget imaginable. I've personally only used hi tech (no gadget) instruments including the early Vox Continental, the Hammond M102 and Hammond B3 all of which I used for gigging around Europe. I still love these instruments (especially the B3), but the downside with these is that they take up a huge amount of space and the B3's require four people to move them - no fun when working basement or attic venues! Although the sounds of these instruments can never be simulated exactly, some of the modern lightweight keyboards get pretty close.

Arranger Keyboards

In my opinion, this is probably the best choice for anyone who just wants to have fun but also retain the option for getting serious and possibly professional. But the variation in quality, features and prices is vast.

Whereas most electronic pianos come with 88 weighted keys, the arranger keyboards *tend* to come with either 61 keys (5 octaves) or 76 keys (6 octaves +) and the keys may be un-weighted, semi weighted or *occasionally* fully weighted.

In addition:

- All have auto accompaniment, but quality and features vary considerably;
- Some have built in speakers / amplification;
- Some have built in sequencers;
- Some have built in samplers.

Casio MZ-X500 Arranger Keyboard (61 notes)

Pricewise, the Casios are excellent value and impossible to beat, but mainly at the top end of their range.

Personally, I wouldn't consider less than 6 octaves which then enables the instrument to be played as a standard piano as an alternative to splitting the keyboard and using the auto accompaniment features. But having said this, the 5 octave Casio MZ-X500 is totally stunning and sells at far less than half the price of anything comparable. This I would consider as a top level to a full-length board - this works well with the PX-5S or the PX-560.

Casio WK 7600 Arranger with internal Amp & Speakers

Arranger keyboards that I've personally owned (all 6 octaves+) include:

- Early Yamaha PSR1;
- Technics (can't remember which);
- Korg i2;
- Roland G70;
- Korg PA-2X;
- Korg SP-500 (fully weighted);
- Casio Privia PX-560 which also has a fully weighted keybed and a synth.

The majority of the above do not have internal speakers / amplification which is the norm for professional equipment. In this event you would also need to purchase an external keyboard amplifier and speaker(s), which needn't have to be an expensive item.

Modules / Controller Keyboards

There are basically two types of modules:

- Sound modules; and
- Backing modules - with sounds.

Sound modules can be connected via midi to enhance the sounds of any midi compatible keyboard or controller. Roland do a good range of these with stunning sounds but they can be expensive.

Backing modules enable any midi keyboard to be used with auto accompaniment. These are ideal for accordionists or any keyboard without on-board auto accompaniment features.

Currently the only backing modules on the market are the Roland BK-7m and a few made by Ketron and Orla. In the past Yamaha have made them and also Korg (the i40m), but these are now only available second-hand - if you can find one.

Roland BK-7m Backing Module

Controller keyboards are generally low priced and light in weight (as they don't actually do anything on their own) and are available with 61, 76 or 88 keys with un-weighted, semi weighted or fully weighted key options. When connected to a sound module they can potentially do and become anything from a superb piano to the best synths etc. But of course, the sounds produced would be no better than the modules used.

Another possible use for a controller would be if you have a good 61 key un-weighted keyboard like a Yamaha Tyros and want the option of a longer or weighted keyboard. In this instance, you would also need a double stand. In fact, a tailor-made stand is available for this specific purpose. You could then have a good arranger keyboard, a fully weighted piano and a two-manual organ all in one, and if you're into organs, you could even add a pedal board.

Probably initially you wouldn't want to go down the controller keyboard route, but it's certainly worth knowing about for future reference.

Auto Accompaniment

All *arranger* keyboards and some pianos / organs have the facility to either use the instrument as a full keyboard (in piano mode) or to split the keyboard at a chosen point and use the upper half for the right-hand melody work and the lower portion with an alternative sound / instrument for bass etc., or auto accompaniment. But note that you'd be struggling in full piano mode with less than 73 keys.

In the auto accompaniment mode, a particular rhythm and style can be selected which will play bass, drums and other instrumentation as soon as a chord is played in the lower portion of the keyboard. As the chord is changed, the instrumentation will follow automatically. In most cases, intros, endings and fill-ins can also be activated at the touch of a button.

This results in the player being in control of a complete multi instrument band / orchestra. Clearly using this option enables even a novice to produce professional sounding work easily. And as a result, many would call this *'cheating'!* Well I suppose if you set the instrument up to do the lot, go off and make a cup of tea and return to take your applause, I suppose it is. My view on this is that if it gives pleasure - *so bloody what!*

BUT, I would strongly recommend that you learn to play both *with* and *without* the auto accompaniment then you will get the best of both worlds. And the exercises and information herein teaches exactly this - for your greatest fulfilment.

Some of what I do personally involves using the auto accompaniment which effectively enables me to play *with* a band without having the commitment of being *involved with* a band. Plus, it enables me to gig solo should I wish to and of course to earn more money. But I mainly, enjoy playing in normal piano mode without the auto accompaniment.

Note that if you are playing with a band, auto accompaniment would never be used.

Sequencers

Most arranger keyboards, synths, workstations and some pianos have one or more built in sequencer(s). This enables you to record, edit and playback chord sequences, styles, fills and variations or even complete songs easily (once you've got your head round it).

Another option is to use an external sequencer via your PC, which actually allows far more control, editing and mixing possibilities. But I have to say that these can be complicated. I currently have Cakewalk Sonar X3 and Cubase, both of which are straining my brain somewhat - *probably an age thing!*

But if you just want to record simple one-track audio files, this can be achieved very easily by using the free Audacity program. There is a link for this at the end of the book.

Harmonisers

If you are into singing along with your playing, some high-end arranger keyboards have built in *'harmonisers'* which creates a harmony to your singing and some can even help correct your crap singing.

This feature is on the Roland G70 as well as the Korg PA series and many others. I can't say that it's a feature that I've ever used myself, but it's interesting nonetheless.

Polyphony

When considering various keyboards, you will come across the words *'polyphonic'* and *'monophonic'*.

A *monophonic* keyboard will only allow you to play one note at a time as in the very early synths - if you play two notes together only one will sound. A keyboard which is say polyphonic to 32 notes will allow 32 notes to be played / sounded at once.

As you *probably* only have ten fingers you may think that this is fine, but when you consider that using the sustain pedal and / or auto accompaniment can increase the need for *polyphony*, 32 notes soon becomes inadequate, so the larger the *polyphony* the better!

Most quality, keyboards have a 128-note polyphony or more, The Casio PX5S, 560 and others have an incredible 256-note polyphony.

Advantages / Disadvantages of Internal Amplification

Most of the lower priced portable keyboards and most home pianos have internal speakers / amplification. If you intend using the instrument for home use only; then this can be ideal. The only possible disadvantage of this is that it makes the instrument physically heavier than it might have been without them, but if you don't intend moving it around too much then this should not cause a problem.

Peavey KB2 Keyboard Amp

Roland KC150 Keyboard Amp

The more expensive portable keyboards tend not to have internal amplification. You may think this odd as it appears that you are paying more and getting less. But as these instruments are primarily produced for the professional (gigging) musician, keeping the weight down to the minimum is useful. and This also leaves the way clear to purchase the right amplification for the musician's individual needs which could vary considerably, governed by the type and size of venues.

If using one of these instruments for home use there are many suitable small amps on the market. In this instance, I would advise purchasing dedicated keyboard equipment or powered speakers both of which should be fine.

Buying Second-hand

Like just about anything, if you buy second-hand you will save a huge amount on the new purchase price and lose a great deal less when you come to sell - *which is inevitable!*

Over the years I've bought several new instruments, but to be honest have lost money on all of them whereas many of the second-hand instruments I've bought, I've used for a few years and often sold for a profit - something I've never got anywhere near doing with a car! And as against cars, musical instruments tend to be very reliable. In fact, I have to say that since 1966 when I bought my Vox Continental organ, I have **never** had an instrument fail on me - *I'm hanging onto a tree as I'm writing this!* The only parts that I've ever needed were a **few** keys that got physically broken on my Hammonds due to a slightly *'over enthusiastic'* playing technique and some valves which were consumables on the Hammonds. But in those days, I always kept a supply of what I knew I was going to destroy.

Common sense dictates that you should use caution if buying on eBay etc., although I have bought this way successfully numerous times. But my advice would be to always view before bidding and check out the seller's ratings in detail. When selling, personally I would never sell on eBay due to their crazy fees, *Gumtree* and *Preloved* have always worked well for me - *and they're free!*

Finally, if you're not sure what to buy, buy low priced second-hand (preferably 6 octaves or more). But always check *discounted* new prices first, and then at least you will minimise your losses if you get it wrong which you probably will! Some of the older top name keyboards incidentally are excellent.

At the time of editing this revised edition the most suitable keyboard to hit the second-hand market is the Casio Privia PX 350 which has a full 88 key hammer action keybed, superb piano sounds and auto-accompaniment, and possibly available for as low as £350 - £400.

Other items that you will need include:

- A stool (preferably height adjustable);
- A stand strong enough to accommodate the keyboard;

- A good quality sustain pedal (preferably with a reverse polarity switch);
- A music stand (included with most keyboards);
- A dust cover for the keyboard;
- Amplification and leads if not included;
- Headphones if you want your family to retain their sanity.

Throughout the book I have included a few of my favourite keyboards, please be assured that these are not *'adverts'* as such. I am not on commission or anything and certainly would not accept any payment for any inclusions. Links for *all* the major manufacturers can be found on my website so that you can get all the up-to-date relevant information in order to make up your own mind as to what suits your needs either now or in the future.

The Legendary Hammond B3

I had the very great pleasure of owning one of these beasts.
A great machine, but no fun humping them into basement or attic venues!

Many digital keyboards get close to reproducing the sound of this beast with only a fraction of the weight. But if you really want the Hammond sound, buy a Hammond!

> "Music is the mediator between the spiritual and the sensual life."
> Beethoven

Your First Exercises

Now before I start explaining the basic rudiments of music theory, these first few exercises can be practiced effectively even without an instrument, so don't worry if you haven't got one yet, these exercises will still be beneficial.

But assuming you have got a keyboard, you need to get yourself correctly prepared as follows.

Correct Hand and Seating Positioning

Firstly, it's a good idea to make sure that your hands are clean and warm. You can achieve this by soaking them in warm water for a while, but then dry them thoroughly. Alternatively, sit on them to warm them up; but if you happen to be sitting on a cold marble slab, nestle your right hand under your left armpit and your left hand under your right armpit for a while which is a method that I used regularly whilst gigging around Europe during the cold winters of the 60's.

The next thing is to be sure that you adopt a correct seating position so that you can achieve the correct hand position. If your seating is incorrect (too low or too high) then your hand positioning will never be correct. I recommend using a height adjustable piano stool so that you can experiment in order to get comfortable. Or of course you may have an adjustable keyboard stand.

Do also take into account the fact that you may need to use the pedals, or at least the sustain pedal, so both feet should be comfortably flat on the floor to begin with.

Your stool should be positioned so that you are seated more or less in the centre of the keyboard - belly button opposite **middle C**, with your back fairly straight but relaxed.

The next pictures illustrate the correct and incorrect hand positions.

 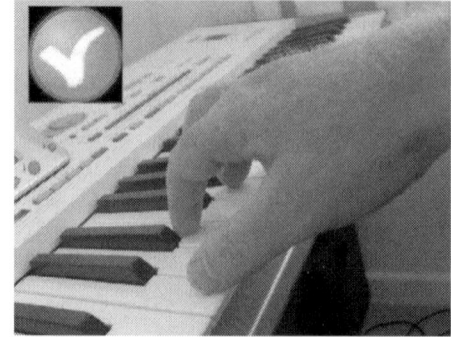

Fingering

As far as music is concerned what most people will call their *'first'* finger is their *'second'* finger as in music the *'first'* finger is always your *'thumb'* (on both hands).

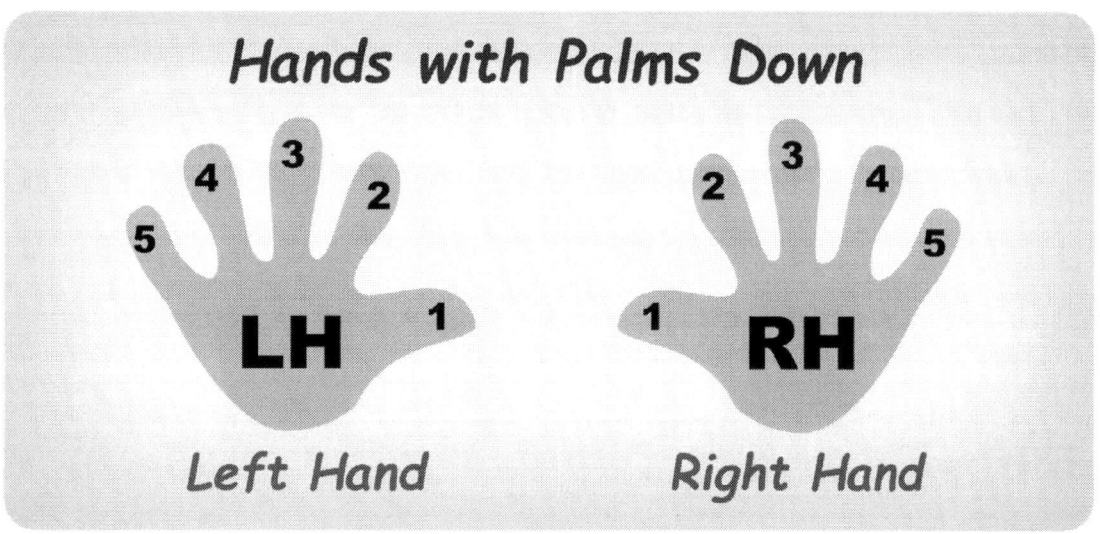

Here We Go

What I'm going to get you to do now will drive your partner, kids, parents, friends and probably even your cat *nuts* - so be prepared! You are going to become a *'perpetual tapper'!* These exercises can be done anywhere, anytime on virtually any*thing* from a table to a steering wheel to your head or even your girlfriend's / boyfriend's leg! But I absolutely guarantee that they will increase your finger strength, independence and flexibility quicker than any other method. Obviously, whenever you can, use a keyboard. But because you can do these anywhere, I will call these the *'tapping'* exercises.

To prepare for your first exercise, proceed as follows:

1. If using a piano or keyboard, adjust your seating position as described previously;

2. Rest the fingers of your right hand (you can do the same with your left hand later) on the keyboard (or surface) in a claw like position with your first finger (thumb) on the white key to the left of two black keys more or less in the middle of the keyboard - **middle C**;

3. Keeping your hand / fingers in this position raise your hand only very slightly so that it's no longer touching the keyboard (or surface). If this is uncomfortable, adjust your seating position;

4. Now begin counting either out loud or in your head: **1 & 2 & 3 & 4 & 1 & 2 & 3 & 4 &** etc.;

5. With each count (but not the *'ands'*) tap your left foot and try and keep a steady rhythm. Now you're ready for exercise 1, but pay attention to the hand / finger position at all times.

Exercise 1

With each tap of your foot, press the keys (or tap the surface) with each finger of your right hand one at a time in a piston type fashion starting and finishing with your thumb as shown in the right-hand diagram below. Speed is of no importance but rhythm is. Take it as slow as you like but keep in time. It's likely that you have started counting far faster than you are able to do this, so simply slow down the tempo.

5 4 3 2 1 2 3 4 (5)
Left Hand x 7

1 2 3 4 5 4 3 2 (1)
Right Hand x 7

When using the left hand, start with the 5th finger, again on a key to the left of two black keys, but the next one down from the one used with the right hand and follow the pattern as in the left-hand diagram above.

Practice this exercise with both hands separately doing each one seven times making the last beat of each segment the first of the next. You will see the significance of *'seven'* later. Gradually increase the speed according to your ability, but remember speed is not important, but accuracy and rhythm is.

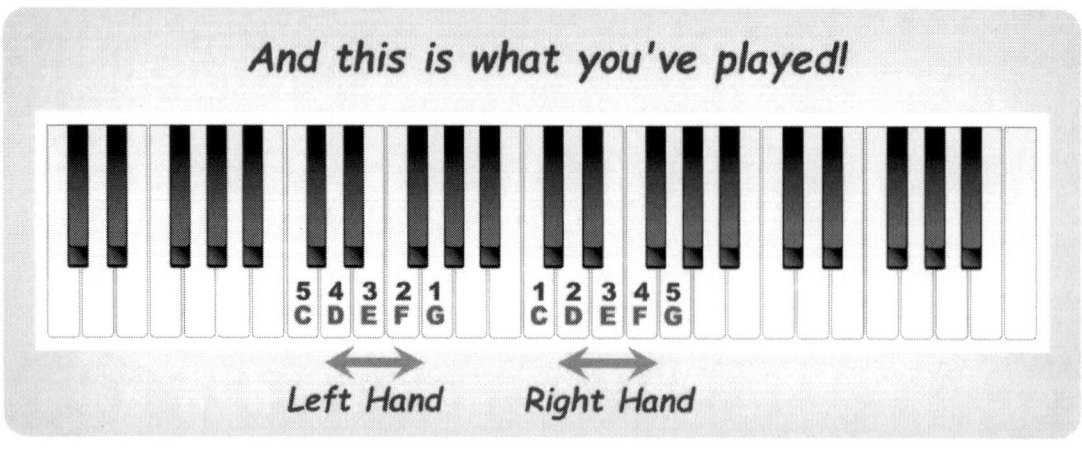

I don't want you to worry about this right now, but in music notation if you play just one segment of the above, you would in fact be playing 9 crotchets, the last of which being the first of the continuum as shown above in music notation for the right hand.

Now as you get a little more proficient, you could double the speed by tapping / playing the notes on the *'and'* beats as well - this would be 9 quavers.

Double it again and it's 9 semi quavers, which is what you should eventually aim for, but you can always alter the tempo to suit yourself.

Each of the exercises has a *'mirror'* version thus enabling every finger in both hands to benefit equally. The mirror version for this first exercise is as follows with the right hand starting with the 5th finger and the left hand starting with the 1st.

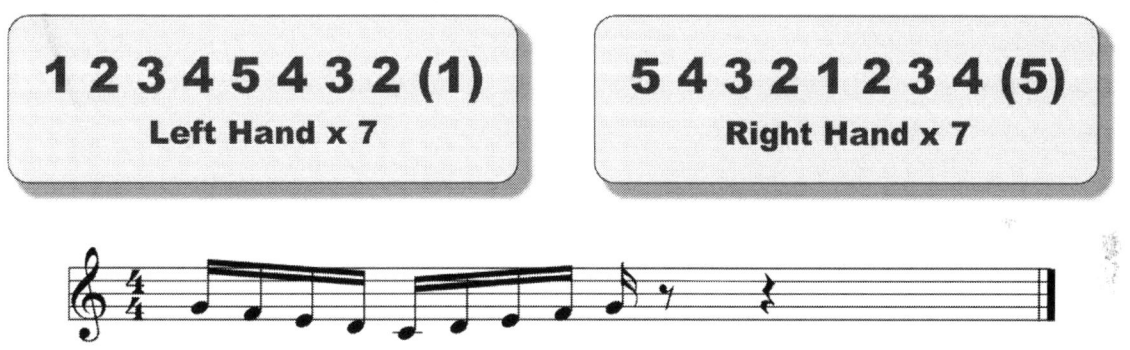

Try these exercises two different ways:

    a) Tapping and releasing each finger fairly abruptly - this is known as *'staccato';* and

    b) Holding each finger down until the next one comes into play - this is known as *'legato';*

    c) Practice with both hands individually and then both hands together.

I'll explain the music notation in detail later, but for the time being just try and get your fingers working which right now is most important and will be for quite some time.

So, when you're ready, move onto the next four exercises which will get your fingers moving in a different order.

Exercise 2

| 5 1 2 1 3 2 4 3 (5) | 1 5 4 5 3 4 2 3 (1) |
| Left Hand x 7 | Right Hand x 7 |

Mirror Version Below

| 1 5 4 5 3 4 2 3 (1) | 5 1 2 1 3 2 4 3 (5) |
| Left Hand x 7 | Right Hand x 7 |

Right hand Music Notation for Normal and mirror version below

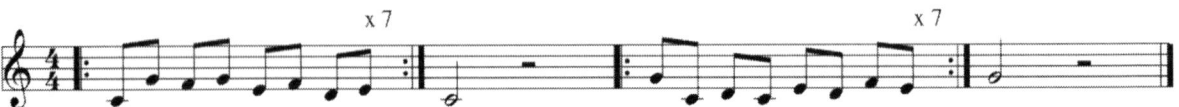

Exercise 3

| 5 1 2 1 3 1 4 1(5) | 1 5 4 5 3 5 2 5 (1) |
| Left Hand x 7 | Right Hand x 7 |

Mirror Version Below

| 1 5 4 5 3 5 2 5 (1) | 5 1 2 1 3 1 4 1 (5) |
| Left Hand x 7 | Right Hand x 7 |

Right hand Music Notation for Normal and mirror version below

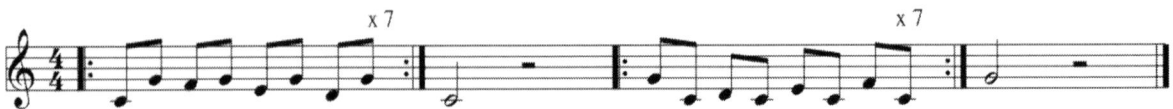

Copyright © Martin Woodward 2011 & 2017

Exercise 4

| **5 4 3 4 2 3 1 2 (5)** | **1 2 3 2 4 3 5 4 (1)** |
| Left Hand x 7 | Right Hand x 7 |

Mirror Version Below

| **1 2 3 2 4 3 5 4 (1)** | **5 4 3 4 2 3 1 2 (5)** |
| Left Hand x 7 | Right Hand x 7 |

Right hand Music Notation for Normal and mirror version below

Exercise 5

| **5 3 4 2 3 1 2 4 (5)** | **1 3 2 4 3 5 4 2 (1)** |
| Left Hand x 7 | Right Hand x 7 |

Mirror Version Below

| **1 3 2 4 3 5 4 2 (1)** | **5 3 4 2 3 1 2 4 (5)** |
| Left Hand x 7 | Right Hand x 7 |

Right hand Music Notation for Normal and mirror version below

Copyright © Martin Woodward 2011 & 2017

Right now, you may understand the above fingering charts better than the music notation, but you must admit that it's getting a bit confusing and remember we are only dealing with five white notes here. But hopefully this has got you tapping and exercising your fingers in order to gain some initial dexterity and flexibility required to progress further.

I appreciate that if you've never done this before, these initial exercises are difficult, particularly between the 4th and 5th fingers, but believe me they work - there are no better!

Later I'll show you more, but remember do them slowly and keep in time.

Even though their greatest importance is to give the initial flexibility and strength to each finger, even when you progress to learn all the scales and arpeggios shown later, never dismiss the importance of the 5 finger exercises. I still do them now after 60 years of playing.

Please continue with these exercises while you are reading the following chapters, I guarantee that you will see the benefits in a very short while. But don't strain your finger muscles too much - do a bit - rest a bit!

The audio link for the tapping exercises is: http://learn-keyboard.co.uk/tapping.html or click on the notation graphics.

Alto Truesonic TS 110a Powered Speaker

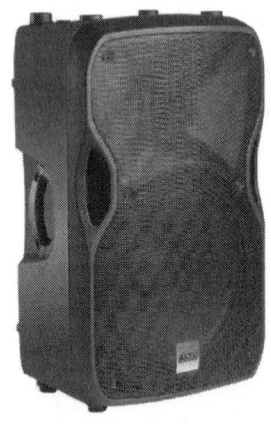 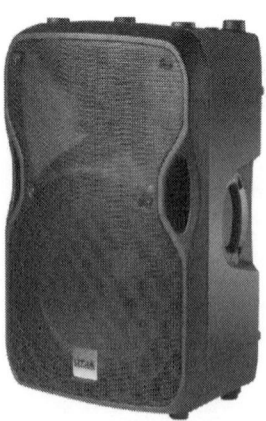

A great alternative to a dedicated keyboard combo amp is powered speakers like these. Although used primarily for PA, these are are great for keyboards and can be used singly or in pairs (for stereo).
These are ideal for home studio and small - average sized gigs.
I have used these!

The Notes of the Keyboard

Now we'll look at the notes of the keyboard and how to identify them.

As already stated, some keyboards / pianos have more keys than others, but this makes no difference in relation to understanding how to play them, as they all have the same basic arrangement of black and white keys.

If you look closely you will see that the black keys are in groups of two then three.

This enables us to find every single note easily. And the first one that you must learn is **'C'** which can be found just to the left of two black keys.

The diagram below shows a four-octave span revealing five **C's** each of which are eight notes apart - hence octave - as in octagon - octopus - eight!

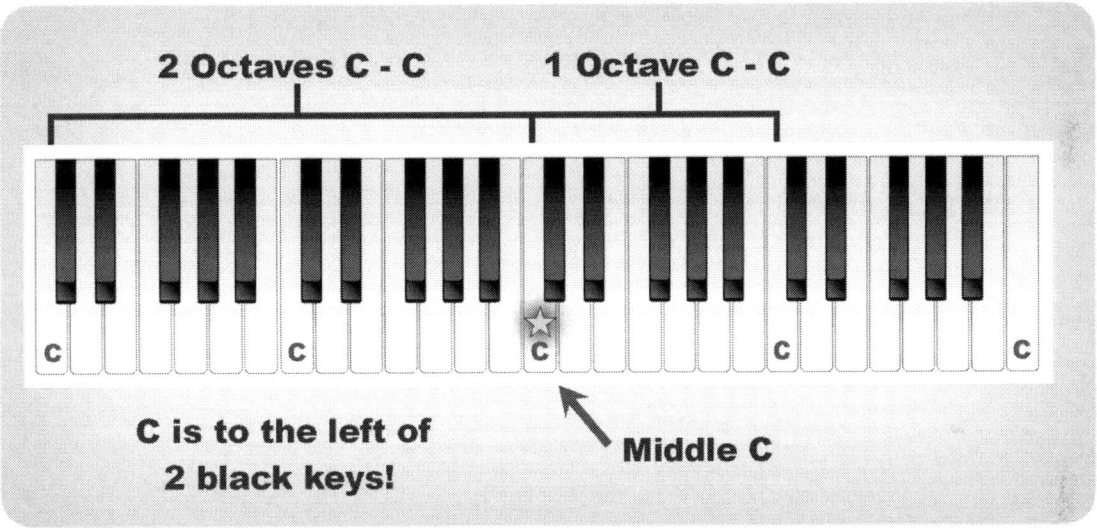

Probably the most important note on the keyboard is **middle C** which is the **'C'** that is more or less in the middle of the keyboard and because it is so important, we are going to put a star on ours as shown.

Now all the notes to the left of **middle C** get gradually lower in pitch and all the notes to the right gradually get higher. And usually you will use your right hand for the higher notes and your left hand for the lower notes.

*So which hand plays **middle C**?*

That's a good question and the answer is that it could be either, but I will explain more shortly.

Now I'll show you what all the other notes are called, but I don't want you to get too confused about all this at the moment. We will be taking it all slowly step by step.

Copyright © Martin Woodward 2011 & 2017

Here's the other notes!

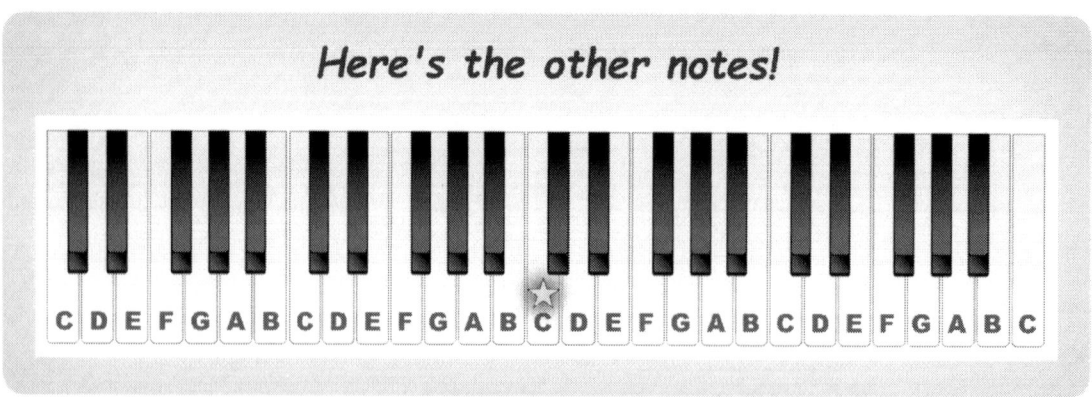

This is mind boggling, how am I going to remember this lot?

Easy, if you split them up into two main groups according to the number of black notes as shown below:

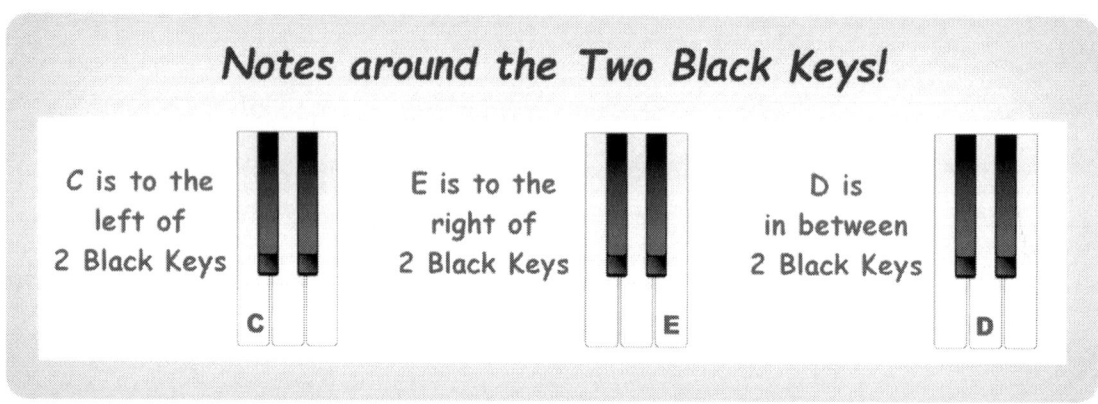

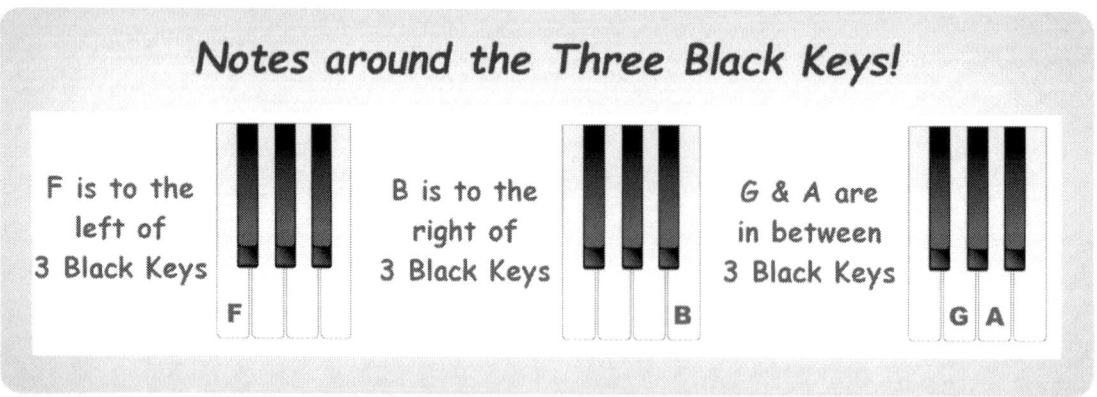

And if you can't remember which comes first **G** or **A** you're probably going Gaga - get it? - GA - GA!!

What about the black ones, what are they called?

Don't worry I've not forgotten them, we'll be dealing with them shortly, but first we'll look at how the keys of the keyboard relate to music notation.

Music Notation

Music notation is basically a glorified *'graph'* using groups of lines called *'staves'* or *'staffs'*, with the *'time line'* being the horizontal axis from left to right and the *'pitch'* being the vertical axis. How long a note is played for is determined by the time element of the note i.e. crotchet, quaver, minim etc. When it is played is determined by how far along the time line it's placed. The pitch of the note is determined by how high or low it's placed on the vertical axis (the stave). Simple - easy peasy - in theory!

As an example, in the diagram below, the first note to be played is **C** which is the lowest pitched note of the phrase and is a *'crotchet'* (don't worry I'll explain all this shortly), followed by **E** and **G** which are higher pitched and played together. They are both *'minims'* which are sustained for twice as long as a crotchet. Then we have **A** which is the highest note of the phrase followed by **G** again both of which are *'quavers'* being timed half the value of a crotchet. And finally, the last note of the phrase is **E** which is a *'semibreve'* which is four times the time value of a crotchet.

The next diagram shows exactly the same phrase in graph form or *Piano Roll* form as used in music recording software. Click on either to hear the phrase, if you want to.

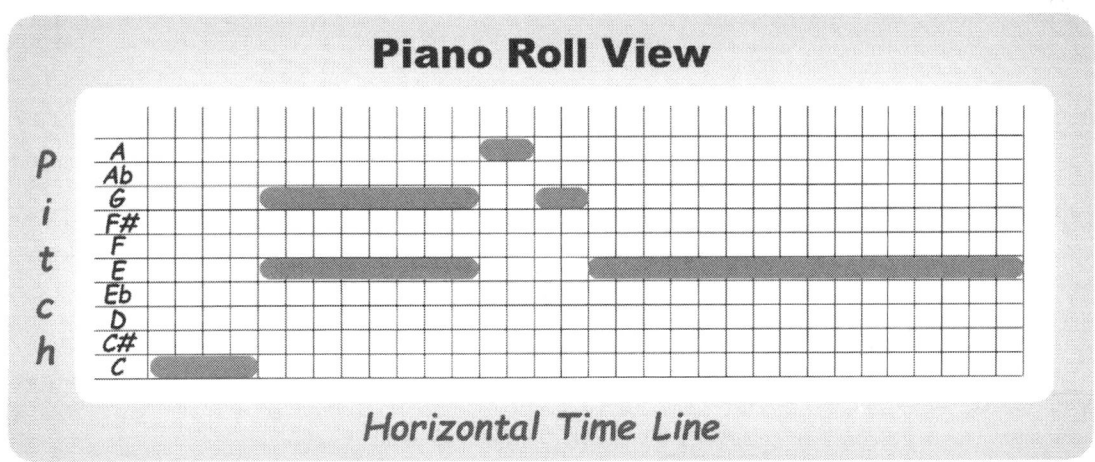

Can you recognise the similarities between the two diagrams?

Undoubtedly any untrained musician would find the piano roll view simpler to understand, and it certainly has its uses when editing recorded music. But look at how much space it takes up compared to the first diagram. And remember this is a very short, one hand phrase. So clearly, learning conventional music notation has to be to every musician's advantage.

In order to extend the vertical axis (in conventional notation) and potentially accommodate more notes, this is split into *'clefs'*. The two clefs used in piano music are the *'treble'* and *'bass'* clefs as shown next and these form the *'grand staff'* (or stave).

Saying: "the two clefs used in Piano music" implies that there are other clefs.

Yes, there are several other clefs used by other instruments and singers, the most common being the *'alto'* and *'tenor'* clefs, but from the piano / keyboard point of view, you can completely put them out of mind, just simply know that they exist and forget about them!

Yamaha CVP 709GP

This has to be my dream machine if money and space were no object!

The Grand Staff

The *'Grand staff'* is made up of two *'staves'* or *'staffs'* of five lines each, the top one being the *'treble clef'* which is mainly used for the higher notes by the right hand and the *'bass clef'* mainly used for the lower notes by the left hand.

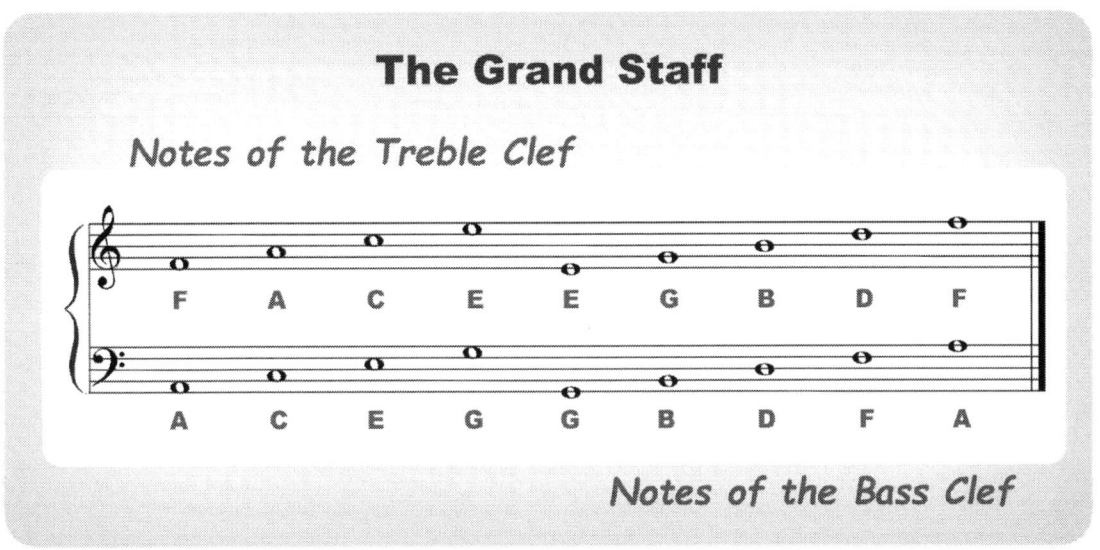

What's the difference between a staff and a stave?

Actually, no-one seems to know for sure, but a staff is a stave - it's just a word, well two words actually, so don't worry about it!

The important thing that you need to learn is that the *'staves'* or *'staffs'* are split into the two *'clefs'* (for piano music) - these are what you need to learn and remember.

An easy way to remember the notes of each clef is to think of them in sections like:

- Treble clef *space* notes **F A C E** - the word *FACE!*
- Treble clef *line* notes **E G B D F** - *Every Good Boy Deserves Favours!*
- Bass clef *space* notes **A C E G** - *All Cows Eat Grass!*
- Bass clef *line* notes **G B D F A** - *Giant Bears Don't Fly Aeroplanes!*

So, which one is 'middle C'?

Well actually **'middle C'** is not in the above illustration, because it falls below the lines of the treble clef and above the lines of the bass clef. In fact, it's exactly midway between both clefs.

The next illustration will show you where it is! Although it is shown in both the treble and bass clefs it is the same note.

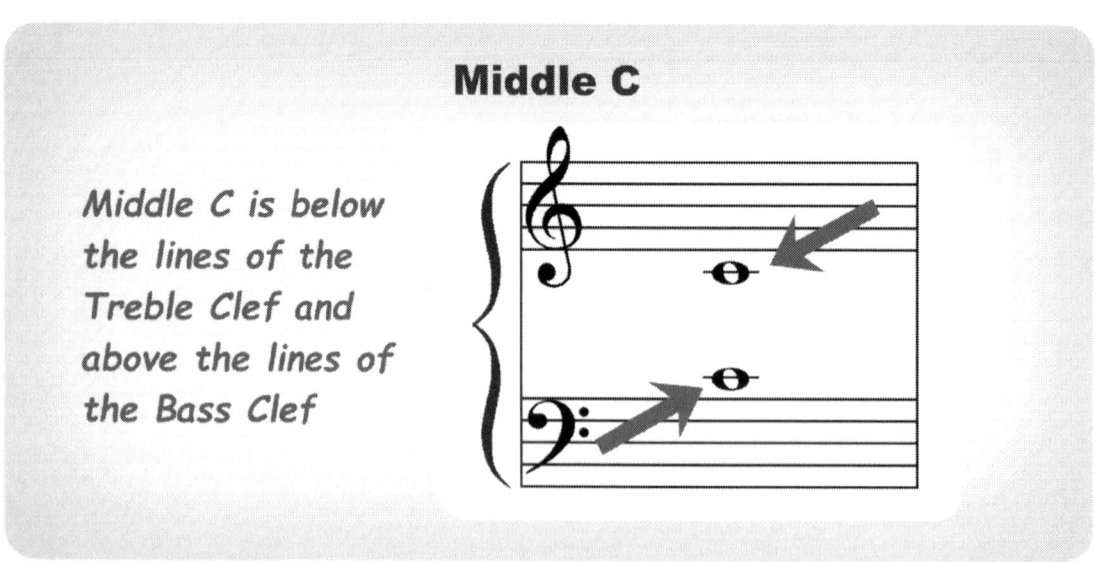

If we bring the two clefs closer together, you will see that there is an imaginary line exactly midway between the two clefs and this is where *'middle C'* lives.

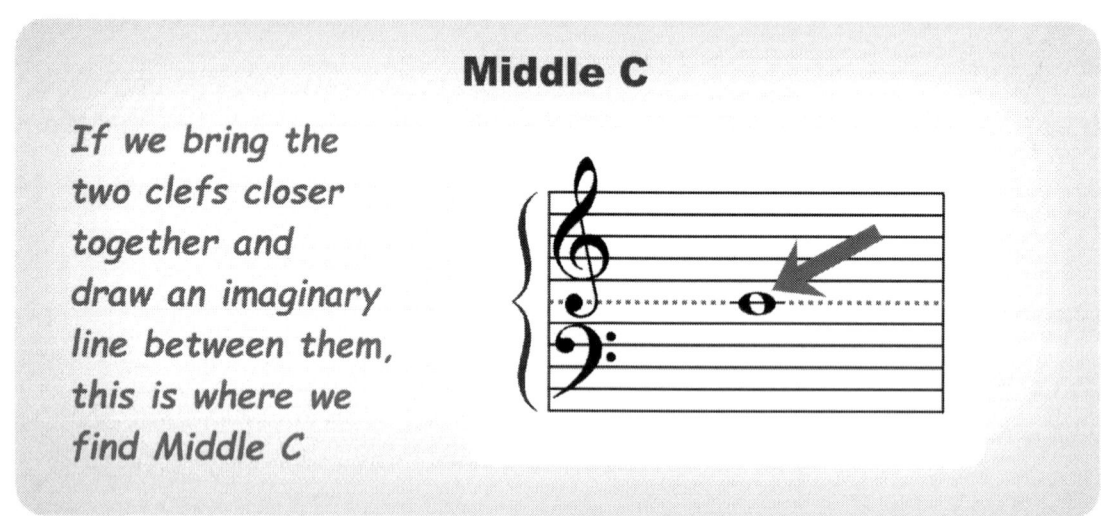

And this is why *'middle C'* has a line drawn through the middle of it. This is called a ledger line and happens with some other notes as well, in fact any time a note goes above or below the clef staff lines.

Now the notes both sides of middle **C** (**B** and **D**) also fall either above or below the clef staff lines which can be seen next.

> *"I have never thought of writing for reputation and honour. What I have in my heart must come out; that is the reason why I compose."*
>
> Beethoven
>
> *Comment: Wisdom from the greatest!*

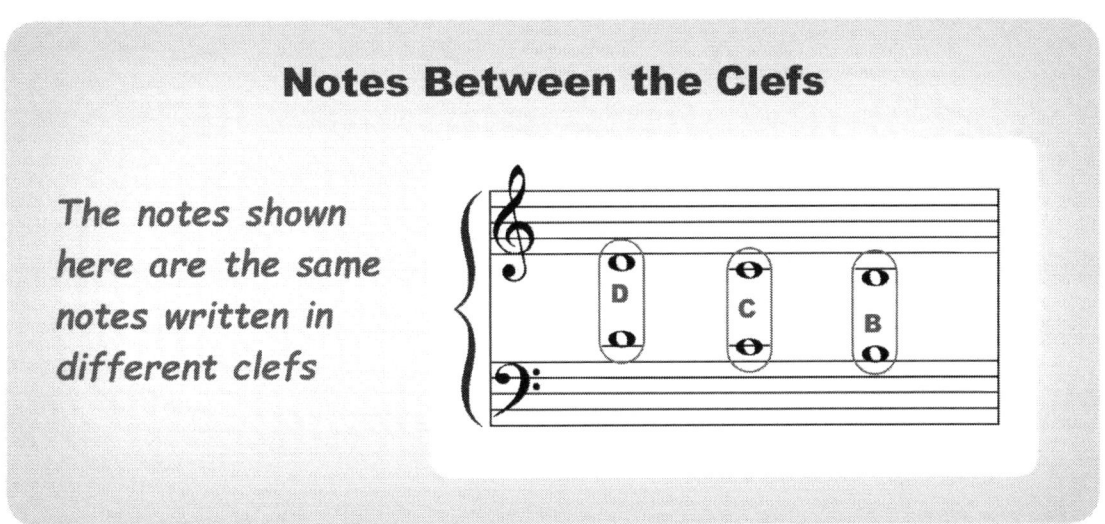

Now there are also notes that fall both above the treble clef and below the bass clef and these in fact would be the top four and the bottom four white notes of a four-octave spread.

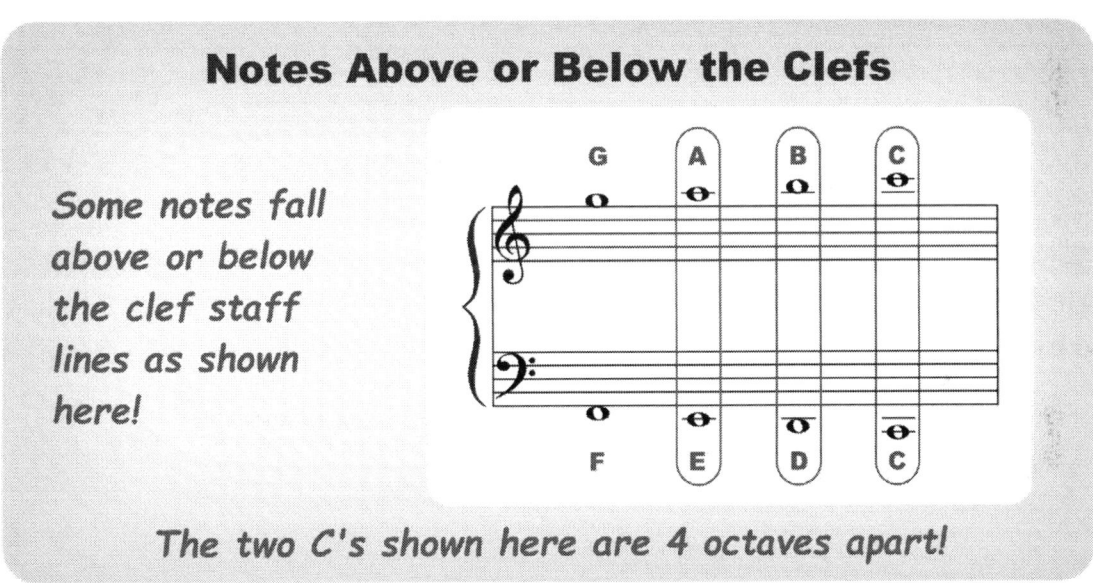

Wow this is getting heavy; I don't think I'll ever understand all this!

Please don't distress yourself, we will be dealing with everything one step at a time and it will all become clear as you progress. But you may occasionally need to review various sections to gain a complete understanding. - Just read on!

> *"I started out with nothing and I've still got most of it left!"*
>
> Seasick Steve
>
> *Comment: Rock on Steve, we all love you!*

How the Notes Relate to the Keyboard

Now we'll look at how the musical notes relate to the keyboard.

This next diagram may at first look a little confusing and difficult to read; and if you are reading this on a tablet, it may not be clear. If you haven't already done so, please go to the rear of the book to get the pdf download link and you will be able to see this much more clearly, even more so by zooming in, in landscape view!

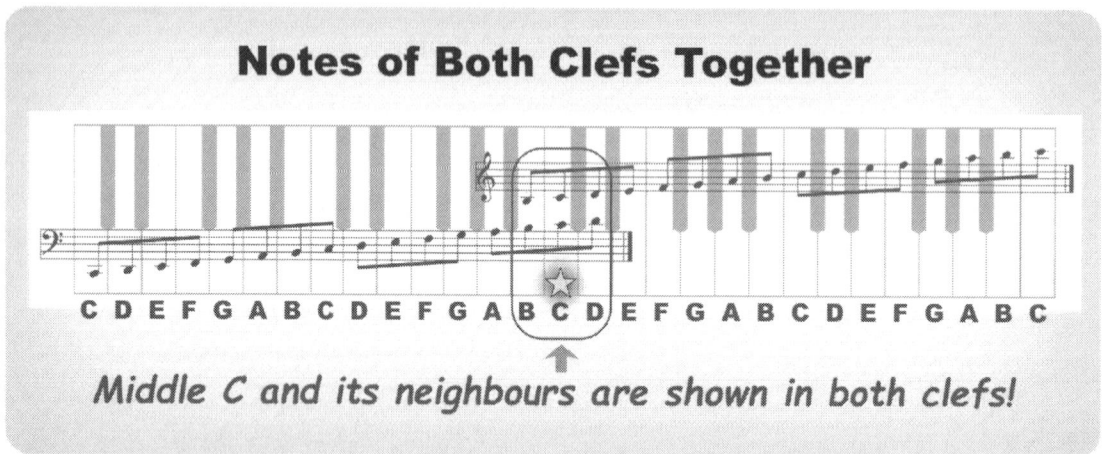

To make this easier to see, below I have split the keyboard into two 2 octave sections, one for each clef, but remember that we have put a star on *Middle C* so that you can always find it!

So, notice that the next two diagrams are actually the same as the above diagram split into two.

It may be useful for you to print out these three diagrams and look at them in detail.

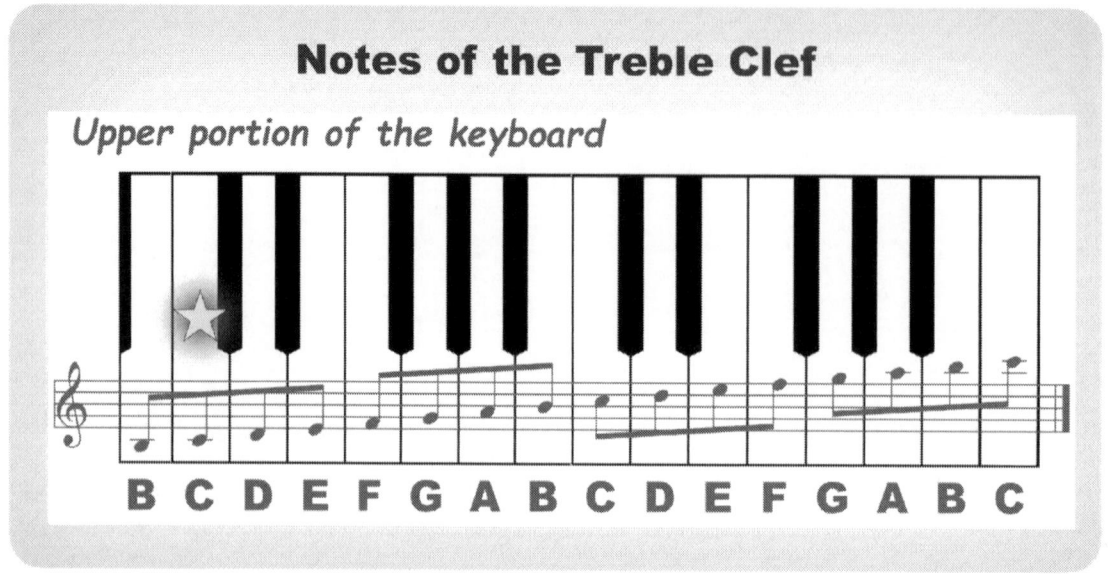

Copyright © Martin Woodward 2011 & 2017

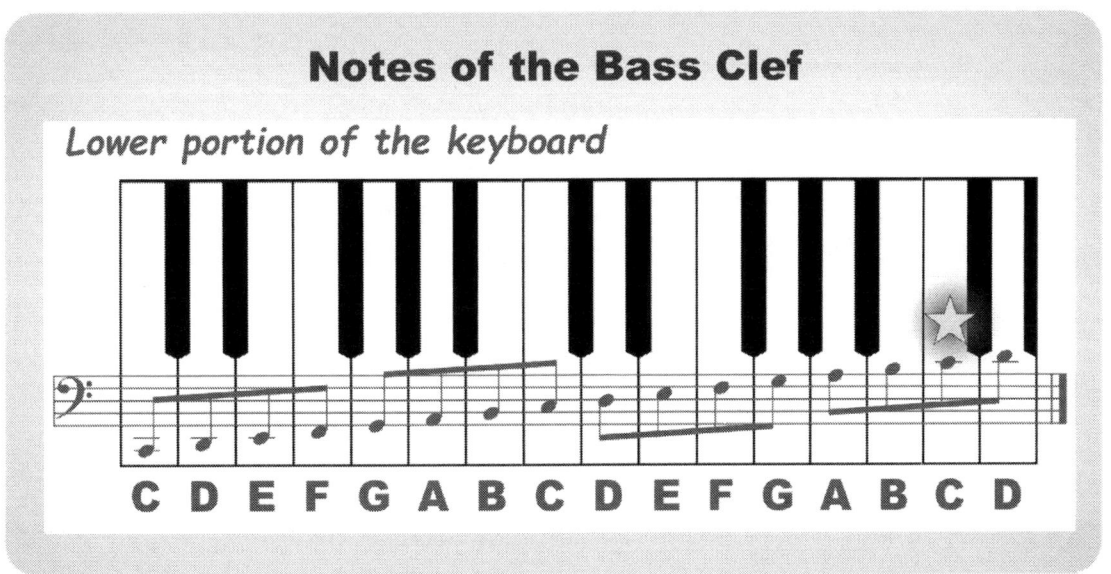

Ok so this shows a four-octave spread, but what happens when the notes are higher or lower than these as on larger keyboards?

Good question! And the answer is that up to a certain point more ledger lines are added, but when there are too many they become impossible to read quickly, so instead the music is written an octave (or more) lower or higher to keep within the clefs and then the *8va, 8vb, 15ma* or *15mb* symbols are used.

As an example, the following two phrases are exactly the same, but on the second one the *8va* symbol is used indicating that the notes should be played an octave higher than written.

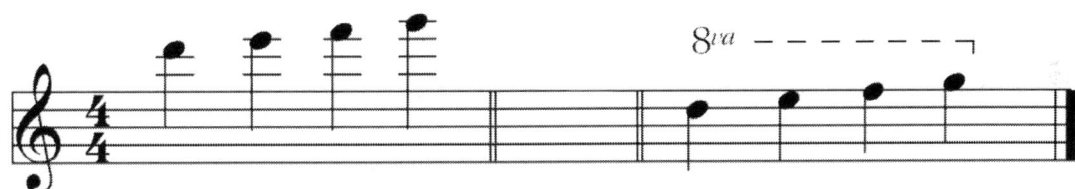

- *8va* = play the bracketed notes one octave higher;
- *8vb* = play the bracketed notes one octave lower;
- *15ma* = play the bracketed notes two octaves higher;
- *15mb* = play the bracketed notes two octaves lower.

To be honest it will probably be a while before you'll need these.

"The beautiful thing about learning is that nobody can take it away from you."

BB King - (King of the Blues)

Sharps & Flats

We've already learnt that the interval from one **C** to the next is an *octave*. And indeed, this is the same interval from **B** - **B** or **G** - **G** etc.

Now the smallest interval in Western music is a *'semitone'* which is the interval from any note on the keyboard to its nearest neighbour be it black or white.

So, the interval between **C** and **B** is a semitone, and also the interval between **E** and **F** as in both cases there are no black notes in-between. In all the other cases, there *are* black notes in-between, so the semitone interval will be to the black note above or below. And as you can see by the diagram below the first black note after **C** is called **C sharp** *or* **D flat**. Note that in some circumstances **B** could also be known as *C flat* (as there are no black notes in between) and **C** could also be known as *B sharp* - but actually this is very rare.

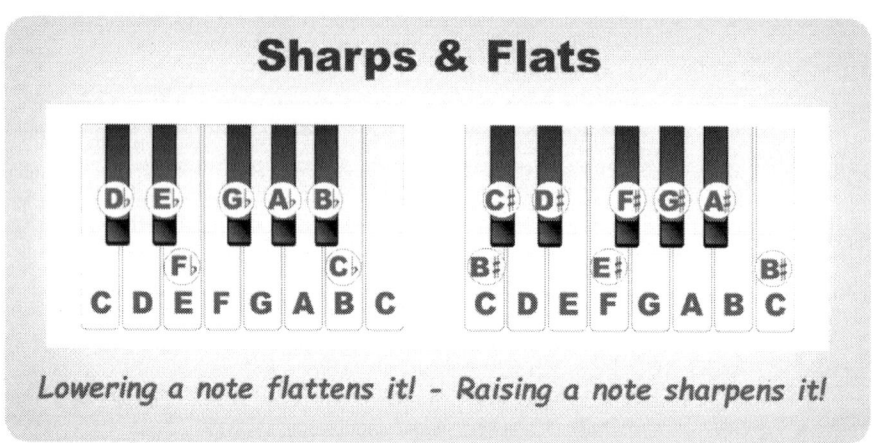

To *'sharpen'* a note is to raise the pitch and to *'flatten'* one is to lower the pitch.

There are also *double sharps* and *double flats* where the pitch of a note is raised or lowered twice as much (2 semitones). But these only occur occasionally in keys heavily endowed in sharps or flats. There are actually only two in this book - in the **G# minor** scales and the **D♭ 7♭ 5** chord in the chord substitution section. It may be years before you come across any more.

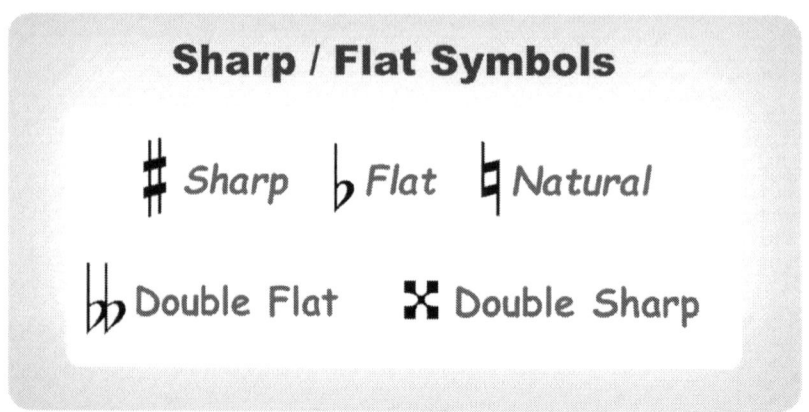

Copyright © Martin Woodward 2011 & 2017

Whether a particular note is known as a sharp or a flat depends on the key signature which will be dealt with later.

Sharps and flats occur in music in two different ways:

- as accidentals; or
- within key signatures (which could also include accidentals).

When they are accidentals, they are simply added to the music as and where they occur as shown below.

In this case any repeats of notes that are *'sharpened'* or *'flattened'* this way remains so for the duration of the bar unless *'naturalised'* using the *'natural'* symbol.

If you look carefully at the last diagrams you will see that both examples are identical. The first one uses **F sharp** and the second uses **G flat** (same notes) to produce the same result.

Why do the black notes have two names? Why not just call them flats or sharps but not both?

Yes, I can see the confusion, but this is because there are *flat* keys and *sharp* keys which we'll be learning about later, along with key signatures.

But first we'll deal with the timing.

Casio Privia PX-560 Piano / Arranger

This little beast takes some beating - especially for the price. This has incredible piano sounds, as well as one of the best keyboard feels out there. It also has other great sounds (all programmable), auto accompaniment and recording features!

I have one of these!

← Timing →

This section deals with time signatures; note values and rests etc. If you are familiar with these, please move onto the next section.

Time Signatures and Bars

Each group of notes is separated into *'bars'* or *'measures'*, which are the vertical lines separating the various notes or groups of notes. The time signature, determines how many notes of what length are to be played to each bar, the first beat of which is often slightly or heavily accented.

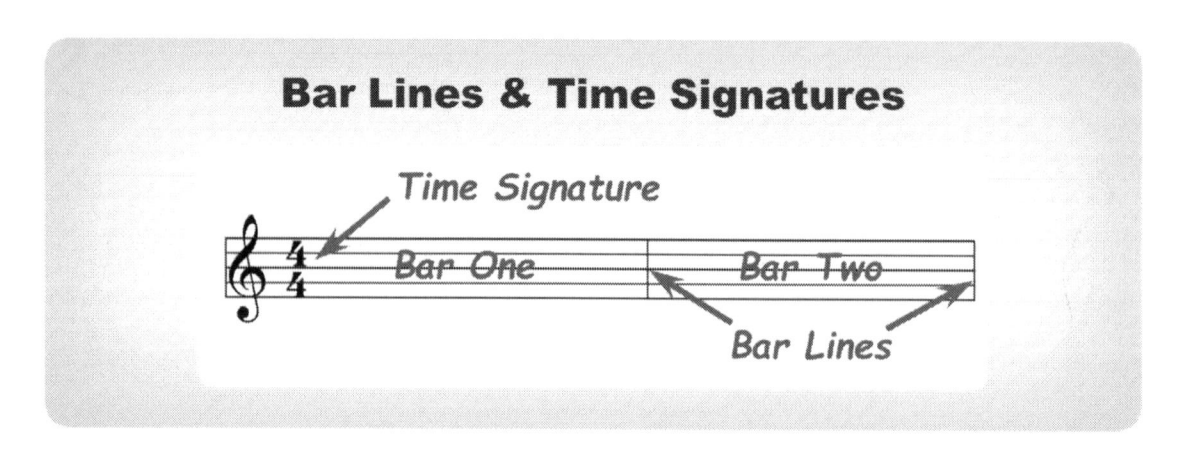

Bar Lines & Time Signatures

The most common time signatures are:

- **4/4** - four quarter notes to each bar. Think or repeat '**1 & 2 & 3 & 4 & 1 & 2 & 3 & 4**' etc., and with your right-hand tap with the '**1 2 3 4**' beats but not the '*ands*'. With your left-hand tap on the '**1 and 3**' beats;

- **3/4** - three quarter notes to each bar (Waltz time). Think or repeat '**1 & 2 & 3 & 1 & 2 & 3**' etc., and with your left-hand tap on the '**1**' beats and with your right hand on the '**2 / 3**' beats;

- **2/4** - two quarter notes to each bar (March time). Think or repeat '**1 & 2 & 1 & 2**' etc., and with your left-hand tap on the '**1**' beats and with your right hand on the '**2**' beats;

- **6/8** - six eighth notes to each bar (two set of three - Jazz Waltz). Think or repeat '**1** 2 3, **2** 2 3 - **1** 2 3, **2** 2 3' etc., (no *'ands'* this time) and tap all the beats with your right hand and the '**1**' and '**2**' beats with your left hand but giving more emphasis on the first '**1**' beat of each pattern. This may seem similar to **3/4** time, but it's generally much faster.

The time signature is always given at the beginning of each piece, and will remain the same throughout unless information is given to the contrary.

The most common time signature without doubt is **4/4** which is also known as *'common time'* and this also has an alternative symbol as shown below as does the **2/2** time signature which is known as *'cut common time'* or *'alla breve'*.

Time Signatures

Common Time — 4/4, C

Alla Breve — 2/2, ₵

Quarter Note Time Signatures — 2/4, 3/4, 6/4, 5/4, 7/4

Eighth Note Time Signatures — 3/8, 6/8, 9/8, 12/8

There are more - **5/4, 7/4, 9/8, 11/8** etc., but we don't need any of these for our purpose right now and by the time you come to need them you will understand them perfectly.

Korg SV-1 Stage Piano (88 keys)

If you're looking for a great looking and great sounding, no gimmick portable piano, this could be the one for you, but you will need an external amp and speaker.

Note Values

The most important note values that you are likely to come across for a while are as follows:

1 Semi-breve = 2 Minims = 4 Crotchets

= 8 Quavers = 16 Semi-Quavers

- The *'semibreve'* also known as a *'whole note'* counts as 4 beats (therefore taking up the whole of a **4/4** bar);

- The *'minim'* also known as a *'half note'* counts as 2 beats (therefore taking up half of a **4/4** bar);

- The *'crotchet'* also known as a *'quarter note'* counts as 1 beat (therefore taking up a quarter of a **4/4** bar);

- The *'quaver'* also known as an *'eighth note'* counts as half a beat (therefore taking up an eighth of a **4/4** bar);

- The *'semiquaver'* also known as a *'sixteenth note'* counts as a quarter of a beat (therefore taking up a sixteenth of a **4/4** bar). As more *'tails'* are added to the quaver family the note values halve. So, four tails will create a 64th note, but we are not going to go into these here.

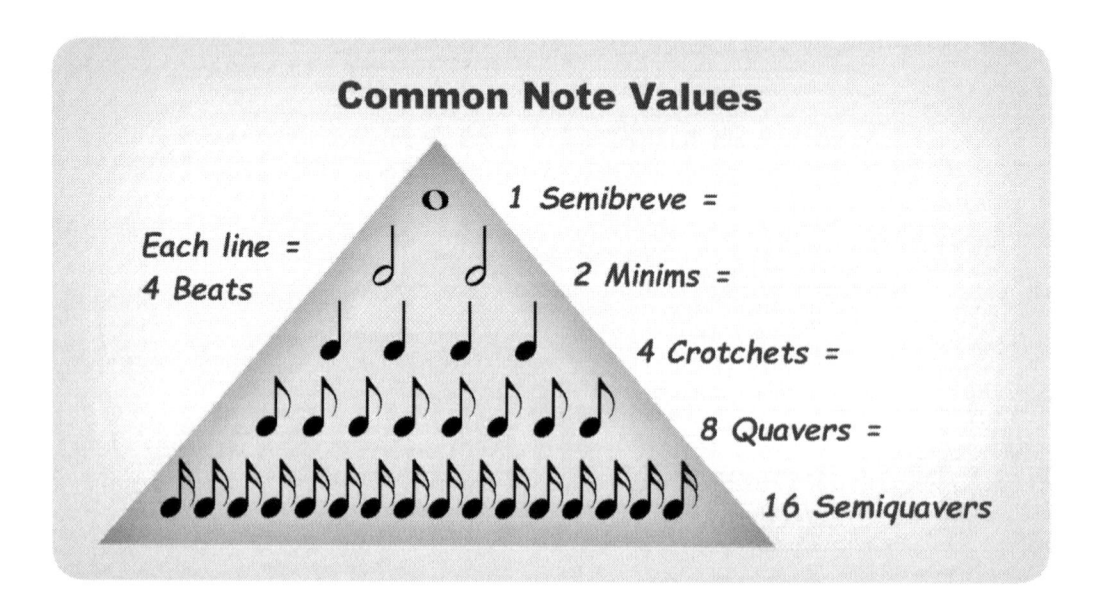

Common Note Values

Each line = 4 Beats

1 Semibreve =
2 Minims =
4 Crotchets =
8 Quavers =
16 Semiquavers

There are longer and shorter notes (and the corresponding rests), but these will do for now.

Rests

Each bar must always compute to the correct value except when *'lead in notes'* are used in the first bar (shown shortly). Therefore, any space where no note is sounded is taken up by a *'rest(s)'* which have similar values to the notes.

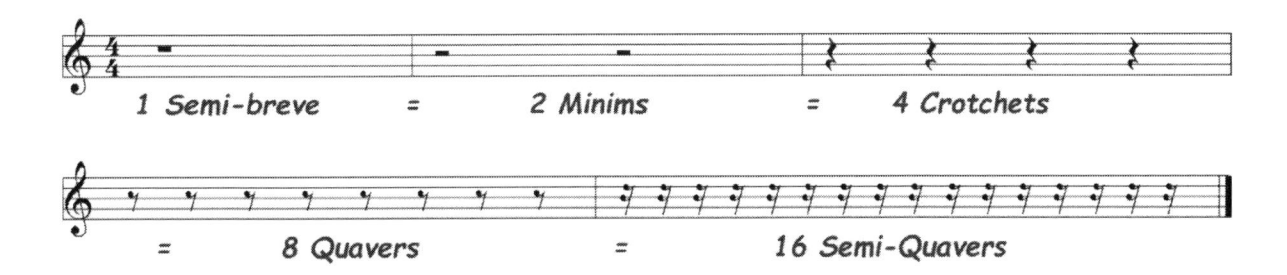

1 Semi-breve   =   2 Minims   =   4 Crotchets

=   8 Quavers   =   16 Semi-Quavers

Note the similarity between the minim and semibreve rests. Although they look similar they are rarely confused as the semibreve takes up the whole bar. I always remember these as a minim *'rests'* and a semibreve *'hangs'*!

*Sorry, I don't get any of this. Could you just explain again exactly what **4/4** timing means?*

Ok, the top '**4**' of the '**4/4**' symbol means that there are four beats to the bar and the bottom '**4**' tells us the value of the beats, and as a crotchet is a quarter of a semibreve, this means that there are four *'quarter'* notes (crotchets) to each bar.

In the case of **3/4** this means that there are three *'quarter'* notes (crotchets) to a bar and **2/4**, two quarter notes to a bar.

In the case of **6/8** the there are six *'eighth'* notes (quavers) to a bar.

Being totally ridiculous, if the time signature was **19/16** there would be nineteen sixteenth notes (semiquavers) to a bar, but such a time signature does not exist in practice - (maybe on another planet). However, time signatures such as **11/8** and **7/4** etc., although a little unusual *do* exist! - I love both of them and use them frequently!

Lead in Notes

Some tunes don't start on the first beat of a bar, in which case *'lead in note(s)'* are used which will make the first bar shorter than the normal bar time. Sometimes (but not always) this is adjusted by also making the last bar a different length to make up the difference. An example of this is shown below which is in fact the first few bars of *'Away in a Manger'*.

Dotted Notes

A single dot after (not over) a note or rest increases its length by 50%. Therefore, a dotted minim for instance would then count as 3 beats instead of 2. Two dots after a note increases its value by 75%, making a double dotted minim count as 3.5 beats.

The next diagram shows examples of how these fit into **4/4** bars.

Dotted Notes   Double Dotted Notes

Groups of a dotted quaver followed by a semi quaver are very common in pop and swing music. A bar of 4 of these followed by a minim (in the next bar) sounds like: **Da D, Da D, Da D, Da D, DAH**. However sometimes these are written as straight quavers but with a note that they should be played in 'swing feel'.

And what about dotted rests?

Yes, there are also dotted rests which work exactly the same.

And what about dots above or below notes?

That means the notes should be played *'Staccato'*, but this is not a *time* element, so doesn't concern us here.

Triplets

Triplets are used when the timing of a group of three notes is divided equally between a beat (or combination of beats). For instance, a *'triplet'* of three crotchets would take up the space of only two and of course the timing of these would change accordingly. Similarly, a *'triplet'* of three quavers would take up 1 beat and not 1.5.

The next diagram shows how they fit into **4/4** bars.

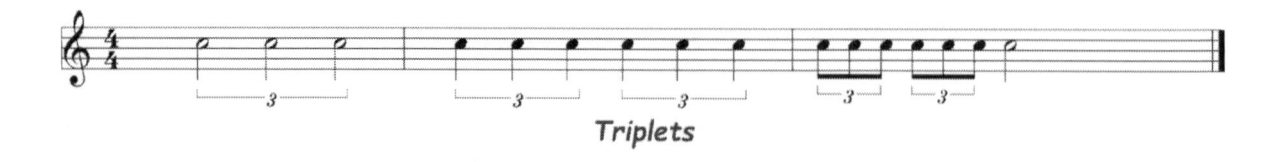

Triplets

At first playing two beats with one hand (in the bass) and three with the other is a bit tricky, but actually you will have heard triplets in many songs and will have sung or hummed along quite easily and naturally.

One well known song with lots of triplets that comes to mind is *'Fool on the Hill'* by the Beatles which is in **4/4** timing.

If converting a complicated solo into music notation it will often be found that groups of 5 or 7 or more notes are divided into a single beat. In this case the appropriate numeral will be seen instead of the '3'. This is often seen in classical music as well as pop and jazz etc.

Tied Notes

Generally, notes are written in a way which allows each beat to be identified easily. In order to achieve this, where necessary certain notes are tied together. In this event only the first note is played, but is held for the length of both *'tied'* notes.

Tied Notes

Notice that bars 1 and 2 of the above are identical and could be written either way whereas the tied notes in bars 3 and 4 *have* to be written as shown as they cross the bar lines - remember each bar must compute to the correct value, you can't have leftovers!

However please don't get these symbols mixed up with phrase marks (or slurs) which look similar but have a totally different meaning.

Grace Notes

A *'grace note'* which is written as a very small quaver usually a semitone above or below the following note, is a very quick slurred note and takes up *'no time'* in the bar time calculation. Again, these are used in all types of music, but extensively in jazz and blues.

The following example shows grace notes, triplets and tied notes.

Grace Notes

Notice that in the last example I've used the *'common time'* '**C**' symbol instead of the **4/4** symbol (as shown earlier). Note that this, as well as the **2/2** *'alla breve'* symbol are purely optional alternatives.

We have used **4/4** timing in all of the examples so far, which should have given you a pretty good idea of how it all works. As we progress, you will see examples of other time signatures.

Using a Metronome

If you have a modern electronic piano or keyboard there will almost certainly be a built-in metronome which can be altered to any specific time value. Note that as well as setting the timing you will also need to set how many beats there are to a bar and the metronome will then *'ding'* on the first beat of every bar and *'tick'* on the others.

If you've listened to any of the links so far, you'll notice that I've added a metronome to them - with the *'ding'* at the first beat of each bar (or measure).

If you are using an acoustic instrument, you will need an external metronome. Electronic versions are widely available and are very inexpensive, but there's something really special about the old fashioned traditional clockwork versions which unfortunately are more expensive. I love them - they come in the same category as cuckoo clocks for me - a touch of nostalgia! - But all they do is tick, tock and ding - no cuckoos!

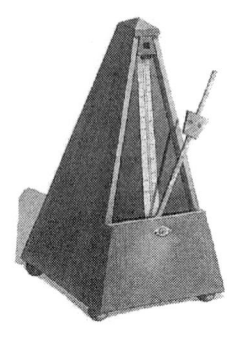

What about when a piece slows down or speeds up?

In this event the no metronome (electronic or mechanical) would be able to cope with the infinite possibilities, but in these events the following terms are used in the music notation:

Italian	Translations
Accelerando -	*Increase speed*
Rallentando -	*Slow down*
Ritardando -	*Slow down*
a tempo -	*Resume original tempo*

There is much more that I could say about timing, but enough has been said for our purposes here.

The audio link for this section is: http://learn-keyboard.co.uk/timing.html or click on the graphics.

5 Finger Exercises in Brief

Ok, so hopefully now you understand a little bit of timing and pitch in relation to music notation. But please remember that the practical finger exercises are of the upmost importance. And one good reason for learning to read basic music notation, is so that you can be taught these practical exercises. If you happen to learn to be able to sight read music somewhere on the way, then so much the better, but do remember that some of the best keyboard players are unable to sight read or even read music at all, Ray Charles and Stevie Wonder to mention two!

I hope you did the *'tapping'* exercises that we started with as the 5 finger exercises are an extension of these and are positively the best exercises that there are. I understand that right now your music reading ability may be very limited. Fortunately, these exercises require only a very limited reading ability, are played on the white notes only and don't require any finger crossovers (which you'll learn later).

The first exercise written here in the treble clef only (right hand) follows the same pattern as the first tapping exercise. But notice that there is a gap between the first and second notes of each section which enables the exercise to ascend progressively up the scale for 7 segments. And notice that this occurs again on the descent starting in bar 8 but between the fourth and fifth fingers (of the right hand).

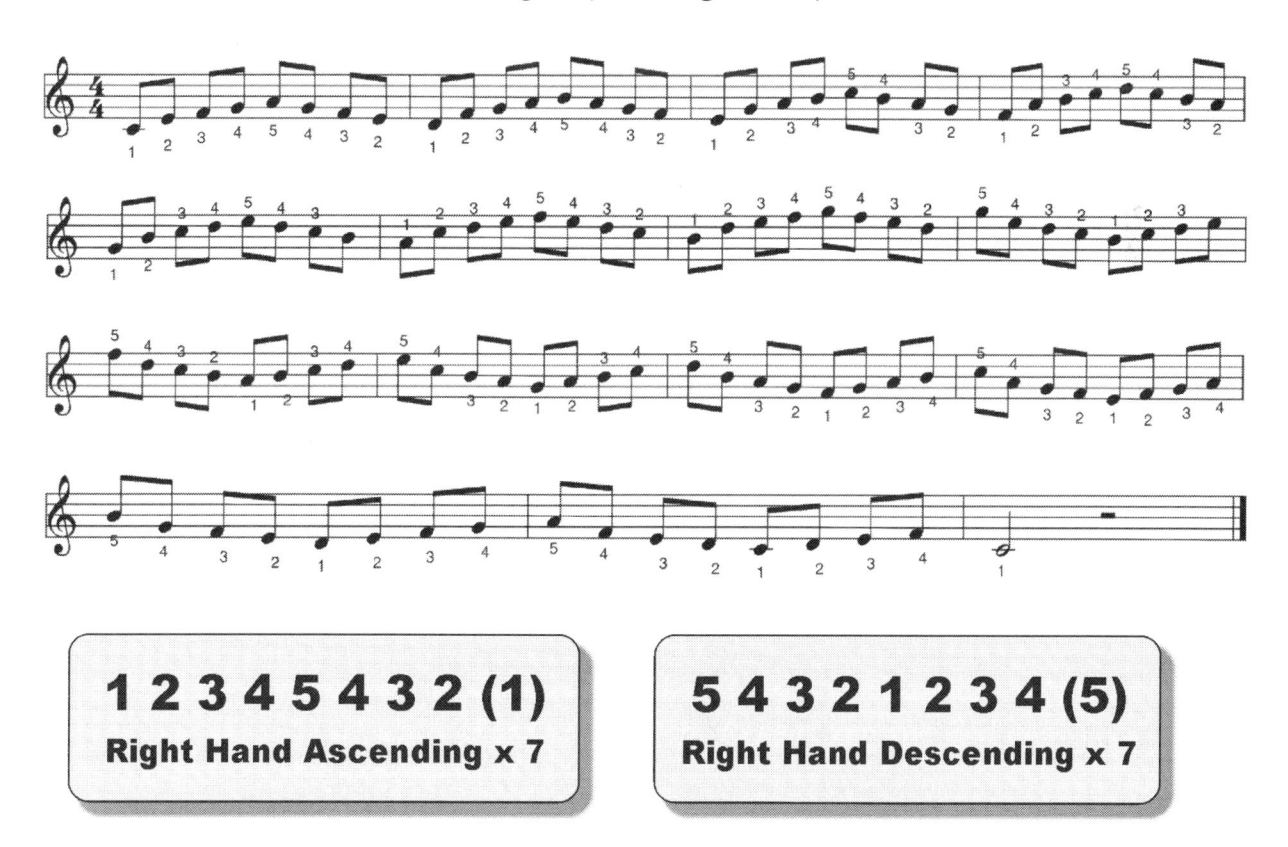

1 2 3 4 5 4 3 2 (1)
Right Hand Ascending x 7

5 4 3 2 1 2 3 4 (5)
Right Hand Descending x 7

In part 2 there are several more of these exercises that should be practiced with each hand individually and both hands together both legato and staccato, but only at speeds that you can handle. Gradually increase the speed according to your ability, but remember that speed is not important - accuracy and timing is!

Please practice the exercises in part 2 in between studying the remaining chapters.

Audio link: http://learn-keyboard.co.uk/5_finger_exercises.html or click on the graphic.

Quick link to Part 2

Casio Privia PX-5S

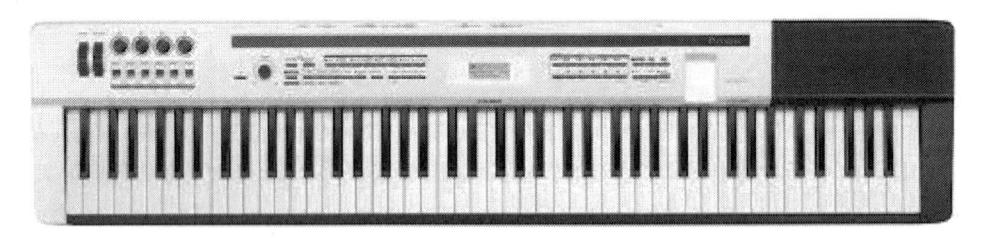

If you fancy a fillet steak for the price of a beefburger, you'll love this little beastie! And before you ask, no it doesn't come with an altimeter or a compass, but it does have a superb piano sound and one of the best hammer action key beds out there; as well as other great sounds, an arpeggiator and recording features.
Don't be put off by the 'Casio' name, this keyboard is up with the best - and can be carried with one arm by a weakling, weighing in at just over 11kg.

I was so impressed that I bought one!

Roland KC110 Keyboard Amp

Add this amp to the above keyboard and you could be making a fortune busking outside your local tube station - as <u>both</u> work on batteries!

Intervals

We've already learnt that the smallest interval in Western music is the *'semi-tone'* and this is the interval from **C - C sharp** (the first black note up from **C**) and going the other way from **C - B** (as there is no black note between **C** and **B**, but the *interval* is just the same). Playing a progression of semitones for one octave or more, starting on any note and returning to the same note is known as the *'chromatic'* scale which you'll see later.

Two or more semi-tones create larger intervals. The interval between **C** and **D** is a tone (two semi-tones) as there is a black note in-between. The interval between **F sharp** and **G sharp** is also a tone, as there is a white note in-between. And the interval between **E** and **F sharp** is also a tone as in this case there is a white note in-between.

Then as more gaps are left in-between the *intervals* become greater and are named as shown below. All the intervals up to an octave are shown here starting on **C**. Continuing beyond the octave the **2nd** plus an octave is known as a **9th**, the **4th** an **11th** and the **6th** a **13th**. Interestingly every interval can be found more than once in every major and minor scale.

Intervals from C

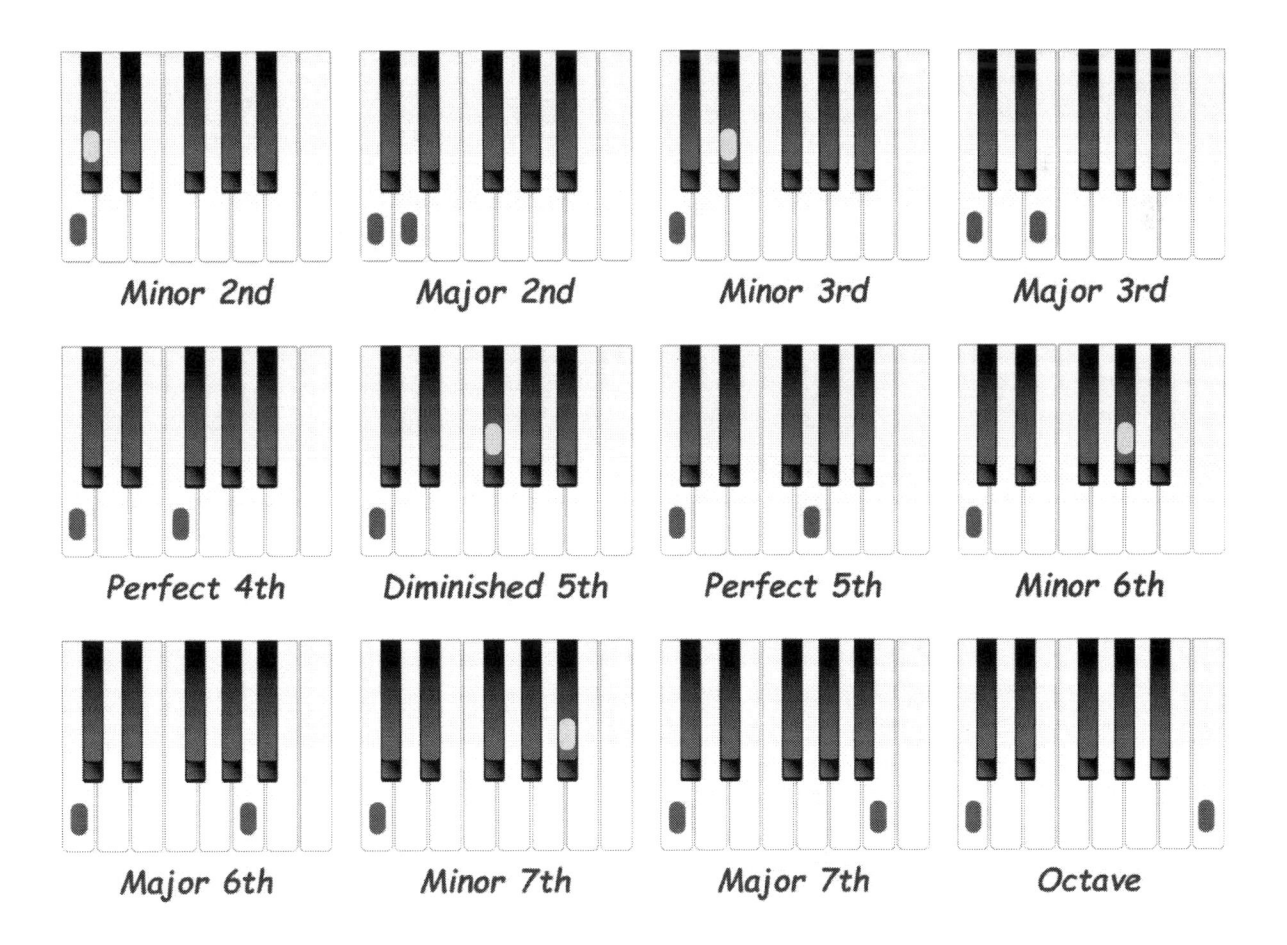

Minor 2nd *Major 2nd* *Minor 3rd* *Major 3rd*

Perfect 4th *Diminished 5th* *Perfect 5th* *Minor 6th*

Major 6th *Minor 7th* *Major 7th* *Octave*

[Musical notation showing intervals: Minor 2nd, Major 2nd, Minor 3rd, Major 3rd, Perfect 4th, Diminished 5th, Perfect 5th, Minor 6th, Major 6th, Minor 7th, Major 7th, Octave]

Note that the **minor 6th** is also sometimes called an **augmented 5th**, and a **diminished 5th** could also be called an **augmented 4th**.

You are advised to learn how these intervals sound played one note at a time from high to low and vice versa and also how they sound played together. There is an audio link on the above graphic, but you should also play these yourself and really get to know them.

Notice how the same notes occur in the **minor 3rd** and the **major 6th**; the **major 3rd** and the **minor 6th**; the **perfect 4th** and **perfect 5th**; the **minor 2nd** and the **major 7th** etc.

Kurzweil PC3K8 Workstation

[Image of Kurzweil PC3K8 keyboard]

As well as being a top of the range music production tool, this is also a superb stage piano with first class piano sounds and keybed! I may well buy one of these!

So why are intervals so important?

Because different intervals form different scales, and different chords etc., and understanding them is essential for composition as well as good theoretical understanding. They are also extremely useful in order to play by ear.

The following chart shows every interval within an octave, in all cases from the lowest note upwards. You may find it useful to print out both charts from this section.

For convenience, I've used **C sharp** instead of **D flat** etc.

Interval Chart

Interval	Notes	Semitones
Minor 2nd	C - C# - D - Eb - E - F - F# F# - G - Ab - A - Bb - B - C	1 Semitone
Major 2nd	C - D - E - F# - Ab - Bb - C C# - Eb - F - G - A - B - C#	2 Semitones
Minor 3rd	C - Eb - F# - A - C C# - E - G - Bb - C# D - F - Ab - B - D	3 Semitones
Major 3rd	C - E - Ab - C C# - F - A - C# D - F# - Bb - D Eb - G - B - Eb	4 Semitones
Perfect 4th	C - F - Bb - Eb - Ab - C# - F# F# - B - E - A - D - G - C	5 Semitones
Diminished 5th	C - F# - C C# - G - C# D - Ab - D Eb - A - Eb E - Bb - E F - B - F	6 Semitones (Tritone)
Perfect 5th	C - G - D - A - E - B - F# F# - C# - Ab - Eb - Bb - F - C	7 Semitones
Minor 6th	C - Ab - E - C C# - A - F - C# D - Bb - F# - D Eb - B - G - Eb	8 Semitones
Major 6th	C - A - F# - Eb - C C# - Bb - G - E - C# D - B - Ab - F - D	9 Semitones
Minor 7th	C - Bb - Ab - F# - E - D - C C# - B - A - G - F - Eb - C#	10 Semitones
Major 7th	C - B - Bb - A - Ab - G - F# F# - F - E - Eb - D - C# - C	11 Semitones

The link for this chapter is: http://learn-keyboard.co.uk/intervals.html .

> *"I'm trying to get people to see that we are our brothers' keeper, I still work on it. Red, white, black, brown, yellow, rich, poor, we all have the blues!"*
>
> B.B. King - (Blues King!)
>
> *Comment: His recent demise was a sad loss to the music world!*

⬅ Keys, Key Signatures & Transposition ➡

The word *'key'* has two meanings in music, one being the physical *'keys'* of the instrument and the other being the *'key'* in relation to the *'key signatures'* and which *'key'* you are playing in.

There are 12 major *'keys'* in Western music (one for each black and white note), each of which has a relative minor. With the exception of **C major** (and **A minor**) each key has a *'key signature'* which shows how many sharps or flats it has.

C major is the only major key without any sharps or flats and therefore has no key signature.

To hopefully explain this clearly, we're going to use a few diagrams showing a simple musical phrase as shown below. This phrase is in the key of **C major**.

The intervals between each note in this phrase are < 2 < 2 < 1 > 1 > 2 > 2 > 1 < 1 (each '**1**' being a semitone and each '**2**' being a tone). Now if we stay in **C major** and begin the phrase a tone higher by starting on **D** instead of **C** (as shown next) this would create a *diatonic* progression as against a transposition and the intervals will be: < 2 < 1 < 2 > 2 > 1 > 2 > 2 < 2. And the phrase would sound completely different due to the different intervals. Play these or use the audio links and hear the difference.

You may think that the second phrase is the first five notes of the **D minor** scale. And yes, it is, but it's also a mode of the **C major** scale which you'll see later when we deal with modes.

If we shove up another degree and start on **E** we'll get the next mode or *'diatonic progression'* which has different intervals again < 1 < 2 < 2 > 2 > 2 > 1 > 2 < 2.

And of course, because of the different intervals it sounds different again!

What does 'diatonic' mean?

Basically, it means using the notes only found in the scale of the key that you're in (**C major** in this case). I'll explain more about this shortly when we talk about chords.

Now if we moved the phrase up a tone from the first phrase but also kept all of the intervals the same (as the first phrase), the phrase would sound the same but at a higher pitch and would be *transposed* one tone higher from the key of **C major** into **D major** which contains some sharps (**F#** and **C#**).

And if we moved this phrase up another semitone (again keeping all the intervals the same) it would be transposed into **E flat major** as shown below.

The reason for transposition is often due to a piece being more comfortable for a singer's particular range or the range of an instrument, and certainly some pieces are easier to play in certain keys, and some just sound better. It's also often used as an embellishment half way through a piece to give it a lift for the finale. An example of this can be heard in *'Beary Glen'* on the front page of my site at http://learn-keyboard.co.uk . This piece starts in **G major** and transposes to **A major** halfway through.

Now, rather than adding accidental sharps or flats as they appear in the notation as shown in the last two diagrams, *'key signatures'* are used instead which are shown at the beginning of each piece. And these mean that all notes corresponding to the sharps or flats in the key signature should be sharpened or flattened accordingly unless otherwise shown, which would be by way of the *'natural'* symbol shown previously, or a change of key signature, which can happen at any time.

The examples shown previously in **D major** and **E flat major** are shown again below in notation view with the key signatures added instead of the accidentals.

Although the second example has three flats in the key signature, only two of these occur in the phrase.

All of the key signatures are shown in the following chart.

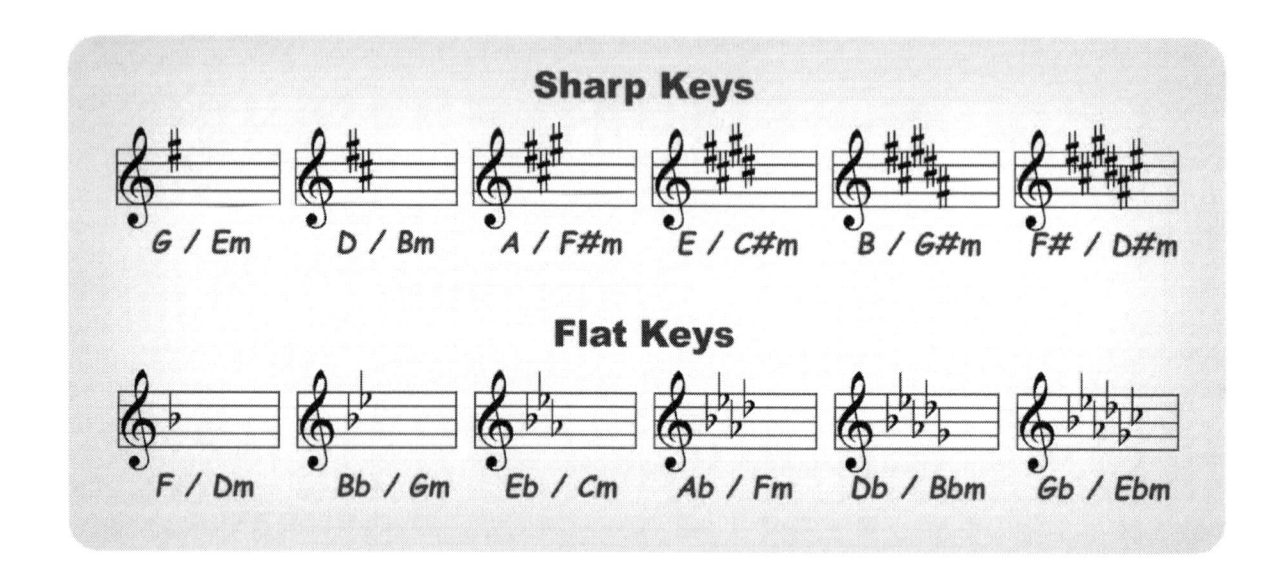

Note that **F sharp major** and **G flat major** (and the relative minors) are the same keys but simply written differently. **C major** and **A minor** are not included in the above chart as they are neither *flat keys* nor *sharp keys*.

I recommend that you learn all the scales in order of how many sharps and flats that they have, which is the order in which they are taught in classical music schools. If you find the thought of this too daunting, don't continue further than you feel comfortable.

Curiously the French word for *'key'* is *'clef'*. Whether this has any significance I don't know - probably not!

Relative Minors

The relative minor of each major key is always a minor 3rd interval below (or major 6th above), so the relative to **C major** is **A minor**. The relative minor always shares the same key signature as of the major key, but will almost certainly have additional sharps, (the 7th and possibly the 6th) as in the harmonic and melodic scales. These are not included in the key signature, but added (as accidentals) where they occur during the piece.

So how do I tell if a piece is in a major or minor key?

There's lots of ways to tell i.e.:

- If there is one sharp in the key signature and the piece starts or finishes on **E**, it's most probably in **E minor** and not **G major**;
- Minor keys often have additional accidental sharps not shown in the key signature which we'll be discussing next;
- You may notice that music written in minor keys is distinctly more *'melancholic'*;
- Usually the first few notes form a major or minor chord or if there's a chord line (as in a fake book) it's a dead giveaway.

In the example below it can be seen that there is an **F sharp** in the key signature; which indicates that the key is either **G major** or **E minor**. As the first few notes in the treble clef form an **E minor** triad and there is a **C sharp** (melodic scale 6th) in bar 3 and **D sharps** in bars 7 & 8 (harmonic and melodic ascending 7ths), it's blatantly obvious (perhaps not to you right now) from the melody alone that this piece is in the key of **E minor** and not **G major**. Furthermore, in the bass clef the first chord is **E minor**!

Don't worry if you didn't fully understand the last paragraph; we will be dealing with scales shortly after which it will make more sense!

The above example is in fact the first few bars of **'Greensleeves'** which was allegedly written by King Henry VIII but was in fact probably written by some poor starving minstrel with a runny nose (hence the title) who had his head removed so that Henry could take the credit! - This was before the days of the Musicians Union!

The link for this chapter is: http://www.learn-keyboard.co.uk/transposition.html .

> *"Put all your soul into it, play the way you feel!"*
>
> Chopin

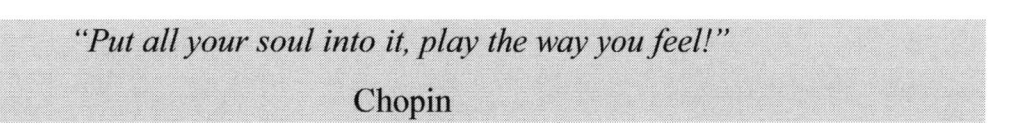

Your First Scales

In order to progress to a reasonable level of skill and theoretical understanding, it's absolutely essential that you know all of the major and minor scales. Running through all of the scales on a daily basis is a superb warm up exercise and only takes a few minutes when you have learnt them.

A Pre-Scale Exercise

In order to play scales effectively, finger crossovers are required.

The most common crossovers are achieved by passing the thumb under the third or fourth fingers ascending and passing the third or fourth fingers over the thumb when descending, as shown in the following photos.

Passing the Thumb under (ascending)

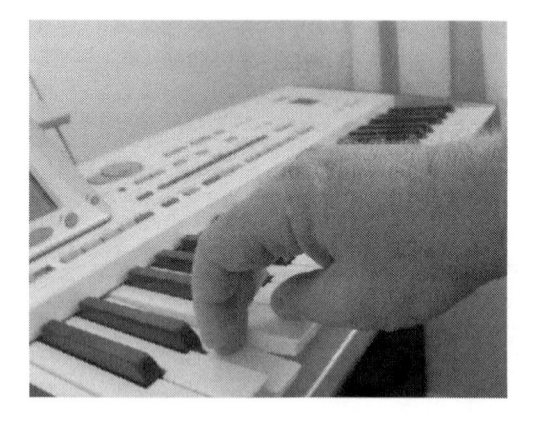

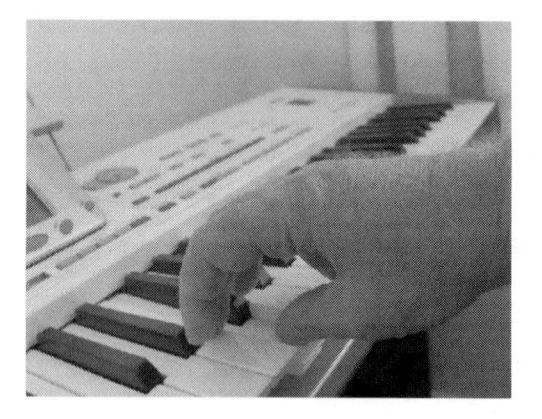

Passing the 3rd Finger over (descending)

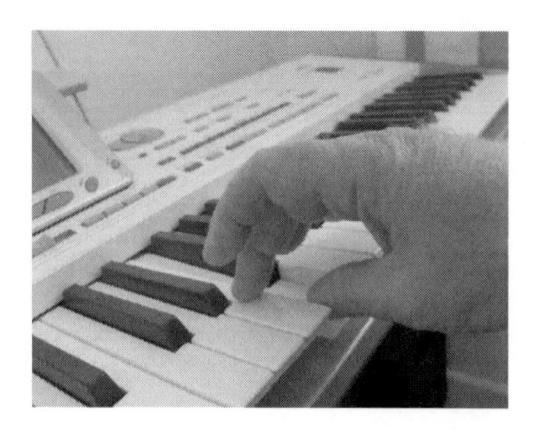

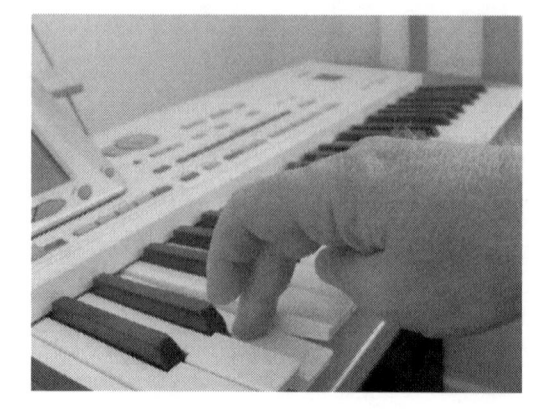

In order to help you learn this technique, I have included this next exercise, but **you must** follow the fingering as stated so that you can practice the finger crossovers.

Practice this slowly and evenly.

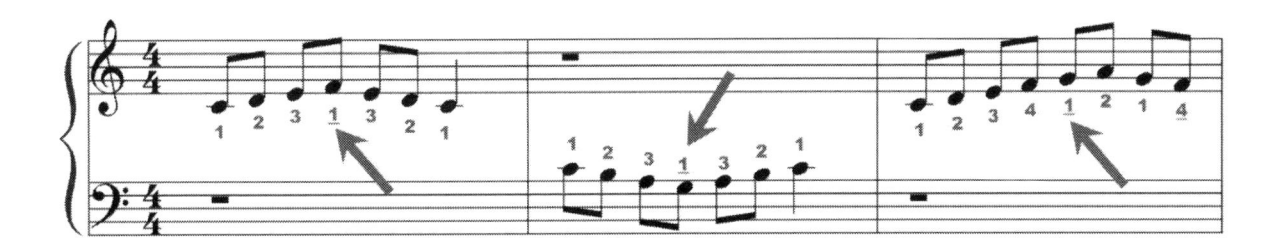

But what exactly is a scale?

A scale is a series of notes played in order usually ascending and then descending for one or more octaves.

There are different types of scales including:

- Major;
- Minor (harmonic and melodic and natural);
- Whole tone;
- Chromatic;
- Pentatonic (major and minor);
- Blues.

What differentiates the various types of scales is the intervals used in their makeup. In this book, we will be dealing with every major and minor scale in every key in keyboard and music notation view as well as the pentatonic and blues scales in the most used keys and more.

To explain further we'll firstly look at the **major** scale.

Click on any of the graphics to hear the audio examples.

The Major Scale

There are 12 major scales, one for each black and white note.

The one thing that every scale has in common is that they all follow the same pattern of intervals according to the type of scale. So, every major scale has identical intervals. The only thing that makes them different is that they start on different notes and consequently are *'pitched'* differently.

For instance, **C major** in its root mode will start on C and **D major** on **D** etc.

Look carefully at the following diagram of the **C major** scale you'll see that the intervals are as follows:

1. **C - D** is a tone (2 semitones);
2. **D - E** is a tone;
3. **E - F** is a semi-tone;
4. **F - G** is a tone;
5. **G - A** is a tone;
6. **A - B** is a tone;
7. **B - C** is a semi-tone.

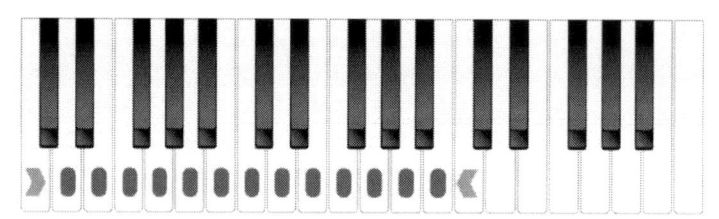

C Major Scale (2 octaves)

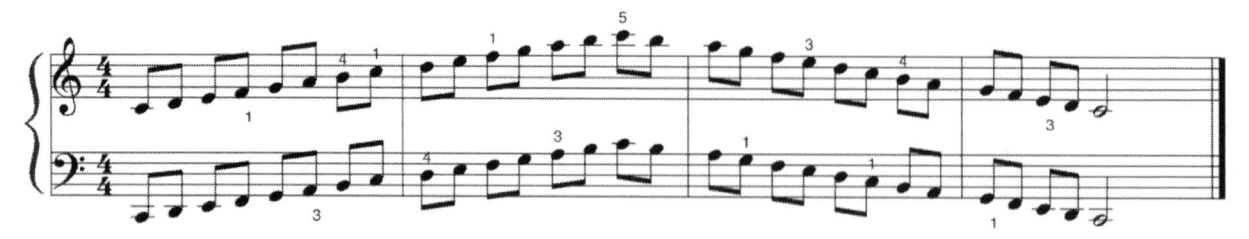

Or to put it another way it's: **2 - 2 - 1 - 2 - 2 - 2 - 1** for a one octave span, which is the interval sequence for every major scale.

So, with a bit of mathematical knowledge you could easily work out every major scale. But to save your brain they're all included herein.

In part 2 you'll see every major scale in every key shown both in keyboard and notation view. In all cases I've included the *important* fingering. Where no fingering is included, it simply follows consecutively.

The degrees of the major and minor scales are named as follows:

- Root - Tonic;
- 2nd - Supertonic;
- 3rd - Mediant;
- 4th - Sub Dominant;
- 5th - Dominant;
- 6th - Sub Mediant;
- 7th - Leading Note or Sub Tonic;
- 8th - Octave (Tonic).

The most important ones to remember are the *'tonic'* and *'dominant'*.

Minor Scales

Each major key has a relative minor which shares the same key signature as the major key. The relative minor can always be found by counting three semitones down from the first note (the tonic) of the major scale. For instance, three semitones down from **C** is **A**, therefore:

- **A minor** is the relative to **C major**;
- **E minor** is the relative to **G major**;
- **B minor** is the relative to **D major**;
- **D minor** is the relative to **F major** etc., etc.

Although the minor keys share the same key signature as their relative major keys, each minor key has one or more additional sharp(s) and these are always shown as accidentals as and when they occur (but never in the key signature). In the harmonic minor scale, there will only ever be one (extra) sharp, which is always the leading note - one semitone down from the tonic (the first and last note of the scale).

So, what is the difference between a major scale and a minor scale?

The difference is caused because of the different intervals. If you've been paying attention you should know that the interval sequence for all major scales is: **2 - 2 - 1 - 2 - 2 - 2 - 1**.

There are two conventional minor scales, the *'harmonic'* and the *'melodic'*, both of which have different interval sequences. The *'natural'* minor scale is simply the major scale beginning and ending on the relative minor, but even this will also have different intervals (to the major scale) due to its different starting position. This is also known as the *Aeolian mode* starting on **A** - in the case of the **A minor natural** scale.

The Harmonic Minor Scale

If you look carefully at the next keyboard diagram showing the **A Harmonic minor** scale you will see that the intervals are: **2 - 1 - 2 - 2 - 1 - 3 - 1**.

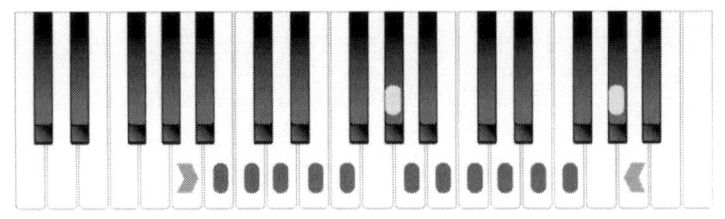

A Harmonic Minor Scale (2 octaves)

If you compare this sequence to the **A major** scale you'll see that the difference is that both the 3rd and 6th notes are flattened by a semitone.

The Melodic Minor Scale

The melodic minor scale has a minor 3rd similar to the harmonic scale, but then ascends with a *sharpened* 6th and 7th (**F#** and **G#** in **A minor**), but then descends with a *natural* 6th and 7th (**F** and **G** natural in **A minor**). It's just a bit more complicated, but well worth the effort to learn. So, the intervals are:

- **2 - 1 - 2 - 2 - 2 - 2 - 1** ascending (from the bottom); and
- **2 - 2 - 1 - 2 - 2 - 1 - 2** descending (from the top), which is exactly the same as the *natural* minor scale shown next.

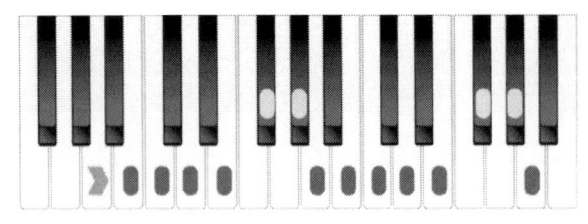

A Melodic Minor Scale (Ascending) 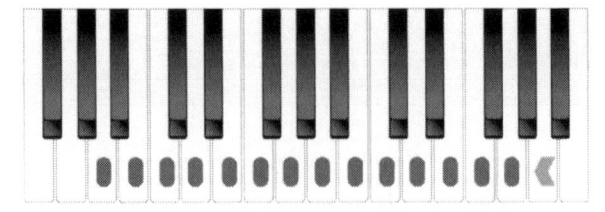   *A Melodic Minor Scale (Descending)*

The Natural Minor Scale

As already mentioned, the natural minor scale is exactly the same as the relative major starting on the 6th note also known as the *Aeolian mode*. All the modes of the major scale will be shown later. The intervals for this scale are: **2 - 1 - 2 - 2 - 1 - 2 - 2**.

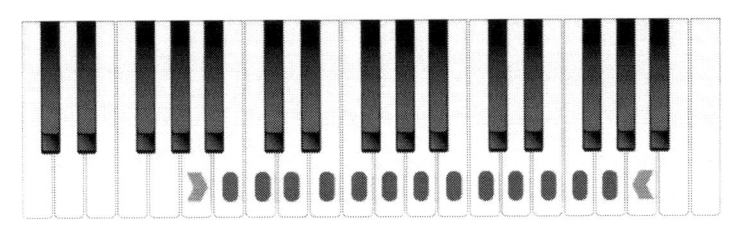

A Minor (Natural) Scale (2 octaves)

Ideally all of the major and minor scales should be practiced with each hand alone and then together for at least two octaves (four is better) both legato and staccato. Don´t try and practice them too quickly, it´s far better to practice them slowly, smoothly and accurately. Speed will come on its own later. All are shown in part 2 in the order that they should be learnt. Once you are familiar with them they can be practiced in any order.

The Whole Tone Scale

As its name suggests all the intervals in this scale are a tone apart. Using this scale can create an *'eerie theme'* although it would become boring after a short while. I wouldn't say that that this is a scale that you particularly need to practice, but needs mentioning nevertheless.

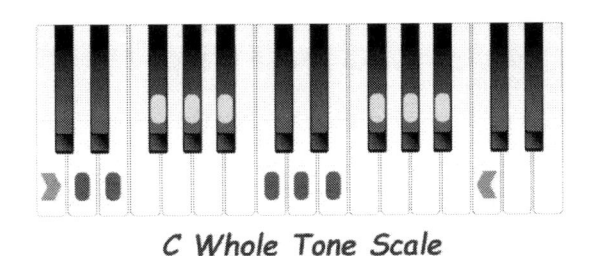

C Whole Tone Scale

The Chromatic Scale

The chromatic scale is one on its own as it hits every note (black and white) in order. It's shown here starting and finishing on **C** for two octaves with left hand and right-hand fingering. The intervals between each note ascending and descending is a semitone.

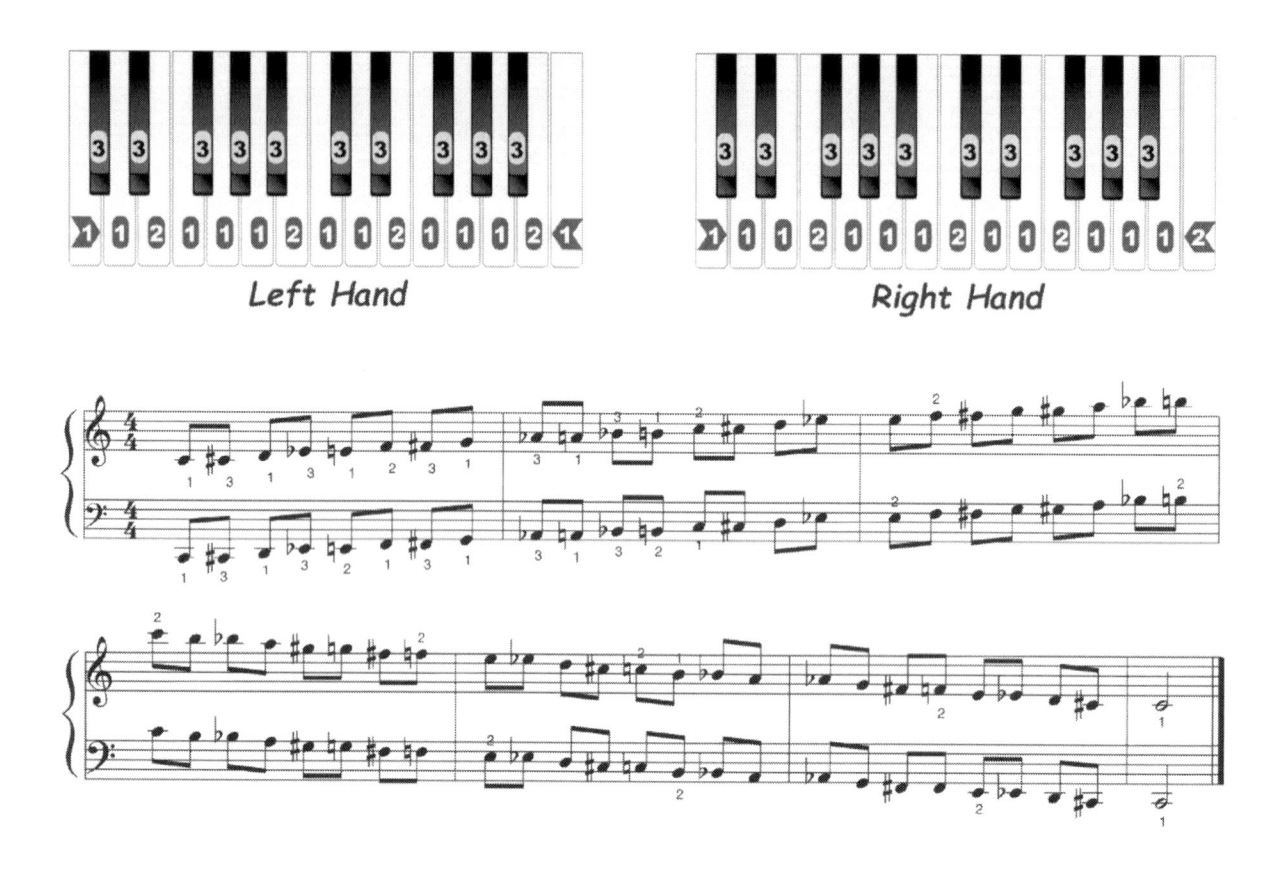

Ideally this scale should be practiced for two or more octaves both staccato and legato starting and finishing on various notes. The fingering remains the same regardless of which note you start on.

The trick to learning this scale easily is to remember where the **2nd** fingers go - **F** and **C** in the right hand and **E** and **B** in the left hand!

Korg Grandstage 73 Keys

At the time of editing this book, this is Korg's latest Stage Piano available with 73 keys or 88. Looks great, but not had a chance to try this yet.

Pentatonic and Blues Scales

The pentatonic and blues scales are commonly used in pop, blues and jazz improvisations. If this is your intention, then the following scales will be vitally important to you.

C Major Pentatonic scale (C6/9)

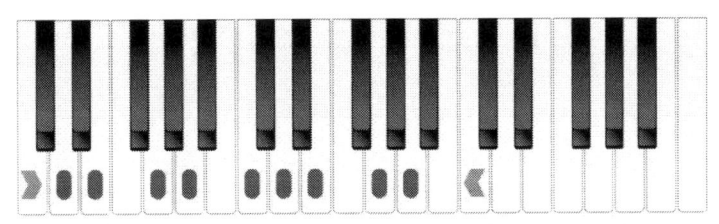

C Major Pentatonic Scale (2 octaves)

The **C major pentatonic** scale is simply a major triad - **C, E & G** with an added **6th** and **9th** - **A & D**. These notes form the **C 6/9** chord.

A Minor Pentatonic scale (Am7sus4)

The minor pentatonic scale is exactly the same as the relative major pentatonic scale (as it has the same notes), but simply starts on the relative minor. The **A minor pentatonic** is constructed using the minor triad - **A, C & E** and then adding the **4th & 7th** - **D & G**. These notes form the **Am7sus4** chord.

Notice that there are no semitones in the major / minor pentatonic scales - only minor 3rds and tones.

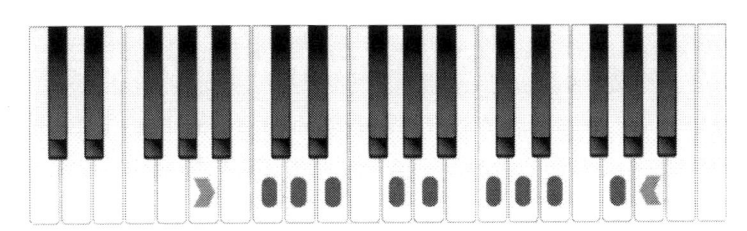

A Minor Pentatonic Scale (2 octaves)

The ♭3rd Pentatonic Scale

This scale is exactly the same as the major pentatonic with the exception that the 3rd is flattened.

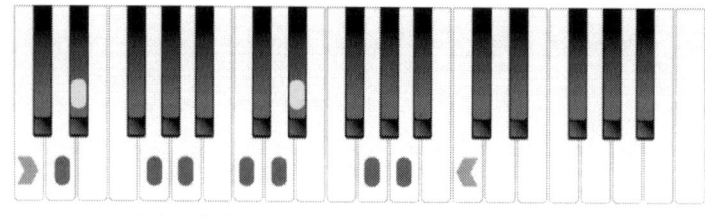

C♭3rd Penatonic Scale (2 octaves)

The Blues Scale

Notice the similarity between the **A Blues** scale and the **Am Pentatonic** scale. Both would work perfectly alright across an **A minor** chord. But interestingly the **'A' blues** scale is also often used in the major key (**A major**) which has no relationship to **A minor** or **C major** at all!

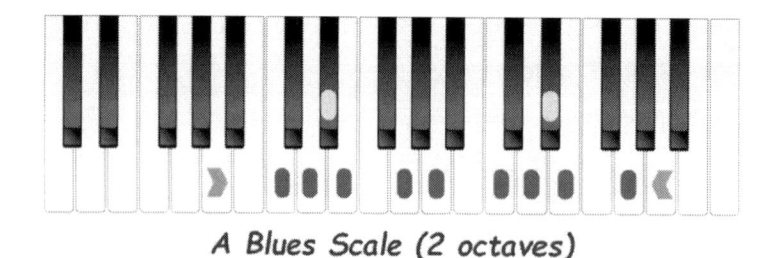

A Blues Scale (2 octaves)

So, to recap and hopefully make this perfectly clear - the major and relative minor pentatonic scales are *exactly* the same as one another except that they start on different notes. The blues scale is the same as the minor pentatonic with an added flattened 5th passing note!

The pentatonic and blues scales are shown in detail in part 2 in the keys in which they are mainly used.

The audio link for this section is: http://learn-keyboard.co.uk/scales_2.html

Quick link to Part 2 (Scales in Full)

⬅ Scale Modes Explanation ➡

As previously mentioned all scales follow the same pattern of intervals. The intervals for the major scale starting on the tonic is 2 tones followed by a semitone, then 3 tones and a semitone: **2 - 2 - 1 - 2 - 2 - 2 - 1** - (sometimes written: **T - T - s - T - T - T - s**). By starting the scale on a different degree, the intervals will be different thereby creating a different sound - these are called modes.

The modes of the **C major** scale are shown for one octave below. Click on the graphics to hear them if you want to

Ionian Mode

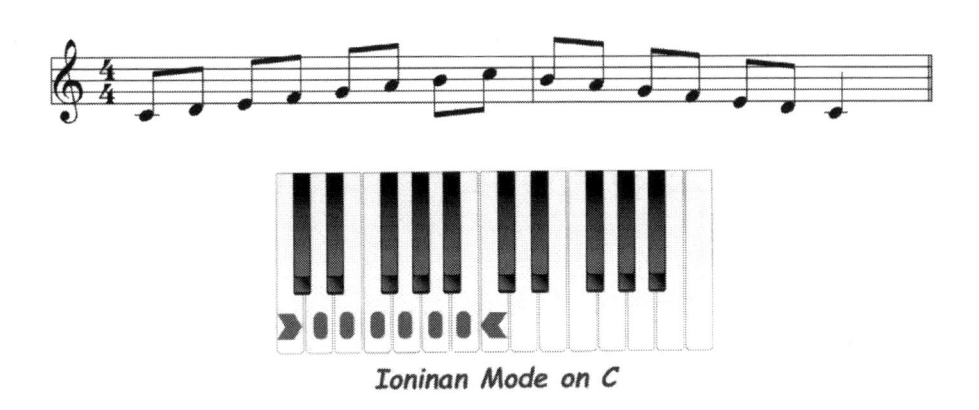

Ioninan Mode on C

The *'Ionian'* mode is the *'normal root position mode'* starting on the tonic and the intervals are **2 - 2 - 1 - 2 - 2 - 2 - 1**. In the key of **C major**, the notes are: **C - D - E - F - G - A - B - C**.

Dorian Mode

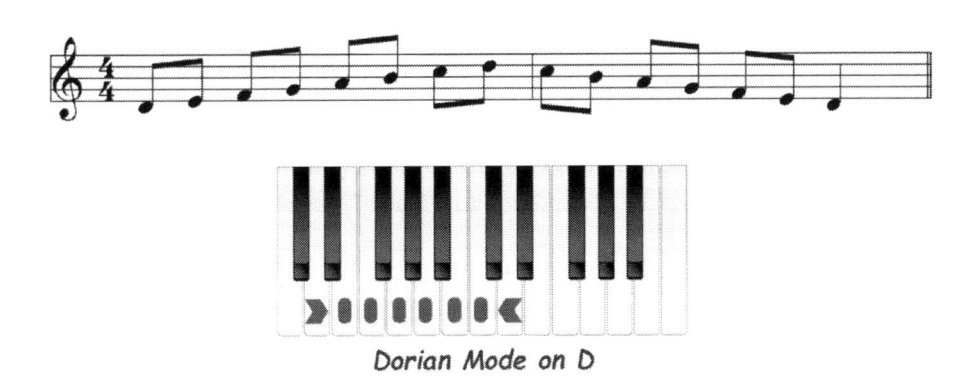

Dorian Mode on D

The *'Dorian'* mode begins on the 2nd degree (supertonic) of the major scale and the intervals are **2 - 1 - 2 - 2 - 2 - 1 - 2**. In the key of **C major**, the notes are: **D - E - F - G - A - B - C - D**.

Phrygian Mode

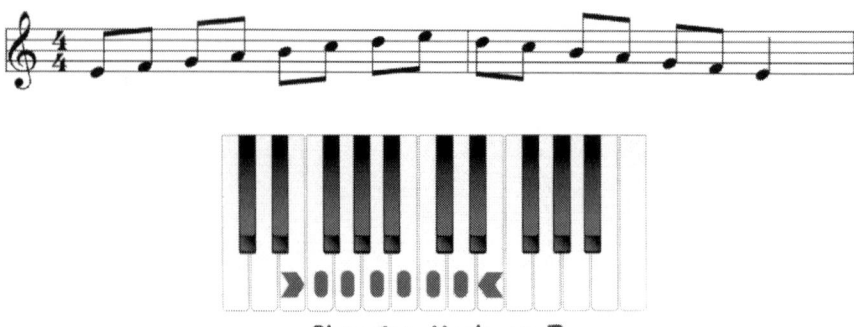

Phrygian Mode on E

The *'Phrygian'* mode begins on the 3rd degree (the mediant) of the major scale and the intervals are **1 - 2 - 2 - 2 - 1 - 2 - 2**. In the key of **C major** this begins / ends on **E**.

Lydian Mode

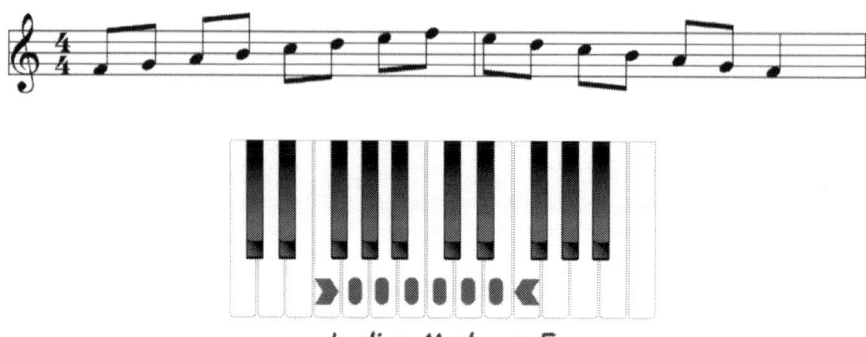

Lydian Mode on F

The *'Lydian'* mode begins on the 4th degree (sub-dominant) of the major scale and the intervals are **2 - 2 - 2 - 1 - 2 - 2 - 1**. In the key of **C major** this begins / ends on **F**.

Mixolydian Mode

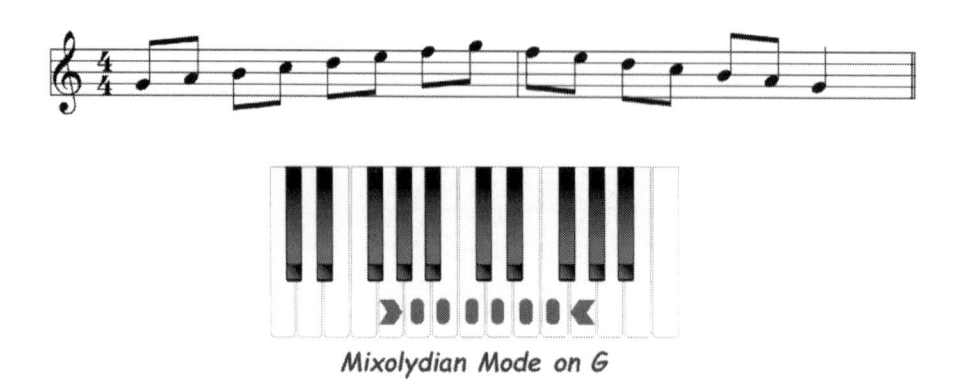

Mixolydian Mode on G

The Mixolydian mode begins on the 5th degree (dominant) of the major scale and the intervals are **2 - 2 - 1 - 2 - 2 - 1 - 2**. In the key of **C major** this begins / ends on **G**.

Aeolian Mode

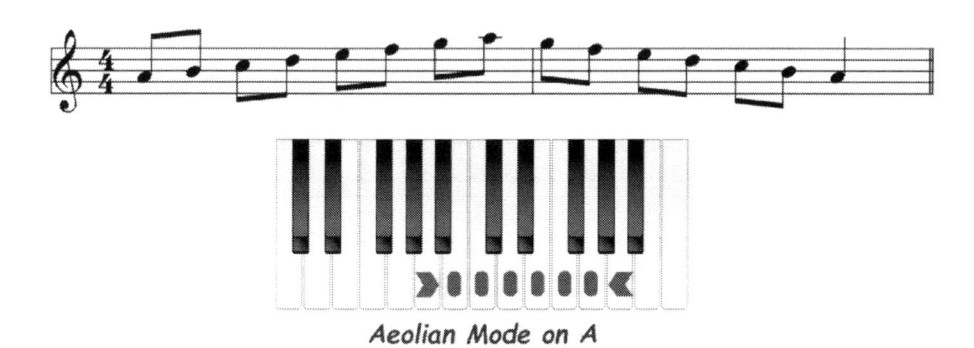

Aeolian Mode on A

The *'Aeolian'* mode begins on the 6th degree (sub-mediant) of the major scale and the intervals are **2 - 1 - 2 - 2 - 1 - 2 - 2**. In the key of **C major** this begins / ends on **A**.

This mode is also the *'natural'* minor scale, in the fact that it starts on the relative minor, but *without* the added sharps in the harmonic and melodic scales. This mode is particularly important for improvising, along with the pentatonic and blues scales.

Locrian Mode

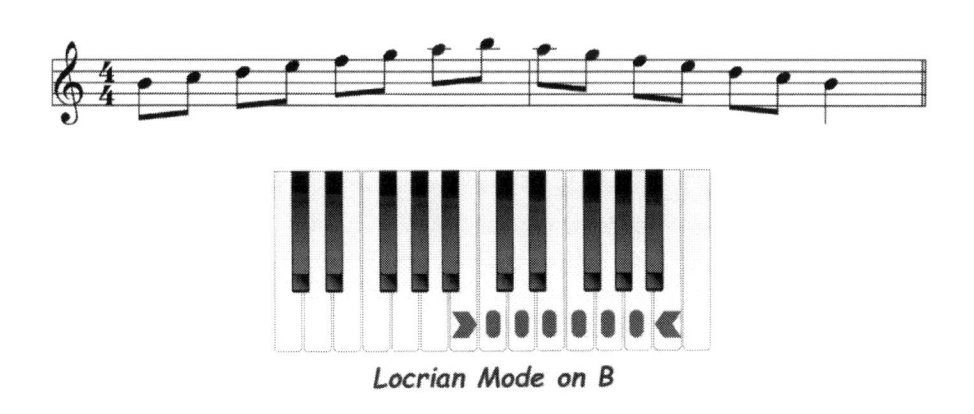

Locrian Mode on B

The *'Locrian'* mode begins on the 7th degree (leading note) of the major scale and the intervals are **1 - 2 - 2 - 1 - 2 - 2 - 2**. In the key of **C major** this begins / ends on **B**.

I wouldn't suggest practicing these until you are thoroughly confident with the various scales in the root (Ionian) mode, but ultimately, they are very important although it doesn't matter whether you remember the names or not!

When you're ready just practice the most important major scales starting on different degrees and you've got it!

I was going to include the two octave examples of all the modes in most keys in part 2, but for fear of boring you senseless, have decided not to. As I have already written these, I will be adding them as a free supplement on my website, so check there if you want them.

Modes of the Pentatonic Scales

It makes no difference whether we use the **major** or **minor** pentatonic scales as they contain exactly the same notes as shown previously and which will be made very clear shortly. But we'll start with the **C major pentatonic** scale in its root position as shown below.

Note that in all modes of this scale there are no semitone intervals - they are always tones (2) or minor 3rd (3) intervals as shown.

Mode 1

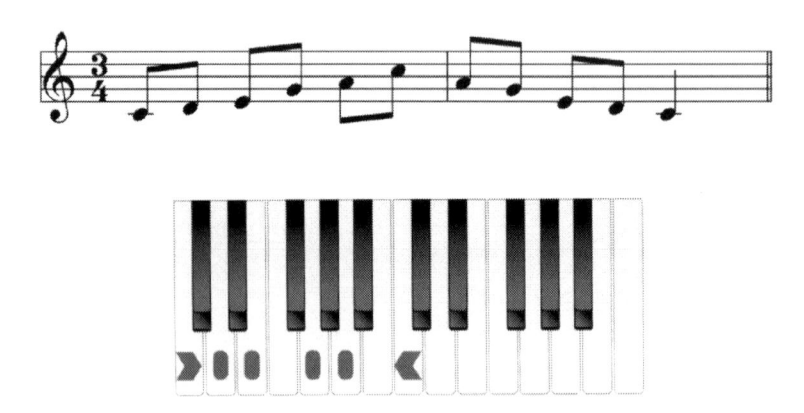

In this first mode (above) the intervals are **2 - 2 - 3 - 2 - 3**. In the key of **C major / A minor** (as shown here) the notes are: **C - D - E - G - A - C**.

Mode 2

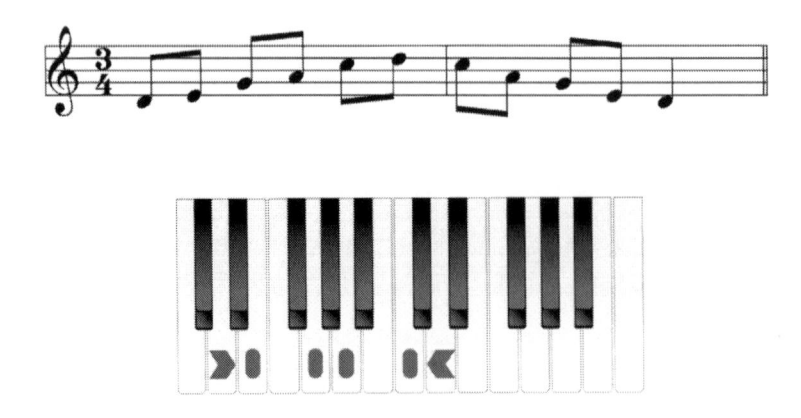

In this mode, the intervals are **2 - 3 - 2 - 3 - 2**. In the key of **C major / A minor** (as shown here) the notes are: **D - E - G - A - C - D**.

Mode 3

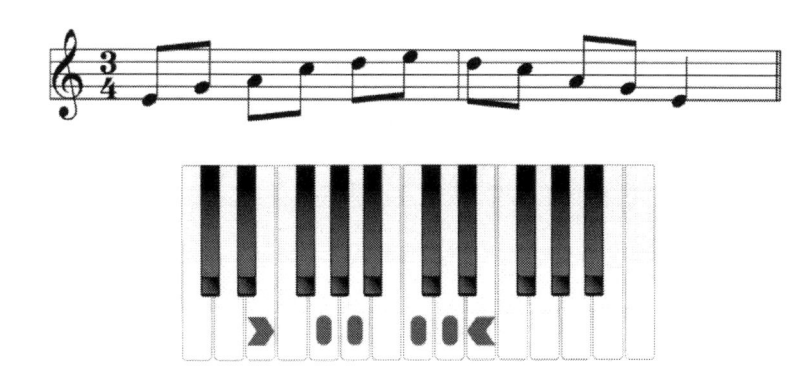

In this mode, the intervals are **3 - 2 - 3 - 2 - 2**. In the key of **C major / A minor** (as shown here) the notes are: **E - G - A - C - D - E**.

Mode 4

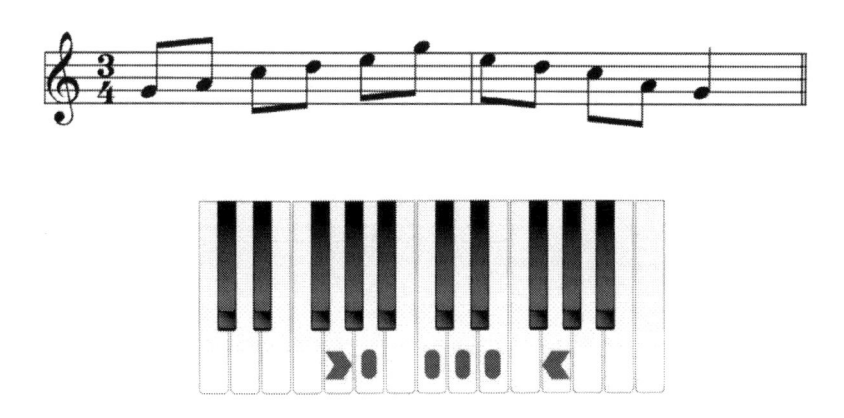

In this mode, the intervals are **2 - 3 - 2 - 2 - 3**. In the key of **C major / A minor** (as shown here) the notes are: **G - A - C - D - E - G**.

Mode 5

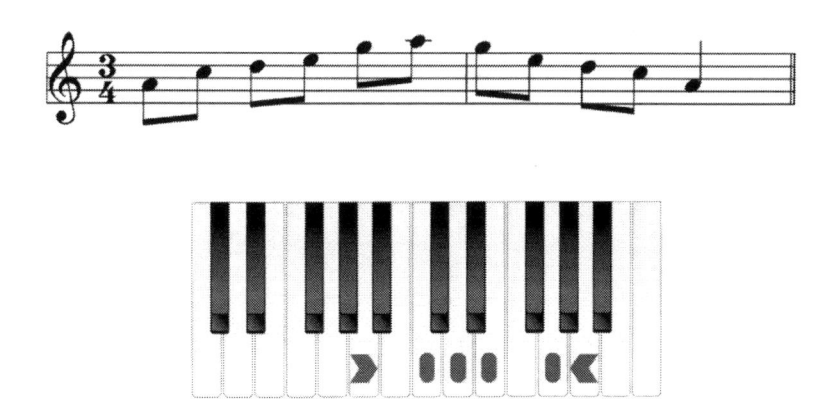

In this mode, the intervals are **3 - 2 - 2 - 3 - 2**. In the key of **C major / A minor** (as shown here) the notes are: **A - C - D - E - G - A**.

This last mode is the root position (mode) of the **Am pentatonic** scale. Never forget that the major pentatonic and the relative minor pentatonic are different modes of the **same scale** and are the notes of the **major 6/9** and **minor 7sus4** chords!

The audio link for this section is: http://learn-keyboard.co.uk/modes_2.html .

Two manual Harpsichord

One of the forerunners to the piano where the strings are plucked instead of struck, which creates a unique sound - I love them! Very few harpsichords are commercially available today, but the sounds can be reproduced on many digital instruments.

> *"Show yourself more human than critical and your pleasure will increase!"*
> Domenico Scarlatti - (Famous for Harpsichord Sonatas)
> *Comment: Wise words from a master! I also love his Sonatas!*

CPS Spacestation V3 Speaker

This thing has to be heard to be believed - stereo sound out of one speaker!
I don't think you could get better for small gigs!

Chord Construction

Every musical piece (in classical, jazz and pop) is formed around a progression of chords, sometimes simple and sometimes very complicated. Either way learning all of the basic chords is absolutely essential and even more so if using auto accompaniment features. Understanding how chords are constructed is essential for correct theoretical understanding - particularly for composition and improvisation.

The basic triad chords are constructed by piling notes of the scale on top of each other a third apart and playing them simultaneously. Using the scale of **C major** and referring to the diagram below you can see that the first and most important chord of the key is made as follows: **C** (root note - the tonic), **E** (3rd note of the scale - the mediant) and **G** (5th note of the scale - the dominant). This is the root position of the **C major** chord.

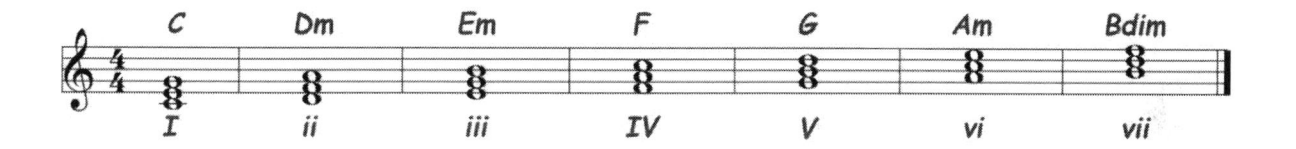

C	Dm	Em	F	G	Am	Bdim
I	ii	iii	IV	V	vi	vii

Moving up the scale, starting on **D**, we achieve a **D minor** triad, and then **E minor**, **F major**, **G major**, **A minor** and **B diminished**. These chords are the *'diatonic'* triads in the key of **C major**, which means that they are all *derived* from the notes of the **C major** scale and as such contain white notes only, (as there are no black notes in the **C major** scale).

Practice these with each hand separately and notice how they sound.

Notice that the difference between a major and minor triad is that the intervals in a *major triad* are a *'major 3rd'* followed by a *'minor 3rd'*, whereas the *minor triad* has a *'minor 3rd'* followed by a *'major 3rd'*. The *diminished triad* consists of two *'minor 3rds'* and the *augmented (+5) triad* has two *'major 3rds'*.

The Roman Numerals shown signify the degree of the scale which each chord starts on. In all cases the diatonic chords of a major scale contain *major* chords at the **I**, **IV** and **V** degrees *minor* chords at the **ii**, **iii** and **vi** degrees and *diminished* at the **vii** degree. Usually (but not always) the minor and diminished chords are signified with lower case Roman Numerals (**ii, iii, vi & vii**).

By adding further thirds above each triad, **CM7** is achieved, then **Dm7**, **Em7**, **FM7**, **G7**, **Am7**, **Bm7♭5**. By adding further notes at third intervals more complicated chords like **9ths** and **13ths** etc. will be created; these will be covered shortly.

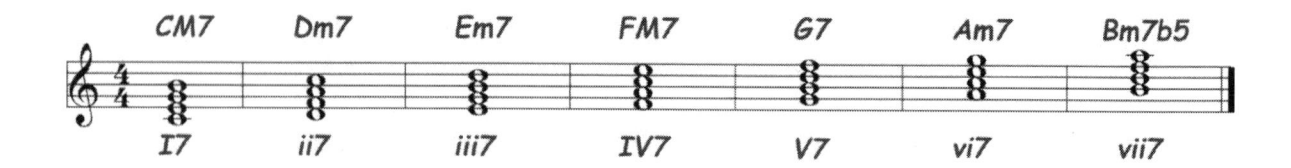

```
    CM7      Dm7      Em7      FM7      G7       Am7      Bm7b5
    I7       ii7      iii7     IV7      V7       vi7      vii7
```

In the keyboard views below I have only shown the **7th** chords; to see the triads, simply omit the 7ths (the last note of each chord). Please also notice that some of the 7th chords are signified with a capital '**M**' and others with a lower case '**m**', this is *vitally important* and will be explained shortly.

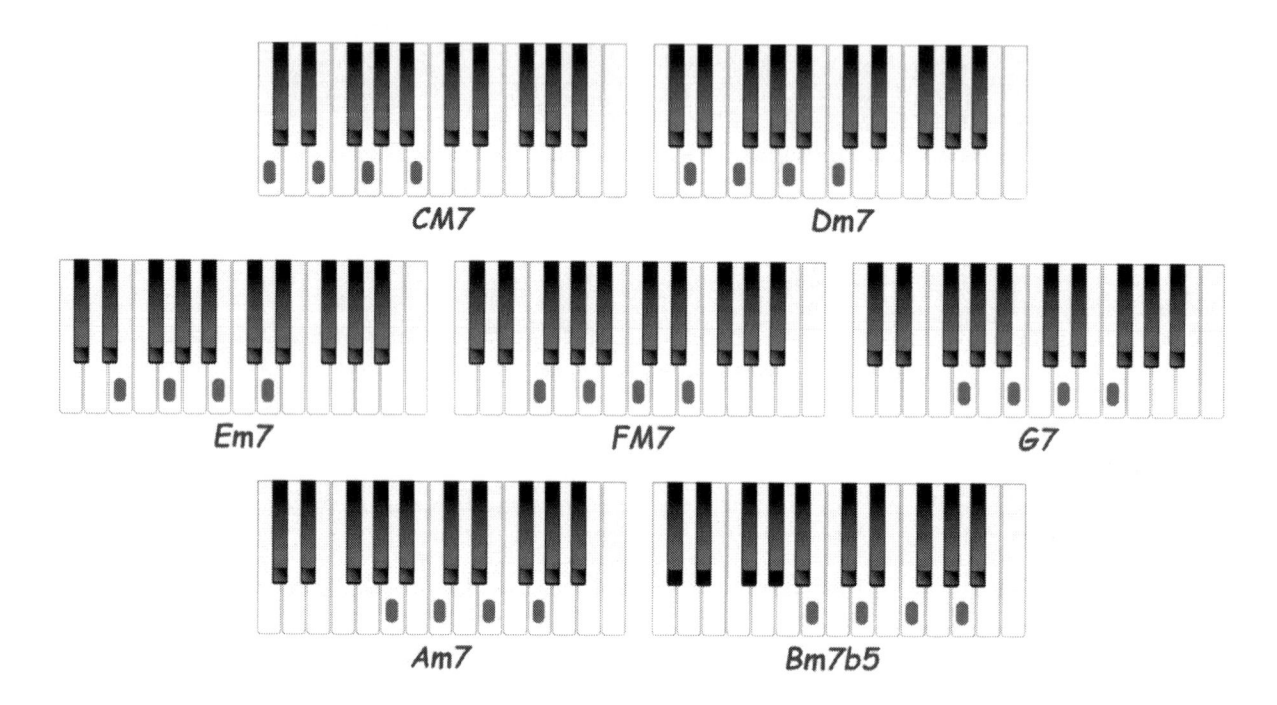

CM7   *Dm7*

Em7   *FM7*   *G7*

Am7   *Bm7b5*

Additional chords can be created from the relative minor scales due to the harmonic and melodic (scales) differences, charts for these are shown in part 2 - quick link.

Note that it's important to remember that while many musical compositions will use only the diatonic chords (found naturally in the relevant scale) and no other, it´s by no means necessarily the case. You can use any chord in any key if you can make it work, but the diatonic chords (as found in the scale) are more likely to work!

A Few Important points about 7th Chords

Major 7th (M7) chords must not be confused with what is generally called a *'normal'* **7th (7)** chord (which really should be called a ***dominant* 7th** but often isn't). **Major 7th** chords have a major 7th (one semitone down from the octave) whereas the *'normal'* (dominant) **7th** chords are the same major triad with a minor 7th (2 semitones down from the octave). **Minor 7th (m7)** chords are like the *'normal'* *dominant* 7th chords but have a minor 3rd. And a **minor** chord with a **major 7th**, would be written **(C)mM7** although I have to say that this one is the least common, but it needs mentioning nevertheless.

Copyright © Martin Woodward 2011 & 2017

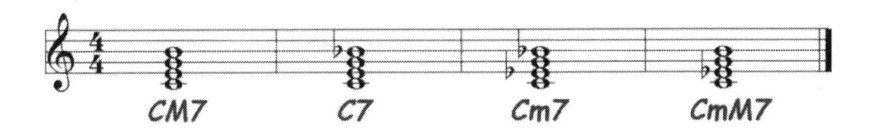

And again, in keyboard view.

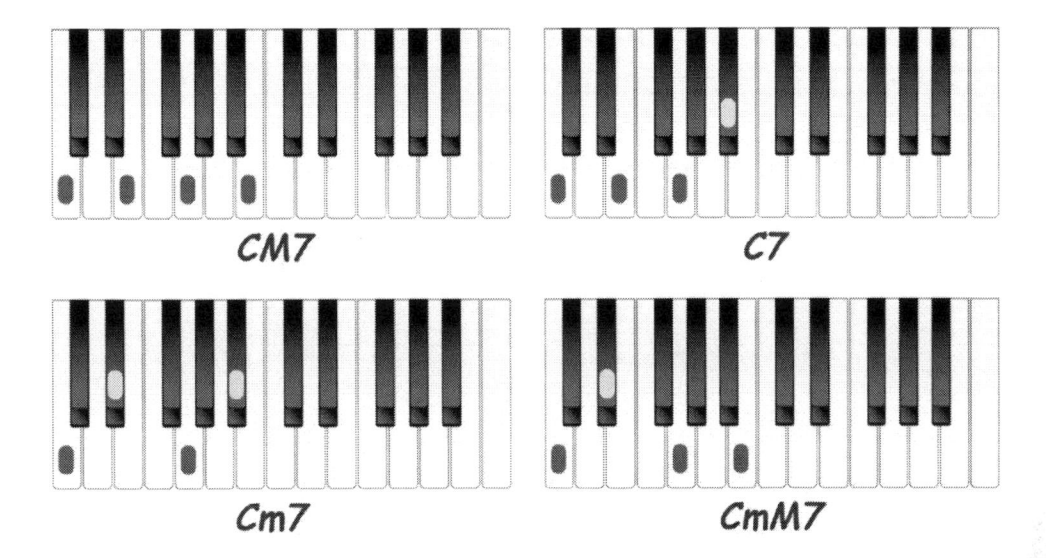

The only *'normal'* 7th chord naturally occurring in the major scales (diatonic) is the *dominant* 7th (which is **G7** in the **C major** scale). The *dominant* 7th chord resolving to the tonic chord (**V7 - I**) is the strongest of all progressions and is used repeatedly in all types of music (classical, pop, jazz etc.). Notice the difference in the sounds of these chords and that they are totally different and can *NEVER* be substituted with one another.

The same applies to **9ths**. What is normally known as a **9th**, is a *dominant* 7th (major triad with minor **7th**) with an added **9th**, but a **major 9th** is a **major 7th** with the same added **9th** and is be written **(C)M9**.

To make this completely clear:

- **C7** is a major chord with a minor 7th;
- **CM7** is a major chord with a major 7th:
- **Cm7** is a minor chord with a minor 7th;
- **CmM7** is a minor chord with a major 7th.

And the only one of the above chords to appear in the notes of the **C major** scale is **CM7** and as such is the only one which is *diatonic* in the key of **C major**.

Play these now and hear the difference.

Suspended 2nd and 4th Chords

The *'suspended 2nd'* (also known as *'sus9'*) and *'suspended 4th'* (also known as *'sus'*) chords desperately want to resolve to the major chord as shown here. These are used extensively in all types of music, but perhaps more so in country music.

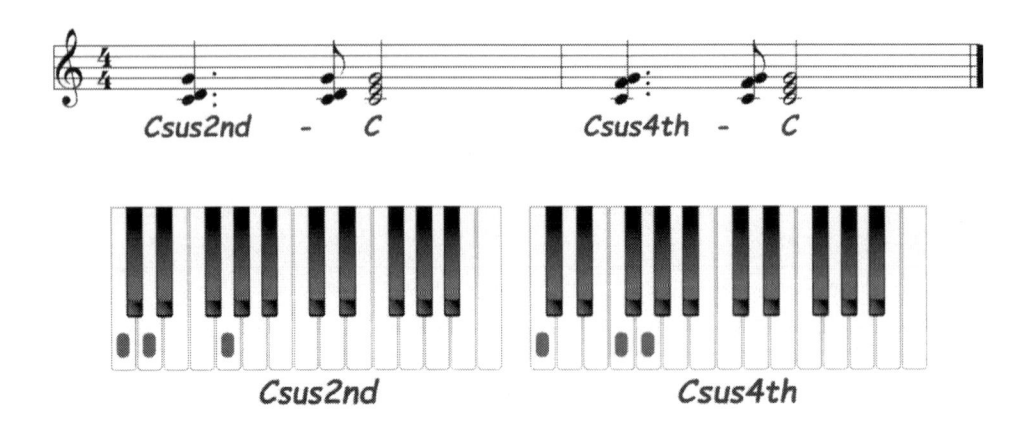

Note that these chords do not have a 3rd and as such are neither major nor minor, but as they *generally* resolve to the major chord, they can perhaps be considered more major than minor, but they could be either.

Diminished 7th Chords

You may be confused about the difference between a true *'diminished 7th'* chord and what is often called a *'half diminished 7th'*, (if not now you probably will be at some point).

Both have the diminished triad which is **B**, **D** & **F** (**B dim**, the only diminished triad in **C major**). You should notice that the triad consists of two *minor 3rd* intervals.

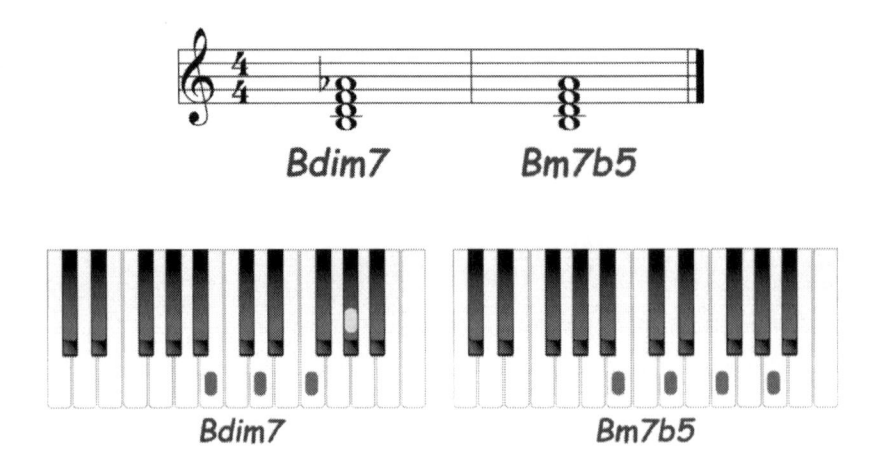

If we add the 7th this will put an 'A' at the top (which is a *major 3rd* interval above **F**) and this is often known as **B (half) dim7**. But this chord could also be known as **Bm7b5** - (**Bm7 flattened 5th**), because that is exactly what it is! Put a **G** at the bottom of this chord and it would become **G9**, which means that **Bm7♭5** could be used as a substitute for **G9** with no problem.

Now instead of adding the **A** (7th) at the top, if we add **G#** (a *minor 3rd* interval above **F**) we will end up with a true *diminished 7th* chord. Although **G#** (**A♭**) is not in the **C major** scale, it is in the relative **A minor**, both in the harmonic and melodic scales and is therefore a diatonic degree in the key of **A minor**.

The symbols shown below are often used to signify the *diminished 7th* and the *half diminished 7th* chords.

Diminished 7th Symbols

O   Full Diminished 7th Symbol
Ø   Half Diminished 7th Symbol

You may notice that the **B, D, F & G#** *diminished* 7 chords are all the same - the only difference being in the bass notes!

A beautiful example of the use of *diminished 7th* chords and arpeggios can be heard in Beethoven's **'Moonlight Sonata'** - a superb timeless piece of music!

Augmented Chords

Augmented chords are often used *'en passant'*, i.e. stepping up from **C - Am** as shown here or from **C - F**.

The *'augmented'* triad consists of two *major 3rd* intervals.

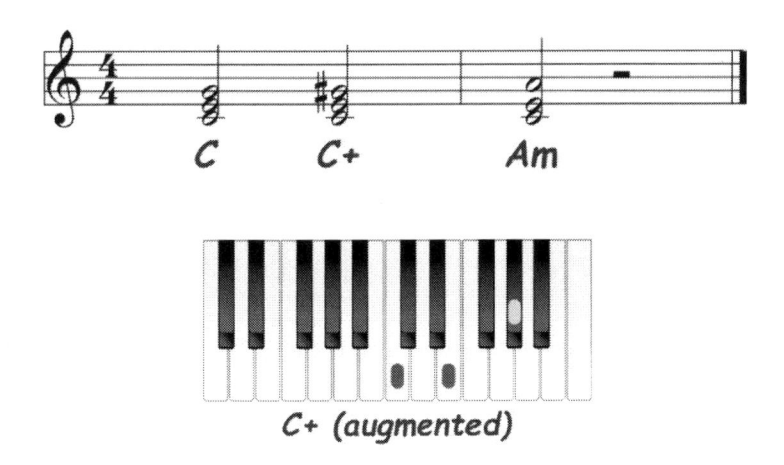

C   C+   Am

C+ (augmented)

But similar to the diminished chords you may notice that **C, E & G#** augmented are all the same chords, being identified apart only by the bass notes.

Copyright © Martin Woodward 2011 & 2017

73

Inversions

By moving the **C** to the top of the first **C major** triad and making the **E** the bottom note, the *'1st inversion'* is created. Similarly, by moving both the **C** and **E** above, the *'2nd inversion'* is constructed. This works the same with full four note chords as well as with triads as shown below.

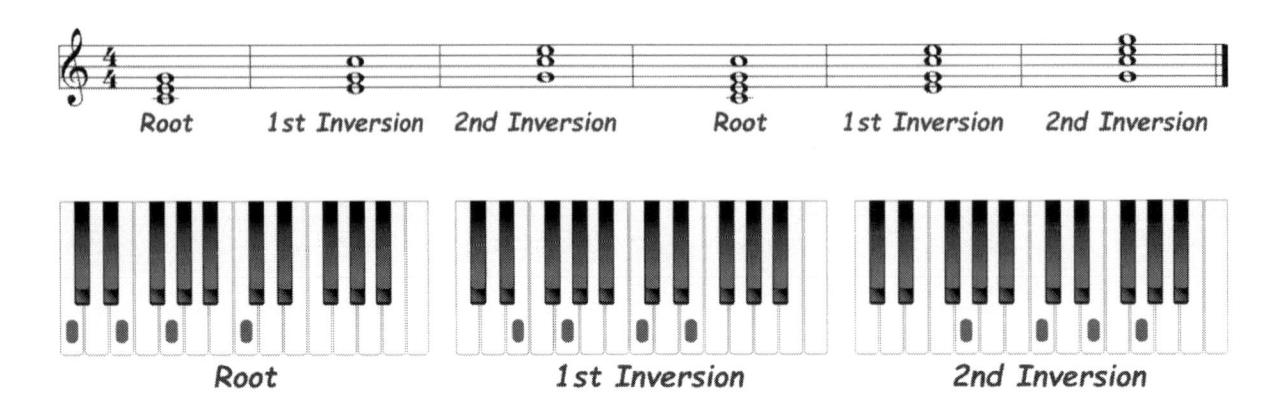

Root   1st Inversion   2nd Inversion   Root   1st Inversion   2nd Inversion

Root   1st Inversion   2nd Inversion

Using inversions can be useful when changing chords with the minimum amount of finger movements. For instance, the **C major** *'root position'* can be altered to an **E minor** triad simply by changing the C to B, or to an **A minor** triad by changing the G to A. And by moving only two fingers a short distance **C major** can be easily changed to **F major** or **G major** as shown below.

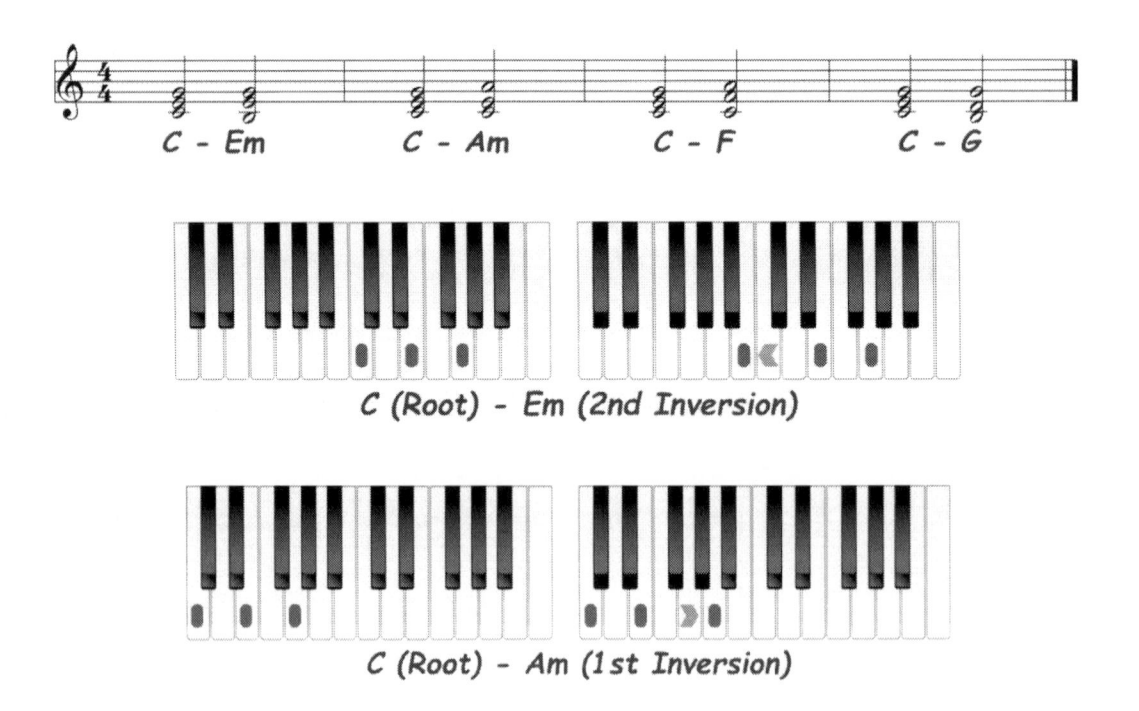

C - Em   C - Am   C - F   C - G

C (Root) - Em (2nd Inversion)

C (Root) - Am (1st Inversion)

Copyright © Martin Woodward 2011 & 2017

C (Root) - F (2nd Inversion)

C (Root) - G (1st Inversion)

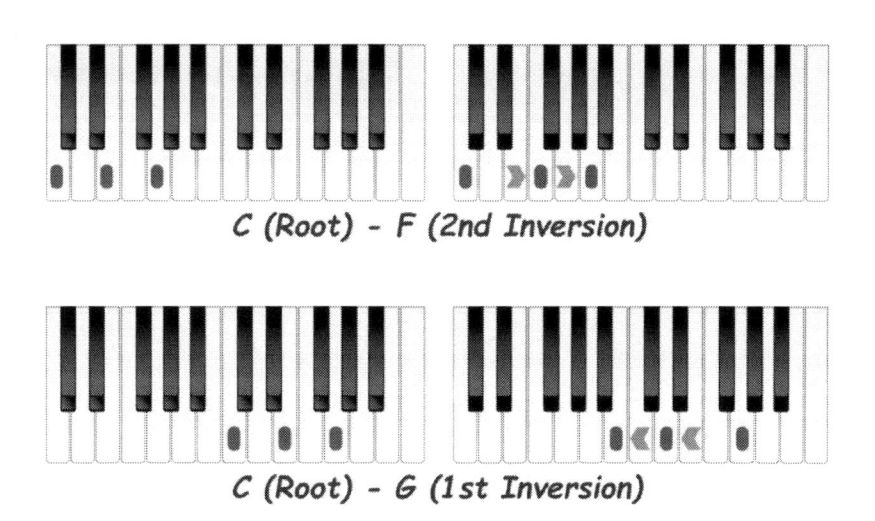

If using auto accompaniment, you'll find that most keyboards will identify the various inversions, but you will almost certainly find that there will also be a function which allows you to choose which note is sounded in the bass which would be the root note by default.

Chord Substitution

As you progress you'll see that many chords are very similar, some even identical and as such can be used as substitutions if required.

For instance, **Am7** and **C6** consist of exactly the same notes - (**C, E, G & A**) and therefore the only thing that could identify them as being different is which note is used in the bass. It's more common (but not essential) to use the root note in the bass. So, remember that every **major 6th** is identical to the relative **minor 7th**.

Similarly, **Am7sus4** and **C6/9** are totally identical and these are very important chords in relation to improvisation as they form the notes of the pentatonic scales.

As already shown **Bm7♭5** can be substituted for **G9** as they are the same chord except for the 'G' as is **Bdim7** and **G7♭9**. Just a few other possible substitutions are shown below.

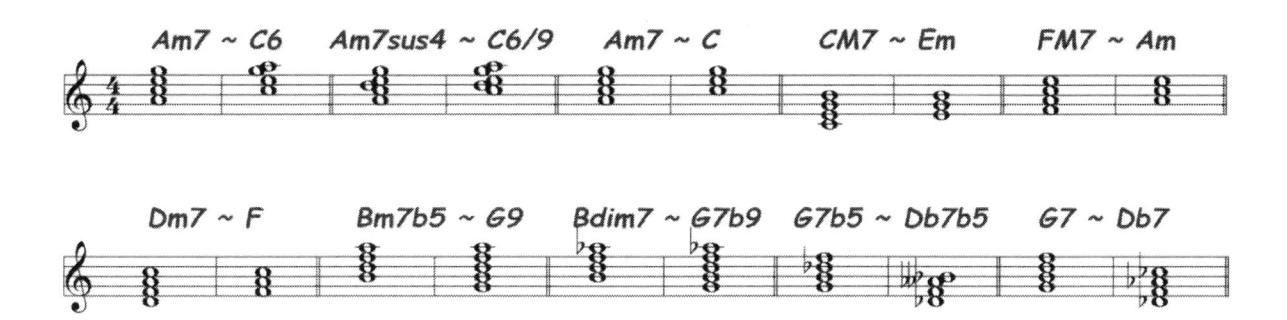

Am7 ~ C6   Am7sus4 ~ C6/9   Am7 ~ C   CM7 ~ Em   FM7 ~ Am

Dm7 ~ F   Bm7b5 ~ G9   Bdim7 ~ G7b9   G7b5 ~ Db7b5   G7 ~ Db7

In fact, any two chords which share at least two common notes can often be substituted. As shown in the last example **G7** and **D♭7** (above) are in fact harmonically as far apart as it gets, but as they share two common notes - **F** and **B** (or

C♭ to be theoretically correct for the **D♭7**) are often substituted particularly as a blues finale - **D♭7 - C**. Note that **G7♭5** and **D♭7♭5** are exactly the same (**C♭** is **B** and **A♭♭** is **G**). And this applies to all **7♭5** chords which are a tritone (3 tones) apart.

You will find that many similar substitutions can be made so don't be afraid to experiment, but always remember that a **'M7'** chord can never be substituted for a normal *'dominant'* **'7'** chord as they have no relationship whatsoever. Similarly, a *'minor'* chord could never be substituted for a *'major'* chord (of the same name, i.e. **Cm** or **C**) for the same reason.

Chord Substitutions as against Chord Alternatives

I feel that I must clarify exactly what I mean by *'substitution'* here, as there is a fear of being misunderstood.

By substitution I mean what you can play *against* what other band members are playing in a way that doesn't clash.

For instance, if the rest of the band (or even your auto accompaniment) was / is playing a **C7** chord and you played a **G minor** - it would work, as most of the **G minor** notes are also in **C7**, the only exception being the **'D'** which would in effect change the **C7** into a **C9** but this wouldn't clash.

But if other band members (or your auto accompaniment) played a **C7** and you tried playing a **CM7** or **Cm7** or **CmM7** etc. against this, it would sound terrible for the following reasons:

- The **'B natural'** in **CM7** and **CmM7** would clash against the **'B♭'** in **C7**; and
- the **'E♭'** in **Cm7** and **CmM7** against the **'E natural'** in **C7**;

Try it and you'll see what I mean.

Now on the other hand what I would call an *'alternative chord'*, is what you might use if you were playing on your own with no auto accompaniment, (maybe composing or arranging) and perhaps choosing a chord to go with the notes **'C'** and **'G'**. In this instance, you would have many potential alternative choices including the four chords that I said previously could never be used as substitutes, i.e. **CM7, C7, Cm7** and **CmM7**. Any of these *could* work because they all contain the notes **'C'** and **'G'** in their makeup. As do **Am7, Gsus4, A♭M7** and no doubt many other chords.

Which chord would be best, would be determined by which chord comes before and after and to a certain extent also the key signature (diatonic chords are more likely to fit). Clearly you would need to experiment.

In all cases the chords must fit the melody notes and any substituted chords must be compatible with one another *and* the melody *and* with what any other band member (or auto accompaniment) is playing.

Extensions Beyond the 7ths

Going back to the **M7** chord extension; if we carry on adding notes to this chord at diatonic 3rd intervals above the root chord, the **M9th**, **M11th** and **M13th** chords would be created as shown below:

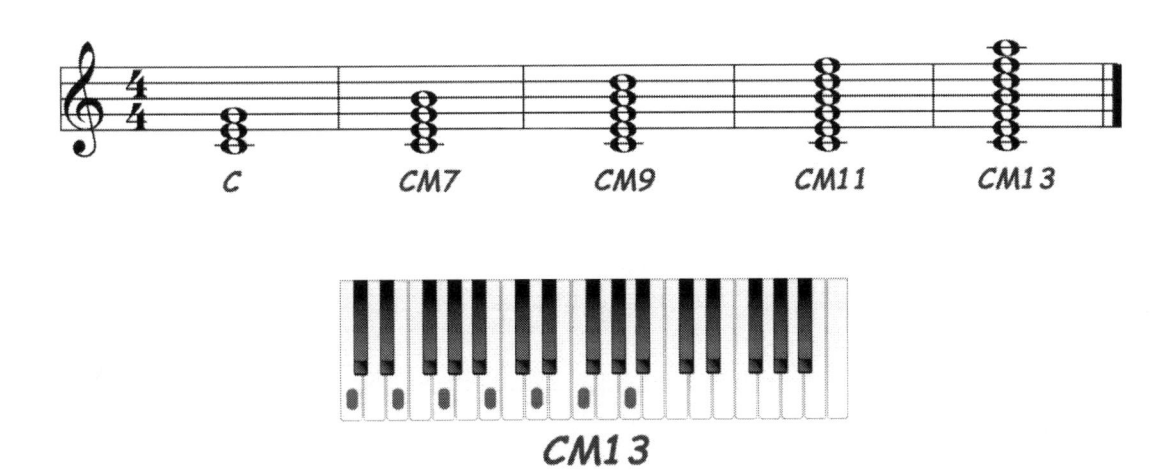

C   CM7   CM9   CM11   CM13

CM13

The fact that the **M7th** is used also makes the **9th**, **11th** and **13th** extensions *'Major'*!

And here's some playable inversions.

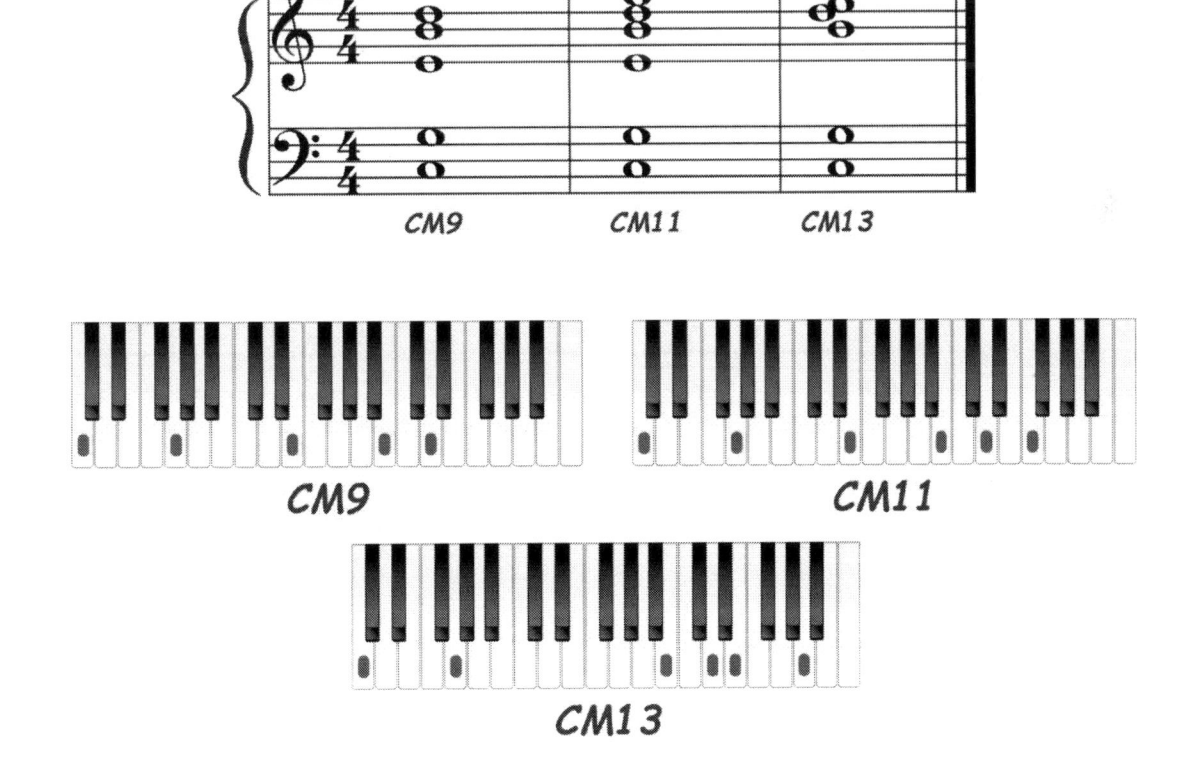

CM9   CM11   CM13

CM9

CM11

CM13

But, I have to say that the **M11th** and **M13th** are very uncommon. The majority of chord extensions are built on the **dominant 7th (V7)** chord which of course is **G7** in the key of **C major**. And the most common extensions created are the **9th**, **11th** and **13th** as shown next.

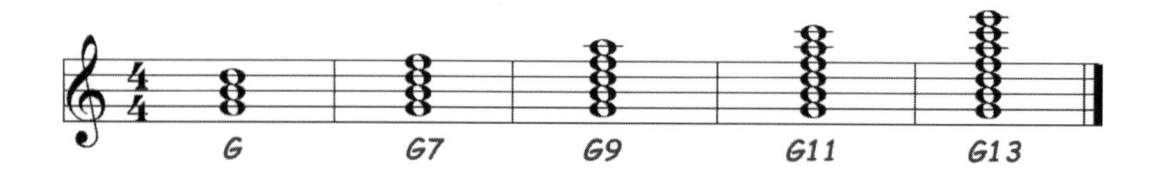

[Musical notation: G, G7, G9, G11, G13 chords in treble clef]

Look carefully and you'll see that **CM13th** and **G13th** are actually different inversions of the same chords and if re-organised are also the notes of the **C major** scale; and as such also contain within them all the other *diatonic* triads and chords of **C major** - think about it!

Here's some playable inversions.

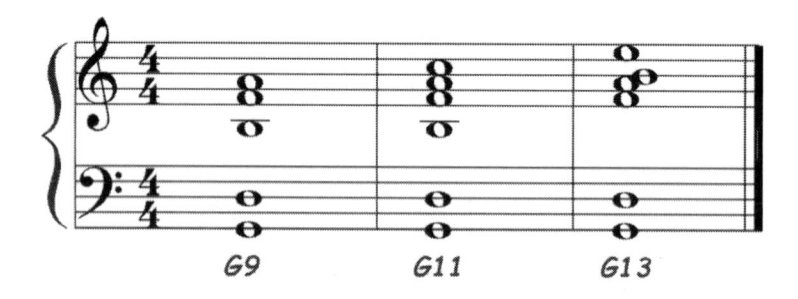

[Musical notation: G9, G11, G13 chords on grand staff]

If playing with a band, you only need to play the right-hand notes as shown here in the treble clef, which although don't include the tonic or 5th *do* create the sounds of the chords - try them - they work great!

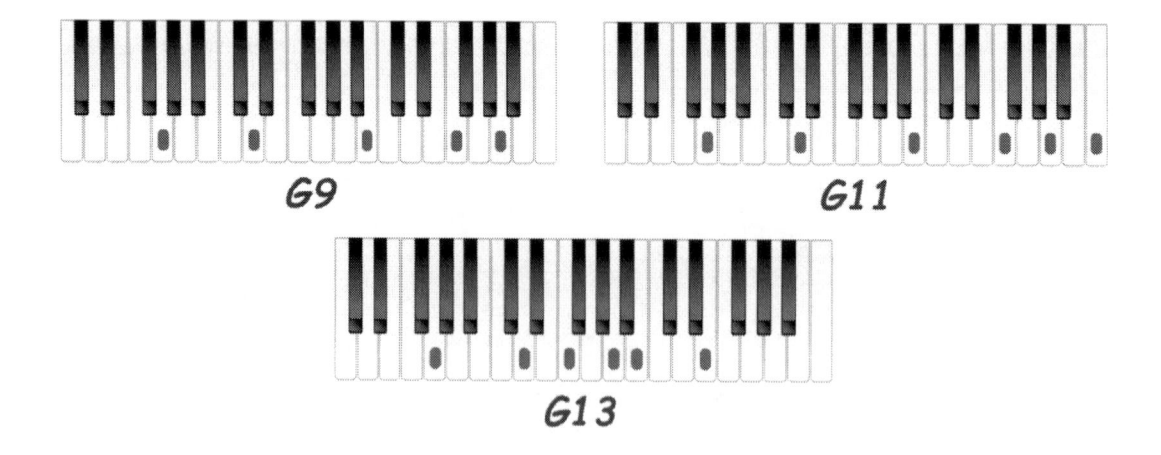

[Piano keyboard diagrams showing G9, G11, and G13 chords]

Notice how the **G13 (V13)** followed by **G9 (V9)** resolves beautifully to the tonic **C major (I)**, shown next.

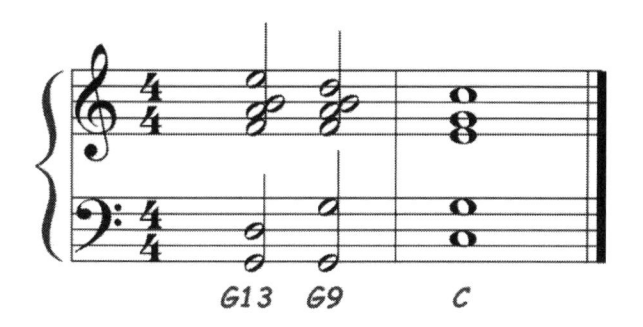

What is the difference between a 6th and a 13th?

Clearly the **13th** is a **6th**. I suppose you could say that a **6th** is a cheap, simple way of playing a **13th** and it works, but the difference is the fact that the **13th** also contains the all-important **7th** and **9th** and is a completely different sounding chord - experiment and hear the difference!

See: http://www.learn-keyboard.co.uk/chord_construction.html for the audio link to this section, or click on the applicable graphics.

Quick link to Part 2 (Chords in Keyboard view)
Quick link to Part 2 (Extended Chords in Keyboard view)

Casio MZ-X500 Arranger / Synth

This little beasty boy is a beauty - only got 61 keys, but what a sound!
This also has incredible recording and editing functions.

I use one of these as a top-level board to my Casio PX-560!

> *"I pay no attention whatever to anybody's praise or blame.*
> *I simply follow my own feelings."*
>
> Mozart
>
> *Comment: - And this is the difference between the leaders and the followers!*

⬅ Chord Fingering ➡

The fingering for the various chords depends very much on whether you are playing triads or full chords and which chord (or passage) is going to follow, and of course to a certain extent it depends on which chord you are playing.

If I was to outline the fingering for each individual chord in every inversion in every circumstance it would bore you senseless apart from taking months to produce.

But what I can do more sensibly is to give you a few valuable *general* examples which work in most instances. But as always, whatever you do - if it works, it's ok.

To keep things simple, we'll start with the **C major**.

If I was asked to play a **C major triad** or a **C major full chord** with my right hand, off the top of my head without thinking, the fingerings that I would use are as follows.

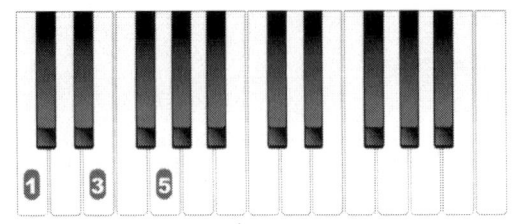

C Major Triad Root Position 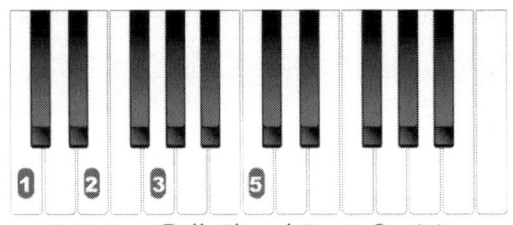   *C Major Full Chord Root Position*

Furthermore, the above fingering would work for every root position major and minor chord. Generally speaking if a scale begins on a black note, you would usually use the 2nd or 3rd finger at the root, but not so with chords - the above fingering would still work for every major and minor root position chord.

Now staying with the root position, as we add the **7ths**, which finger that is used at the top (the 7th) is determined by whether it's a white note or not as shown below.

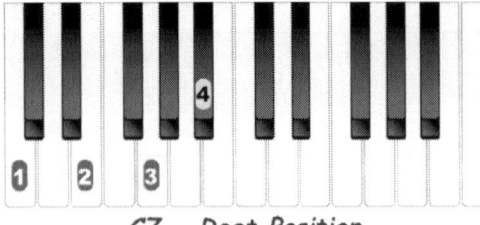

C7 - Root Position 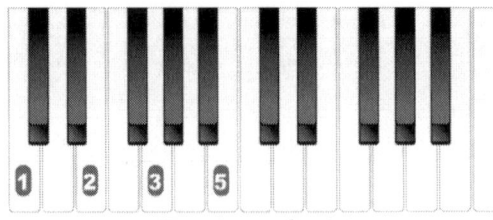   *CM7 - Root Position*

And if we look at **G7** and **GM7** as below, you will see that it's the other way around with the 5th finger being used on the **G7** and the 4th on the **major 7th** as it's a black note.

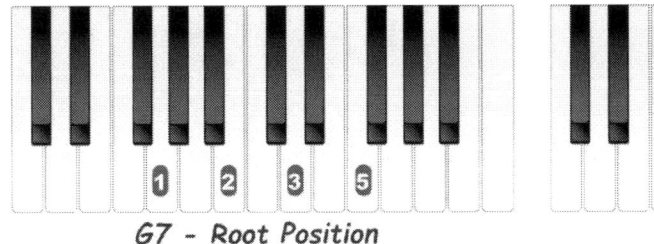

G7 - Root Position 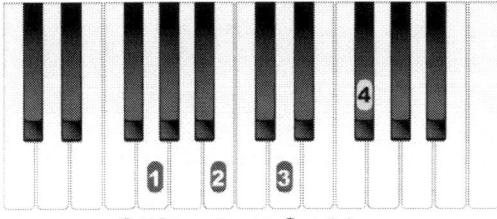   GM7 - Root Position

I must stress that these are not *'rules'*, just *'guidelines'*. If you feel more comfortable using your 5th finger on the black 7th keys, then do so. But in all cases when the span is a full octave as in the full (4 note), chords then the 5th finger will *generally* be used at the top on both white and black notes.

Ok, so now we'll look at some alternatives which are commonly used when changing to other chords. The example below shows the **C major triad** changing to **F major** - the common **I - IV** progression. By using this fingering, a smooth change can be made, particularly if sustaining the **'C'** throughout.

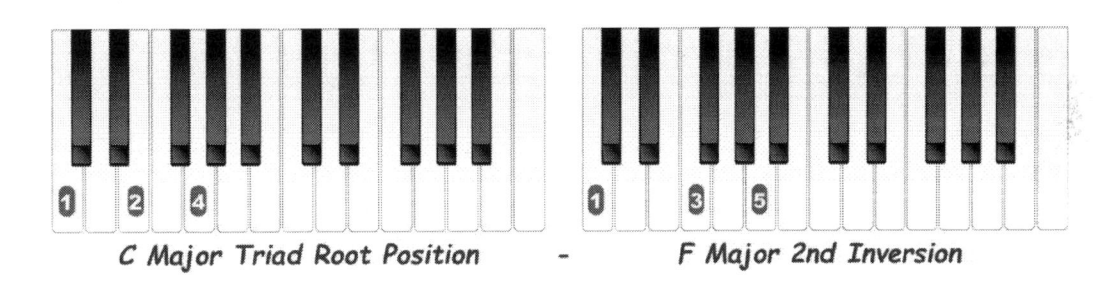

C Major Triad Root Position   -   F Major 2nd Inversion

But for **C minor** to **F minor**, the fingering would alter as shown next. This is ***not*** because the chords are minor rather than major, but simply because of the way the black notes fall.

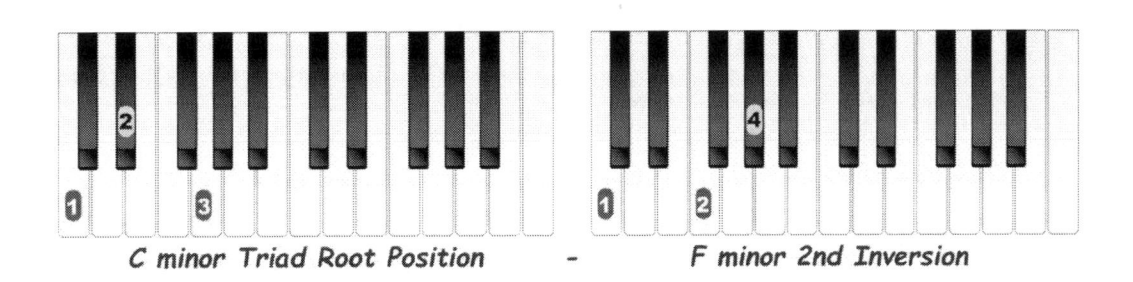

C minor Triad Root Position   -   F minor 2nd Inversion

"Music is everybody's possession!"

John Lennon

Notice that the fingering for **E major** to **A major** is exactly the same due to the black notes falling in the same relative positions - remember it's nothing to do with the major / minor difference!

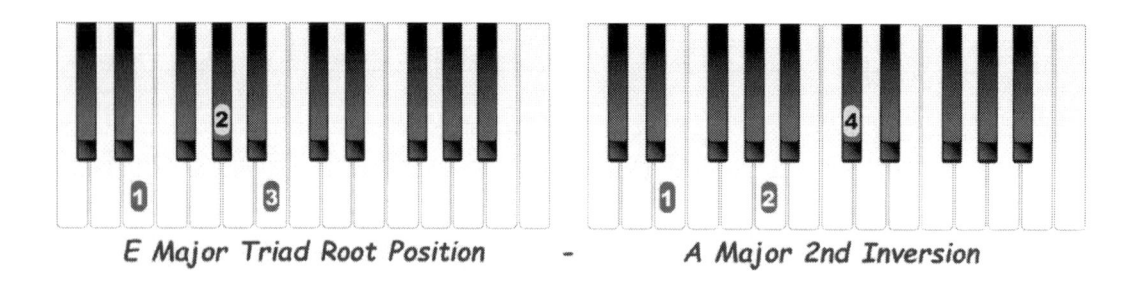

           E Major Triad Root Position   -   A Major 2nd Inversion

Another most common progression is the **I - V** as shown below using **C major** *'root position'* to **G major** *'1st inversion'*.

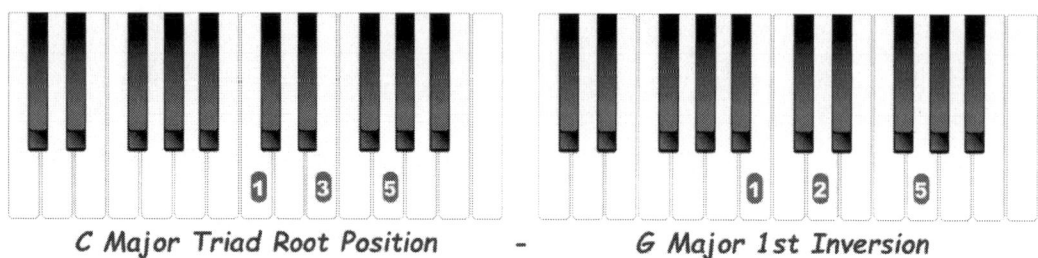

           C Major Triad Root Position   -   G Major 1st Inversion

If progressing to the *'2nd inversion'* as shown next, notice that using a different fingering on the first triad is more suitable.

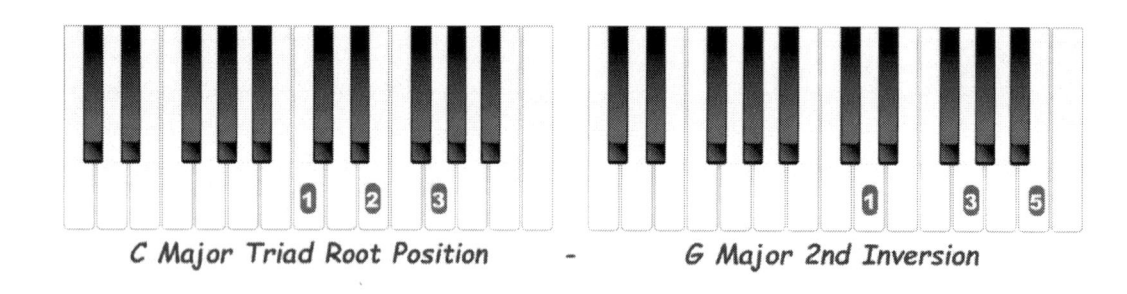

           C Major Triad Root Position   -   G Major 2nd Inversion

In all the progression examples given, note that at least one of the notes between the two chords remains the same, which assists a smooth transition. Obviously, this is not always possible, but whenever it is, it's a good idea.

Another way of ensuring a smooth transition is to *'place'* unused fingers over one or more notes of the next chord in preparation. For instance, the 5th finger could be hovering over the **'B'** in the last example which means only the 1st finger has to do any movement!

And finally, the root positions of the **C diminished 7th** and **C augmented** triad.

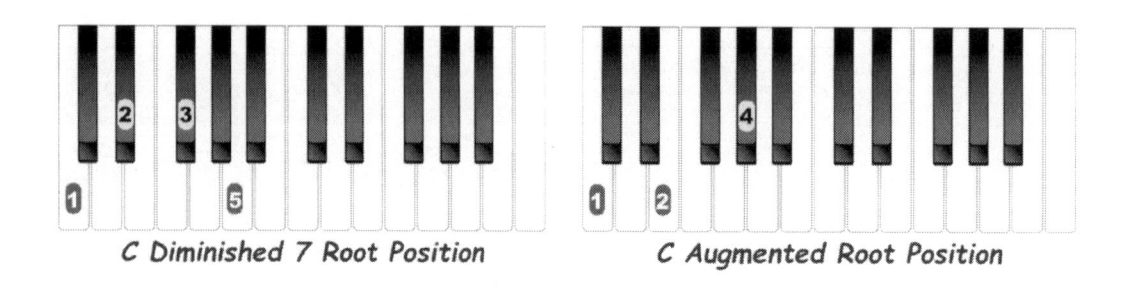

           C Diminished 7 Root Position   C Augmented Root Position

Copyright © Martin Woodward 2011 & 2017

Left Hand Chord Fingering

Now obviously your left hand is going to be completely different. The same sort of variations will apply - but differently. You might think that the fingering is simply *'mirrored'*, but it's not, as although your hands are mirrored, the keyboard is not!

Here's the same chords and progressions but with suggested **left-hand** fingering.

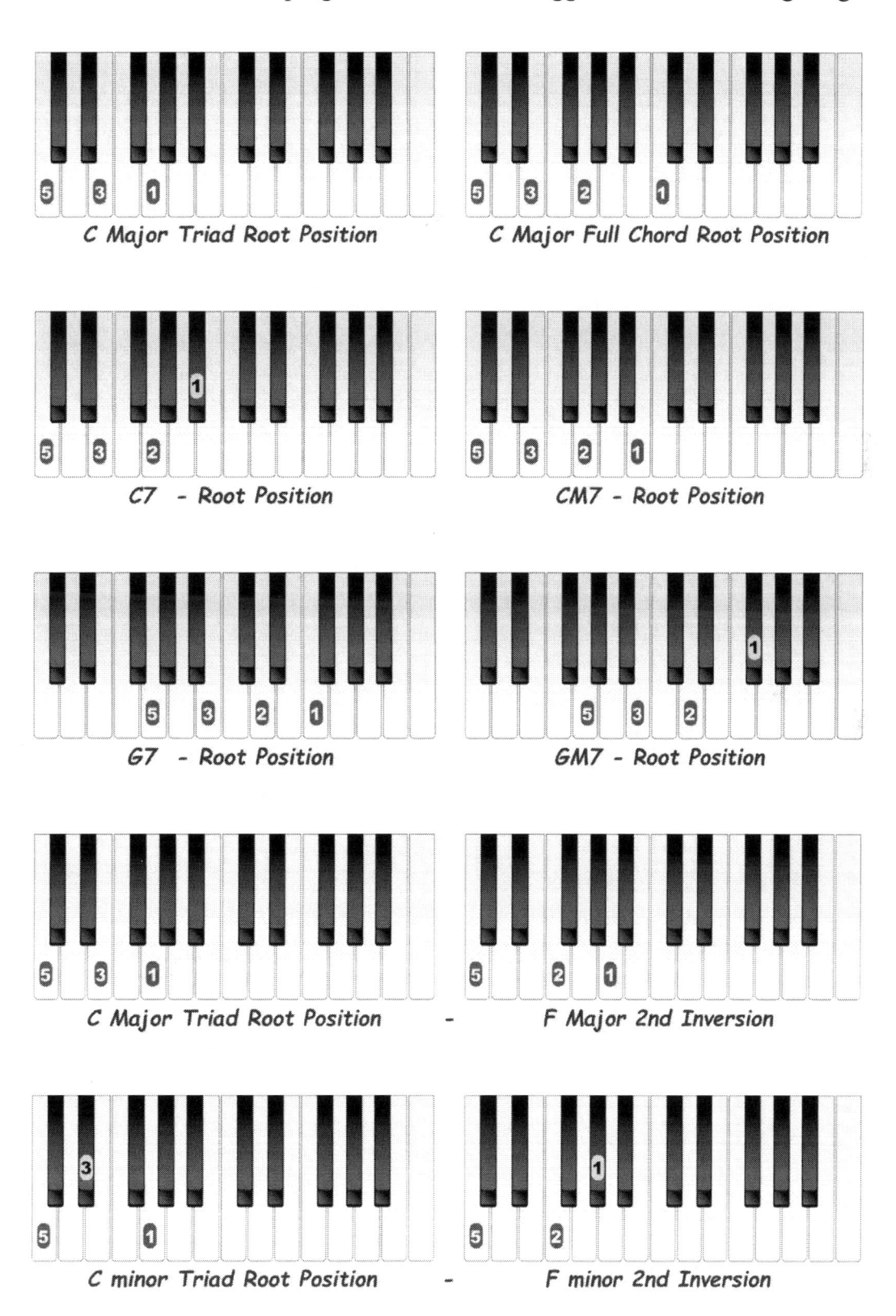

C Major Triad Root Position

C Major Full Chord Root Position

C7 - Root Position

CM7 - Root Position

G7 - Root Position

GM7 - Root Position

C Major Triad Root Position   -   F Major 2nd Inversion

C minor Triad Root Position   -   F minor 2nd Inversion

Copyright © Martin Woodward 2011 & 2017

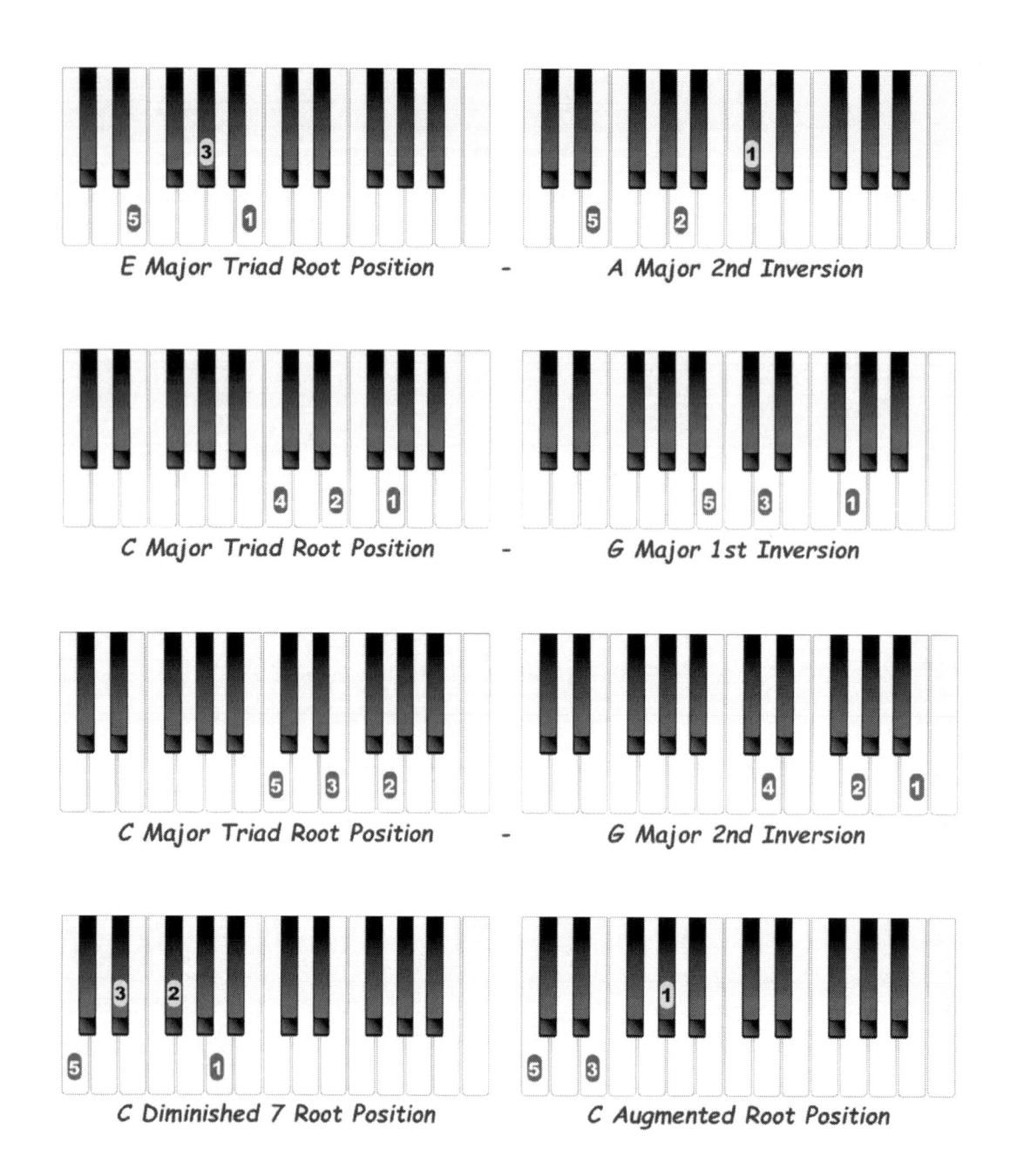

E Major Triad Root Position   -   A Major 2nd Inversion

C Major Triad Root Position   -   G Major 1st Inversion

C Major Triad Root Position   -   G Major 2nd Inversion

C Diminished 7 Root Position   -   C Augmented Root Position

If you've been paying attention, you will have noticed that there are not so many variations with the left-hand fingerings as with the right hand. This is something that surprised me, and that I was not consciously aware of until I wrote this section.

Anyway, so hopefully now you've got the idea and can now relate all this information to other chords. But remember it's not written in blood, these fingerings work well for me, but to be honest I've seen other really good musicians who use what appears (to me) to be crazy fingering, but it works for them.

There are no audio files for this chapter.

> "Music is the one incorporeal entrance into the higher world of knowledge which comprehends mankind but which mankind cannot comprehend."
>
> Beethoven

⬅ Chord Sequences ➡

As already mentioned, every musical piece is constructed around a sequence of chords which may be extremely complex or very simple consisting of as few as two or three chords. But do remember that just because a piece may be complex with many chords this would certainly not necessarily make it more pleasing to listen to. In fact, very often simple is best! Even some of the greatest classical compositions are based around only a few chords.

You've no doubt heard the term *'three chord wonders'* referring to songs with only three chords, and if this is the case you can more or less guess that they will be the **tonic (I)**, the **subdominant (IV)** and the **dominant (V)** - **C**, **F** and **G** in the key of **C major**.

The most common sequence using these three chords is the *'12 Bar Blues'* which is shown below, but note that there are many variations of this.

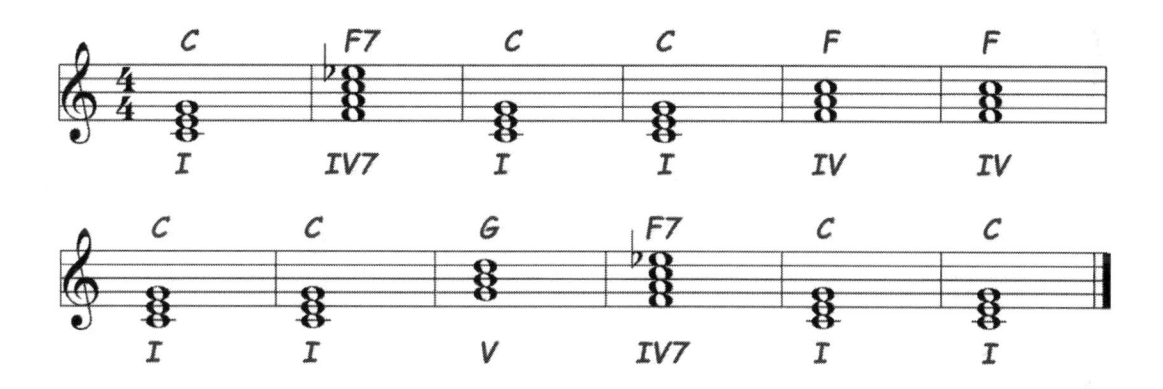

Whether you are aware of it or not you will have heard this sequence thousands of times.

As seen previously, the strongest of all progressions is **V7 - I** (**G7 - C** in **C major**) and the second strongest is **IV - I** (**F - C**), hence the reason that these three chords are used so often. Now if you think about it, **I - IV** (**C - F** in **C major**) is also a **V - I** progression in the key of **F major**. Or to put it another way the progression is the interval of a perfect 5th descending or a perfect 4th ascending, which amounts to the same thing.

If after making this progression (**G - C**), we continue with this interval again, we'd get **C - F**, then **F - B♭**, **B♭ - E♭** etc. Carry on doing this and it will take you through the *'chromatic circle of 5ths'* as shown below. And this takes us through the full spectrum of major chords and keys and eventually returns to **C major**.

Copyright © Martin Woodward 2011 & 2017

85

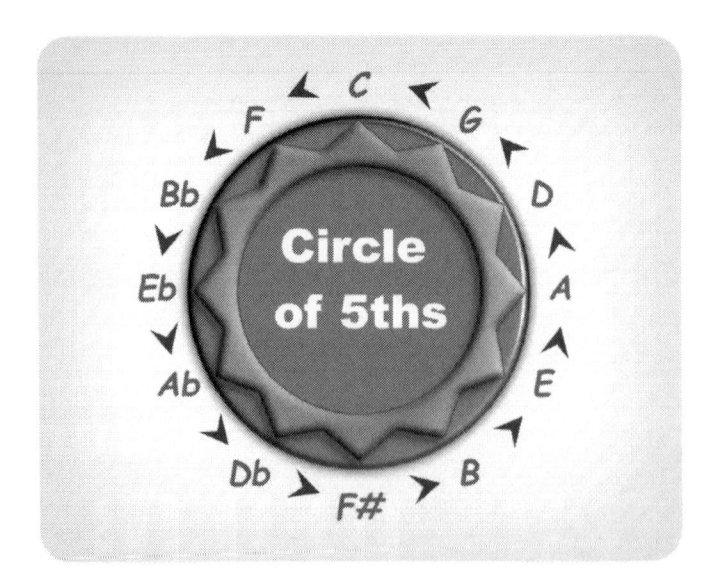

Portions of the circle of 5ths are used in numerous compositions due to the strength of the resolutions. But as the full circle goes through every key, it's doubtful that the *full* circle would be used.

Below is the circle of 5ths again in music notation form, although in every case I've added the dominant 7th before each resolution (which makes the resolutions stronger). Listen to this and you should not fail to notice that each dominant 7th chord *wants* to resolve to the next chord in the circle (a 5th below).

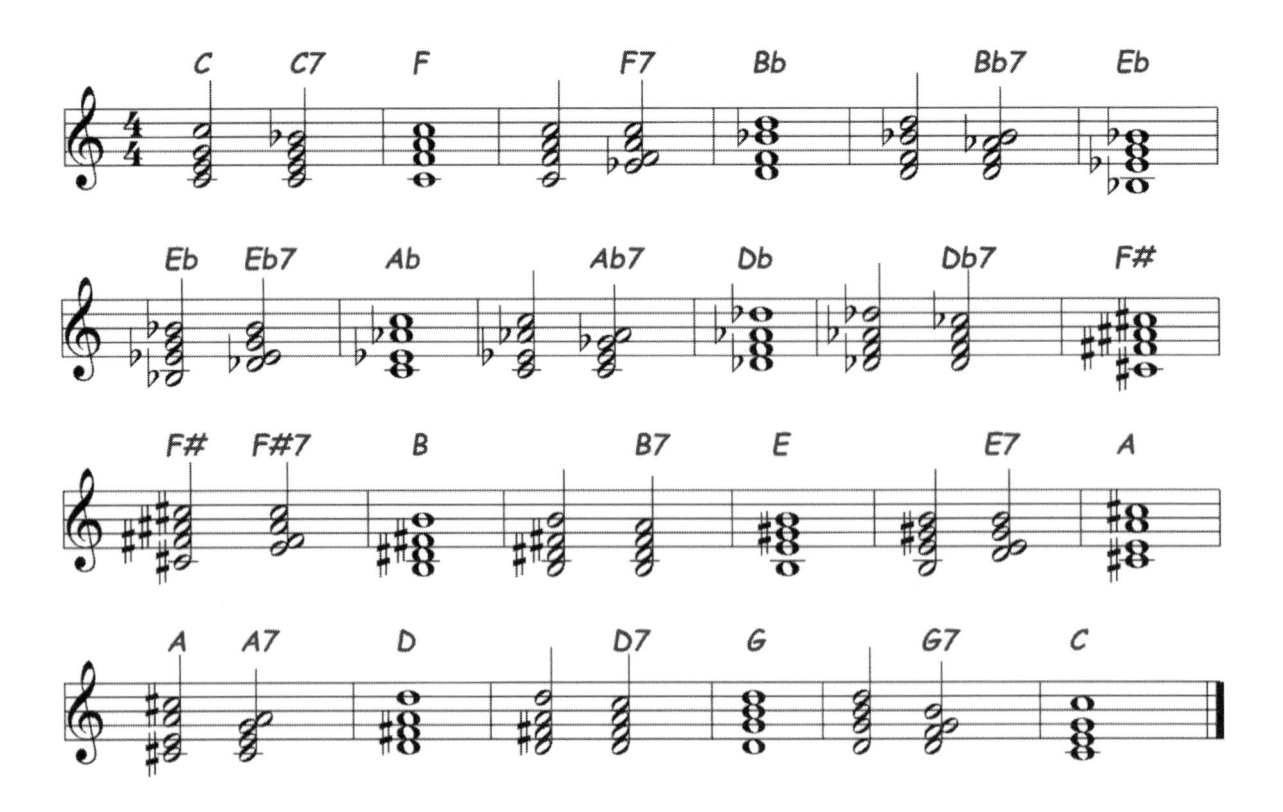

To see all of these chords in keyboard view, please see the charts further on.

Now, by making a very small modification to the circle and using chords only found in the scale we end up with the following *diatonic* resolutions which you'll hear extensively either in total or partially in all types of music from classical to pop.

The next two examples are in **C major / A minor** and the slight modification incidentally is that the interval from **F - B** is a **diminished** (or flattened) **5th**. All the others are **perfect 5ths**. Also, we've used the minor and diminished chords as they appear in the scale, shown previously in the chord construction chapter.

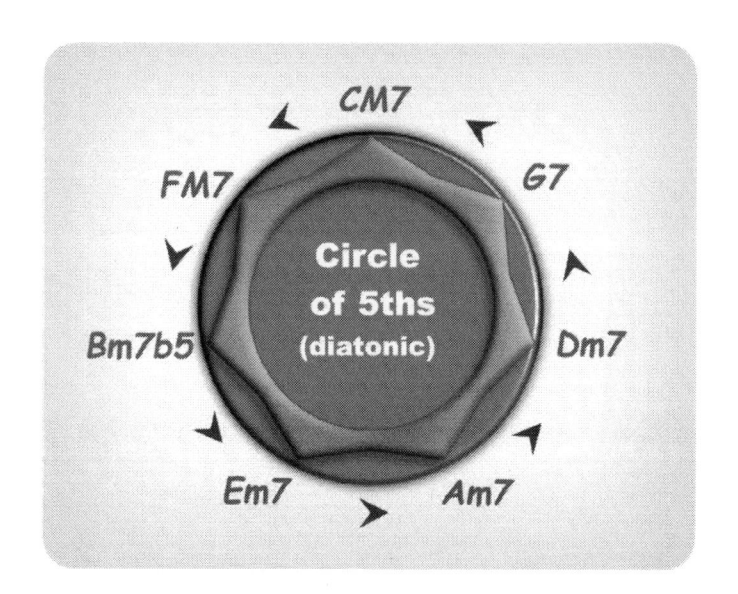

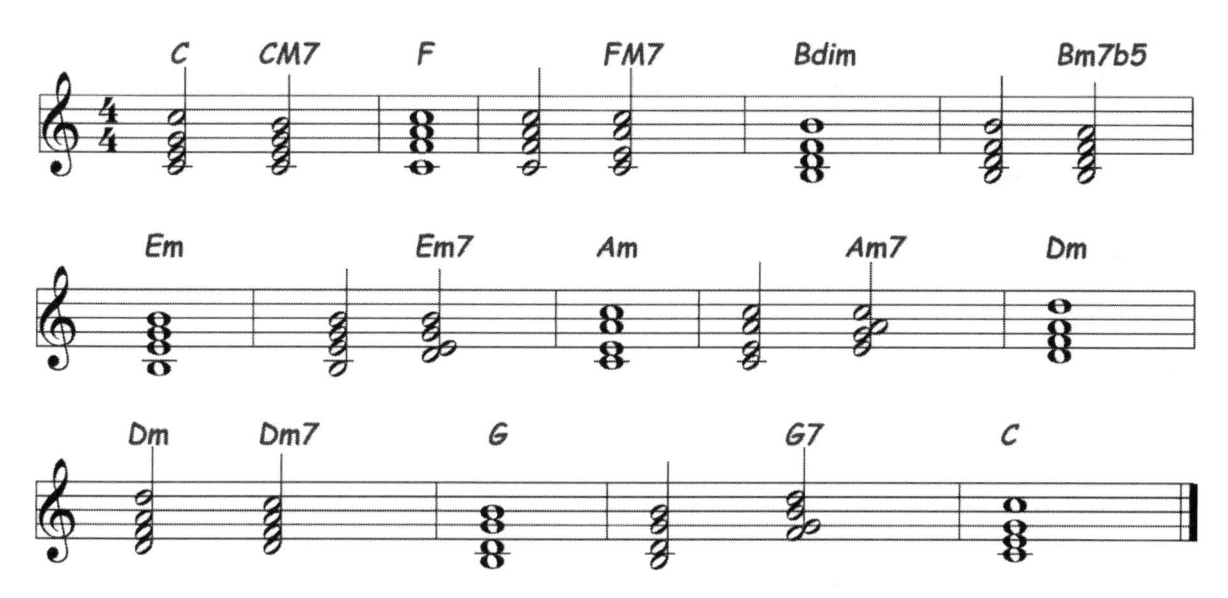

The extra (alternative) chords in the *'minor'* circle below, are due to the differences in the melodic / harmonic scales. Again, these were shown in the chord construction chapter.

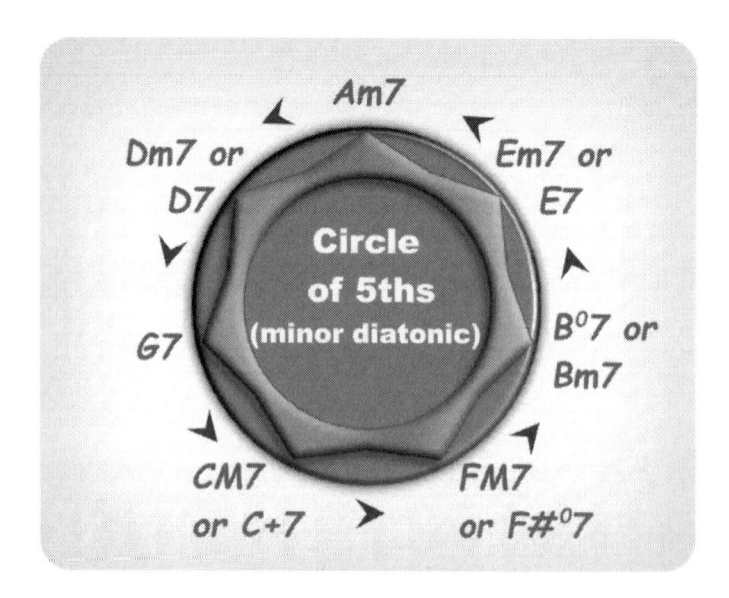

The notation example below shows just one of the several possible variations.

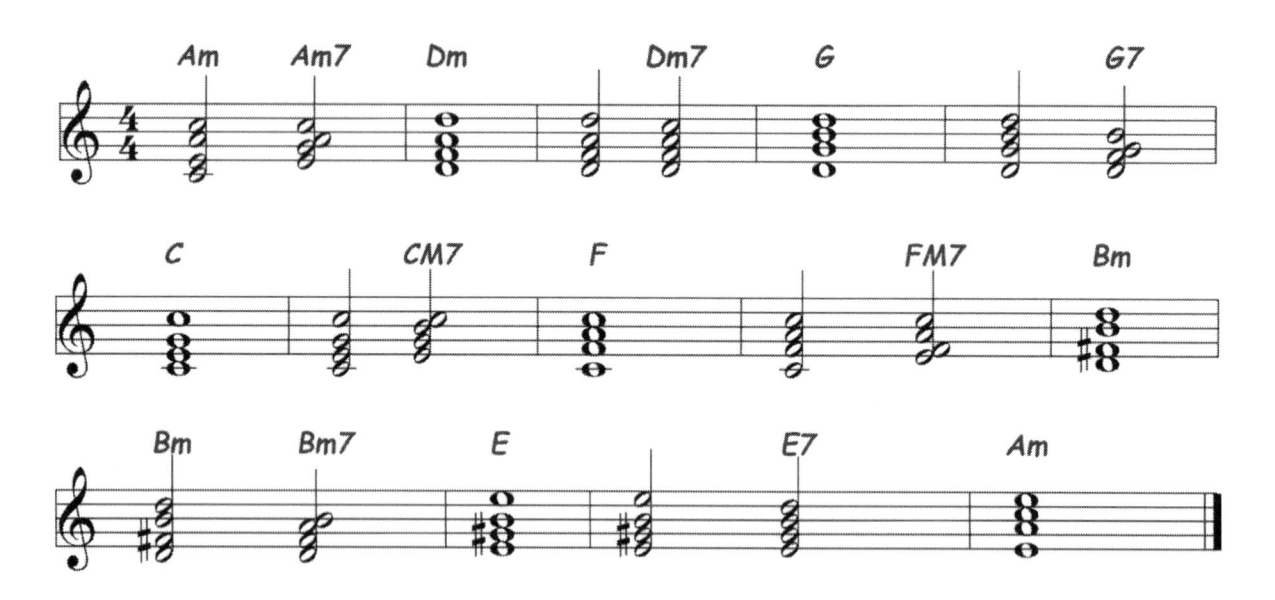

Other very common sequences (shown below) are **Dm7 - G7 - C - (ii7, V7, I)** and **C - Am - Dm7 (or F major) - G7- (I, vi, ii7, V7)**, both of which incorporate a portion of the circle of 5ths which is why these sequences are so strong. Try and notice how often part of the circle is used in other compositions - it's very common.

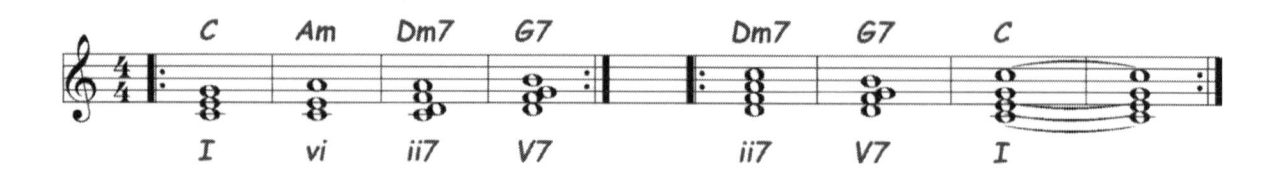

The audio link for this section is: http://learn-keyboard.co.uk/chord_sequences.html

⬅ Arpeggios & Broken Chords in Brief ➡

An *'arpeggio'* is simply a *'broken chord'*, although the Royal College of Music describes these differently, an *'arpeggio'* being as shown below (**C major** - 2 octaves).

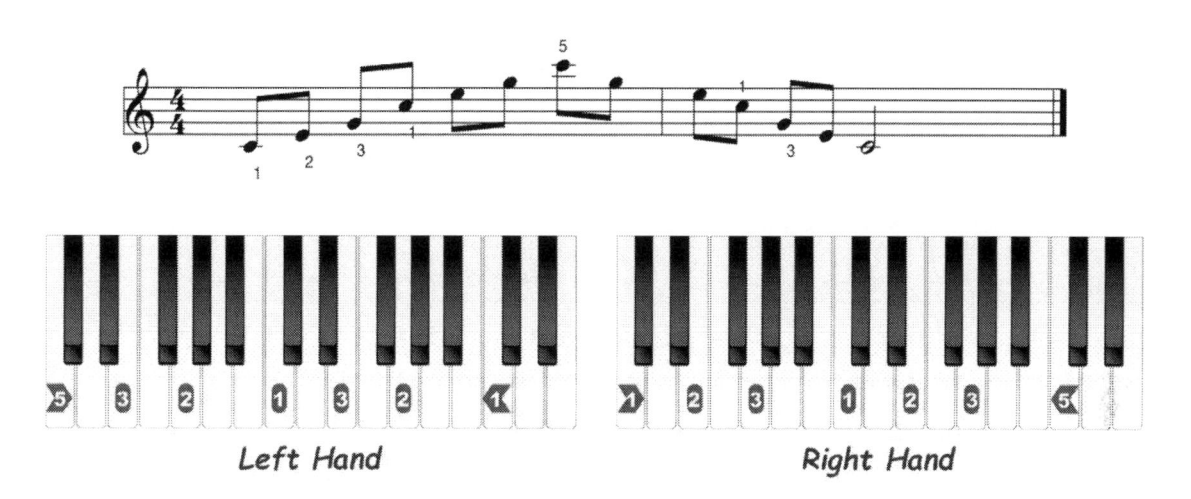

Left Hand *Right Hand*

And a *'broken chord'* as shown in the next diagram (**C7** - 2 octaves).

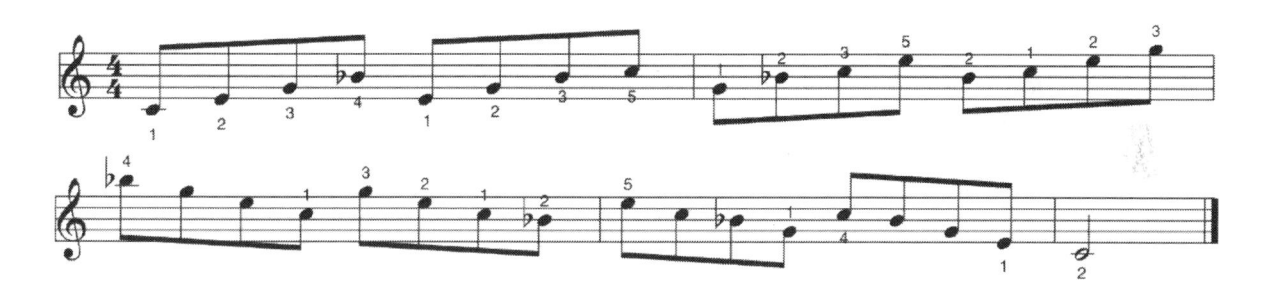

Both of these they are especially important for a number of reasons:

a) They are often used (in different ways) in the left hand (classical and modern);

b) They are often used in bass patterns;

c) They are excellent finger exercises;

d) They are an extremely important tool to help with composition and improvisation.

It's absolutely essential that you know and practice every arpeggio in every key major / minor with both hands together and separately, remembering that speed is not important but accuracy and fluency is! All of these and other useful exercises are shown in part 2.

Similar to the scale exercises, it's also useful to practice these starting on different notes as shown here (**CM7** arpeggio on **E**).

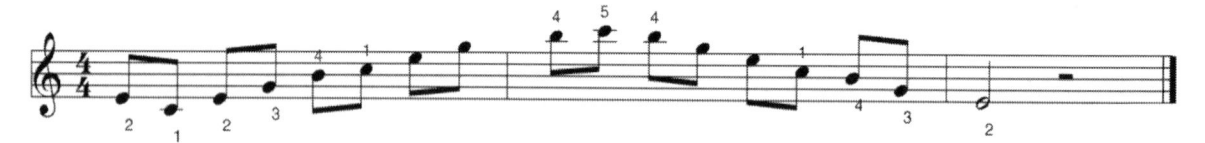

Another extremely useful (and important) way of practicing them is to split the arpeggio / chord into triplets as shown here (**C major**).

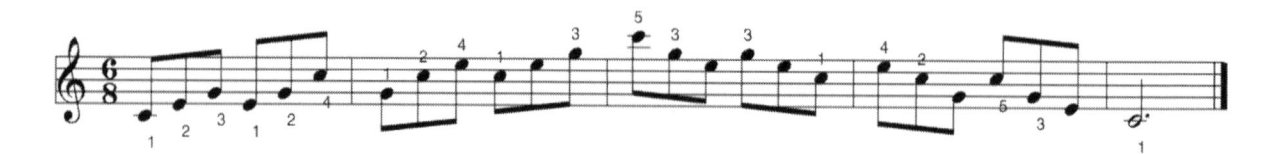

Other useful and similar versions are the **7th**, **m7th** and **M7th** arpeggios as shown next in keyboard view.

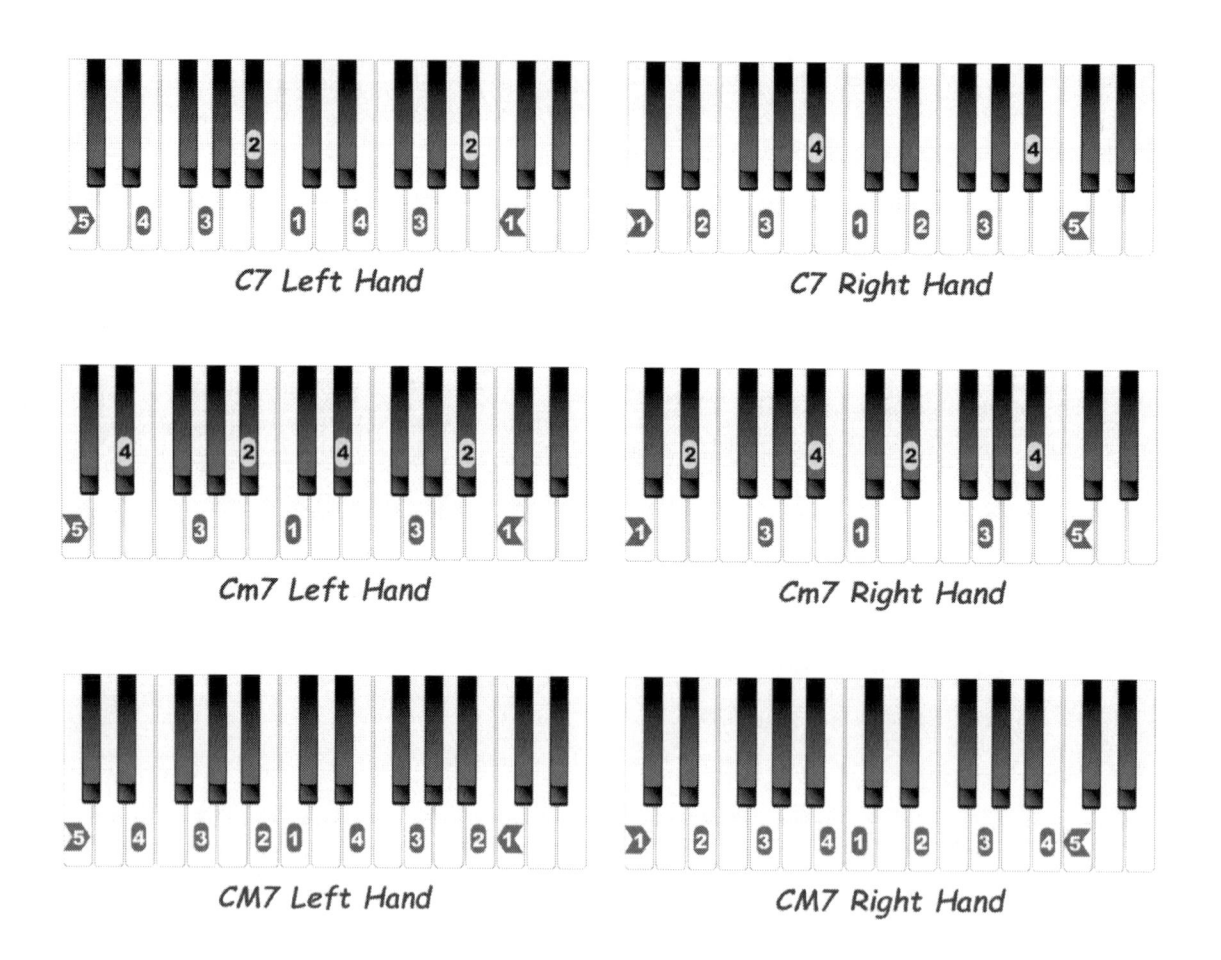

C7 Left Hand

C7 Right Hand

Cm7 Left Hand

Cm7 Right Hand

CM7 Left Hand

CM7 Right Hand

These can be heard by clicking on the graphics, however these are not shown in part 2, but all the chords from which they are derived are.

The audio link for this section is: http://learn-keyboard.co.uk/arp_brief.html

Quick link to part 2 (Arpeggio Exercises).

Important Musical Terms

There are an enormous amount of musical terms and symbols, many of which apply only to certain instruments. Following are the most common terms applicable to the piano / keyboard.

Staccato

Generally, notes are played *'legato'*, which means that the second key is played *as* you are releasing the first, thereby creating a smooth transition. But some notes need to be struck deliberately detached or disconnected. This is known *'staccato'*. All the scales and exercises should be practiced both *legato* and *staccato*.

In music notation, notes which should be played *staccato* have a dot over or under them as shown here:

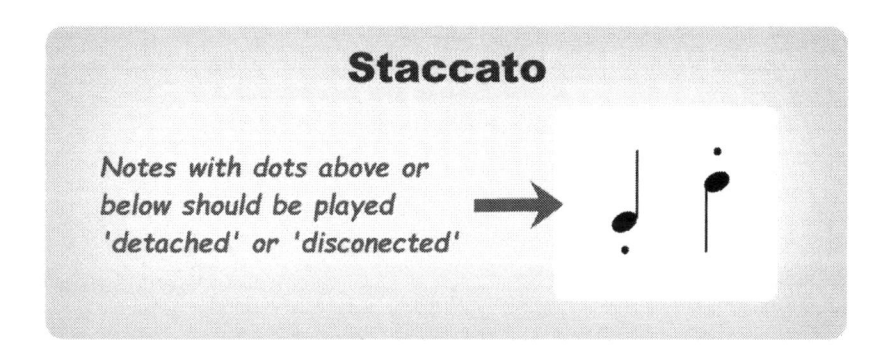

Staccato

Notes with dots above or below should be played 'detached' or 'disconected'

So, a dot over a note means it should be played staccato and if the dot is after it means that half as much again should be added to the time length - Yes?

Absolutely correct! The correct placing of a *'dot'* makes a huge difference!

Marcato

The *'Marcato'* symbol as shown below indicates that the note should be accented.

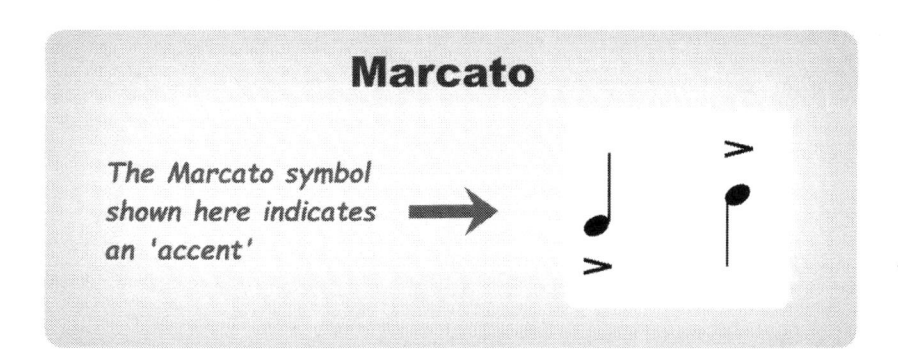

Marcato

The Marcato symbol shown here indicates an 'accent'

Fermata

The *'Fermata'* symbol as shown below indicates a *'pause'* and thus interrupts the general tempo of the piece.

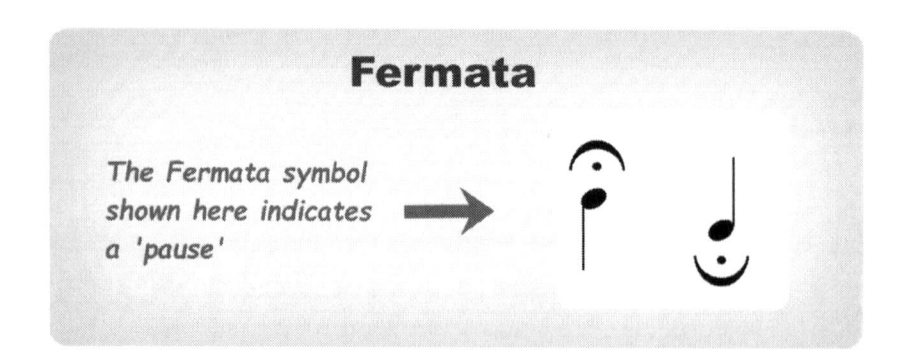

The Fermata symbol shown here indicates a 'pause'

This symbol is used in one of the pieces to follow which is entitled **'Falora'**.

Repeat Last Measure

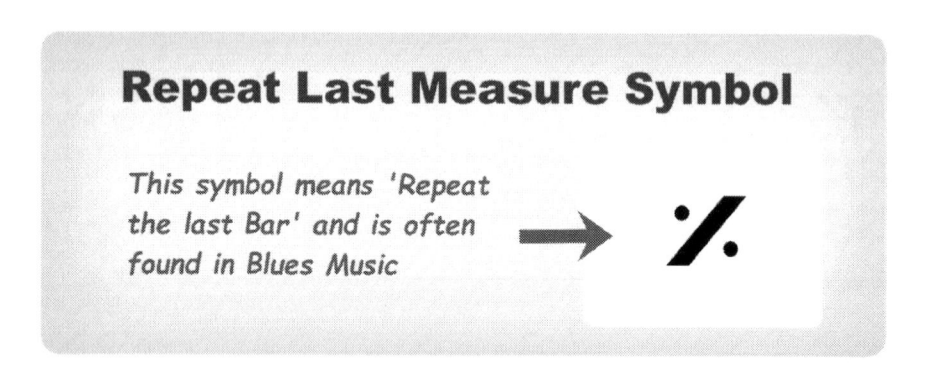

This symbol means 'Repeat the last Bar' and is often found in Blues Music

This symbol is used where one or more bars is an exact duplication of the previous one(s). As this is often the case in *'Blues'* or *'Boogie Woogie'* music, this is where they are mostly seen, as shown in the example below.

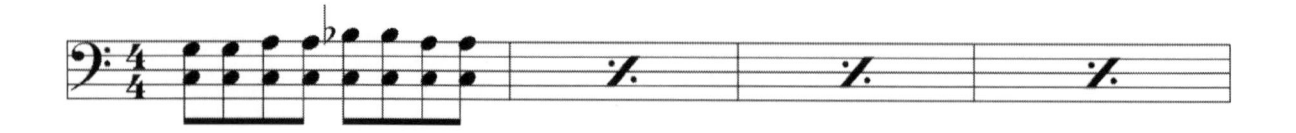

Navigational Symbols

Just like navigating through a website, finding your way through a piece of music is not always straight forwards. In order to minimise the number of pages and consequently save the amount of page turns, certain navigational terms and symbols are used. These are all used very frequently in all types of music, so understanding these is essential.

Navigational Markers

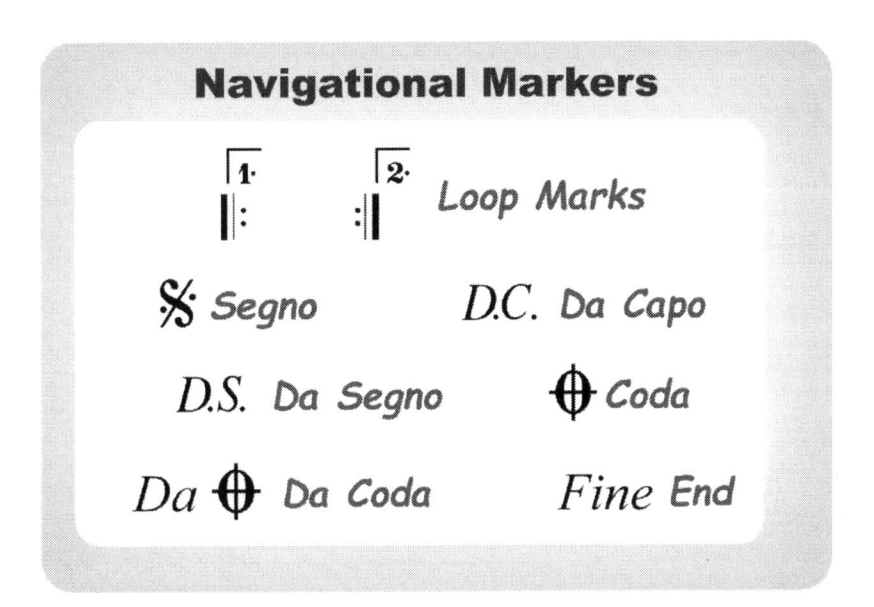

(Loop Marks, Segno, D.C. Da Capo, D.S. Da Segno, Coda, Da Coda, Fine End)

Segno

The *'Segno'* sign is simply a reference mark and used in conjunction with the Da Segno (*D.S.*) marker.

Coda & *Da* Coda

The *'Coda'* is an end section marked by the *'Coda'* sign and used in conjunction with the *D.S.* and *D.C.* markers unless the instruction *Da Coda* appears which means *'go to the Coda'* after any repeats.

Fine

The *'Fine'* sign means *'end'* and is often found in the middle of a piece, meaning that the piece would end there after further instruction from either the *D.S.* or *D.C.* markers. You will see examples of this later.

Da Segno

The marker *'D.S.'* means *'go to the sign'* and is used in three ways as follows:

1. *D.S.* - jump forward or back to the *'Segno'* mark;
2. *D.S. Al Fine* - jump to the Segno mark and finish at the *'Fine'* mark;
3. *D.S. Al Coda* - jump to the Segno mark and then proceed to the *'Coda'*.

Da Capo

The marker *'D.C.'* means *'go to the beginning'* and is used in three ways as follows:

1. *D.C.* - go back to the start;

2. *D.C. Al Fine* - go back to the start and then end at the *'Fine'* mark;

3. *D.C. Al Coda* - go back to the start and then proceed to the *'Coda'*.

Loop Section

As you progress will come across some *'loop section'* symbols. The first one (below) means that the whole piece should be repeated from the beginning.

The next one means that the bar (or bars) between the markers should be repeated.

And this one means that the piece should be repeated from the beginning, using the bar marked '1' the first time and the one marked '2' the second time.

These symbols are used extensively in the practice pieces to follow.

Dynamic Symbols

Dynamic Symbols

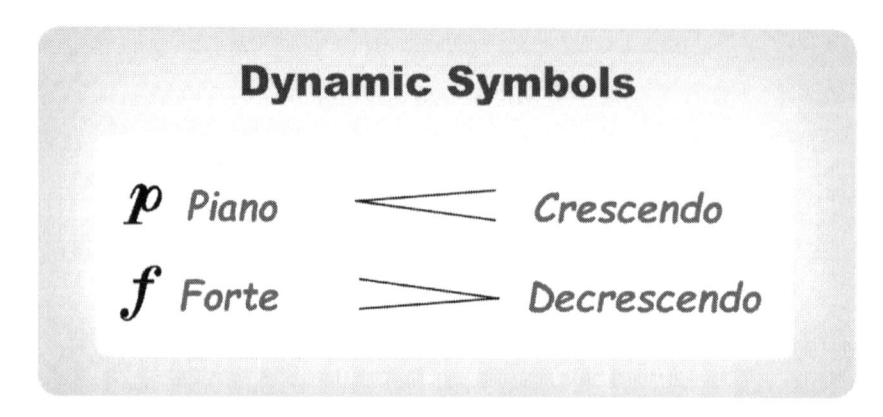

p Piano   < Crescendo

f Forte   > Decrescendo

There are many dynamic symbols, but these are the most common in relation to the piano / keyboard.

Italian Words		Translations
Crescendo (cres.)	-	Gradually becoming louder
Diminuendo (dim.)	-	Gradually becoming softer
ppp - pianissississimo	-	Very, very soft
pp - pianissimo	-	Very soft
p - piano	-	Soft
mp - mezzo piano	-	Moderately soft
mf - mezzo forte	-	Moderately loud
f - forte	-	Loud
ff - fortissimo	-	Very loud
fff - fortississimo	-	Very, very loud
poco a poco	-	Little by little

Embellishments

The following embellishments are mainly found in classical music, although the *'Arpeggio'* is common in all types of music.

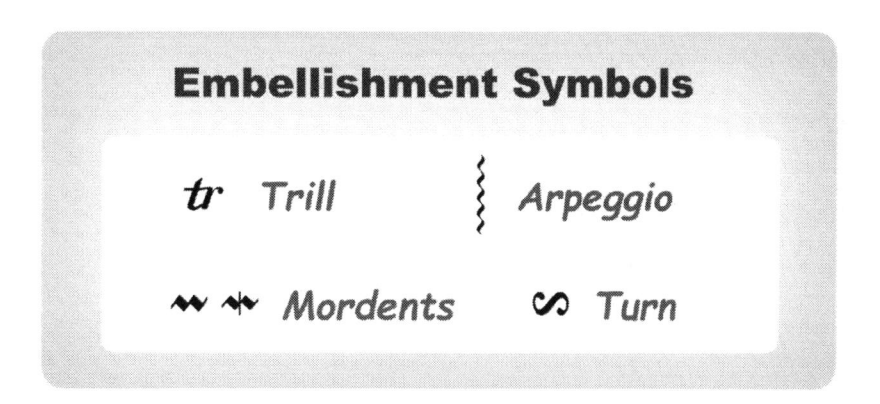

Embellishment Symbols

tr Trill   Arpeggio

Mordents   Turn

Trill

The first diagram below shows what is written and the second how it should be played. However, the *'trill'* or *'shake'* as it's sometimes called is rarely *exactly* as written in the second example; it may start off slowly and then increase in speed. It's also open to interpretation by the individual musician.

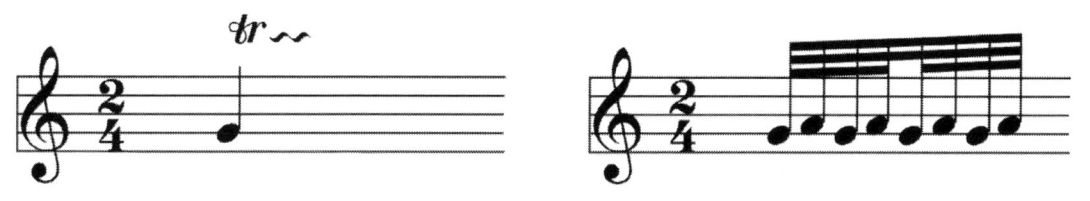

The note immediately above in the scale is used unless a sharp, flat or natural sign is used to signify otherwise.

High Mordent

The *'high mordent'* does a quick *alternation* between the written note and the next note above in the scale as shown below.

Low Mordent

The *'low mordent'* (or *'inverted mordent'*) is the opposite of the above and alternates between the written note and the next note below in the scale as shown below.

Both the high and low mordents are mainly found in classical music and rarely in any other type.

Arpeggio

The *'arpeggio'* symbol mustn't get confused with the arpeggio exercises which you'll learn shortly, although the term basically has the same meaning - *'broken chord'*!

The notes should be played from the bottom in sequence, sustaining each note as they are played. This is how it would be played on a harp which is where the word originated from!

Phrase Marks

Phrase marks are used to join short musical sections or *'ideas'*.

> **Phrase Marks**
>
> *Phrase marks are used to join groups of notes into phrases.*

A similar indistinguishable mark is called a *'slur'* and mainly used by bowed or woodwind instruments, but they are still used to mark a 'phrase'.

But please don't get these confused with *'ties'* (as shown in the second rhythm section), which look similar but are **totally** different.

Sustain Pedal Symbols

Without doubt the *'sustain'* (damper) pedal is the most used pedal, and if you have an electronic keyboard, it may indeed be the only one that you have.

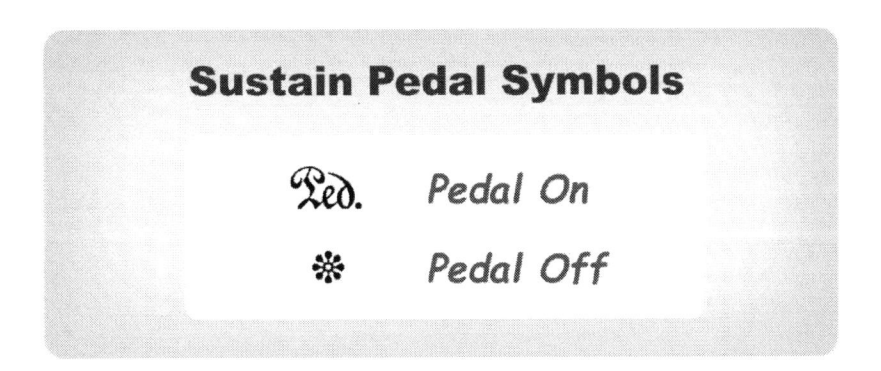

> **Sustain Pedal Symbols**
>
> 𝒫𝑒𝒹.   *Pedal On*
>
> ✸   *Pedal Off*

The *'una corda'* (soft) pedal is generally used at the discretion of the musician to increase the timbre of softly played notes.

The *'sostenuto'* pedal is generally only found on grand pianos (mainly American) and is again mainly used at the discretion of the musician in order to sustain certain notes while leaving others unaffected.

There are many more symbols and terms that you may need to know in the future, but right now I'm trying to limit these to the minimum so as not to strain your brain any more than necessary.

But, without doubt the most important thing is actual practice on the keyboard. Hopefully, you can manage this for at least 30 minutes once or twice a day. But if you can manage more than this, then so much the better!

There is no external audio link for this chapter, but you can hear the loop sections by clicking on them.

Yamaha MOXF6 Workstation (61 keys) - Very Hi Tech

This is a great value workstation which has most of the sounds of the mighty Motif for a fraction of the price. This also has a stunning arpeggiator as well as being bundled with Cubase recording software - but very hi-tech!

I have used one of these with my Privia PX-5S which gave me the sounds from both instruments (which could be played on either); a full hammer action keybed on the Privia for piano pieces and a semi weighted keybed on the MOXF6 for fast organ / synthesizer stuff etc. - a brilliant combination.

Another really interesting thing about this keyboard is that it's KARMA compatible. If you don't know what this is check out the website at http://www.karma-lab.com . This has been described as auto accompaniment with a mind of its own!

"It's easy to play any musical instrument: all you have to do is touch the right key at the right time and the instrument will play itself."

Johann Sebastian Bach

Comment: - I bet a few struggling beginners would like to kick him in the nuts for saying that!

⬅ Putting it all Together ➡

Ok so let's look at a summary of what we've done so far:

- 5 finger exercises and the tapping exercises (don't forget these when you are not near a keyboard);
- Scales - major, minor (harmonic and melodic), chromatic, pentatonic and blues;
- Chords - major, minor, diminished and augmented with extensions (**7ths** etc.);
- Arpeggios and broken chords.

Now I don't suppose for a minute that you've managed to learn all of these yet, but try and work through a portion of each section in part 2 according to your ability. If you practice every day as suggested you will become proficient whatever your age or previous ability - I guarantee it!

But of course, all the exercises and scales that I'm getting you to practice are only tools to improve your understanding and technique and are a means to an end to playing real compositions - or perhaps even creating your own or maybe for improvisation.

The scales and other exercises were originally created by the old masters in order to give equal practice to both hands. But as a general rule each hand will have a different purpose determined by:

- The style of playing (classical, jazz pop etc.);
- Whether or not you are soloing;
- Whether you are accompanying a singer;
- Whether or not you are playing with a band;
- Whether or not you are using auto accompaniment.

When playing solo; broken chords and arpeggios are often used as left-hand accompaniment to the right-hand melody. Following are a couple of very different examples of this. Remember that we are using the bass clef here!

Notice in the first example (above) that the broken chords are: **C major** root position followed by **F major** second inversion and **G major** root position and are all very *'close'* as against the next example (below) which uses the same chords in a *'wider'* span. The former is seen often in classical music and the latter in more modern music.

As always there are numerous variations of both of these.

Other very common left-hand passages include the *'walking bass'* patterns as shown below (over a **C7** chord).

Or a pentatonic minor pattern (**A minor**) below:

Casio GP-500BP

I can't understand why anyone other than an absolute 'purist' would want an acoustic piano when there are keyboards like this around which have the authentic feel and sound of an acoustic as well as being a lovely bit of furniture!

And one of the many boogie woogie style riffs as shown in the next example (over **C** / **C6** and **F** / **F6** chords), usually used in the *12-bar blues* sequence.

But initially you may want to keep things as simple as possible in the left hand particularly if you right hand is *busy*. This can be as simple as a sustained triad on the first beat of the bar or a repeated tonic and fifth on each beat or every other beat as shown below.

If accompanying a singer or playing with a band, it's likely that your right hand would be playing chords / arpeggios and other embellishments while your left-hand compliments these by playing **octaves** or **10ths** (if you have big enough hands).

If using the auto accompaniment feature with the keyboard split, simply play the appropriate chords with your left hand in this section and the melody with your right hand in the upper section, which in most cases is much easier. But as stated earlier for your greatest fulfilment, learn to work both with and without the auto accompaniment.

The audio link for this section is: http://learn-keyboard.co.uk/putting_together.html or click in the graphics.

> *"Dope never helped anybody sing better or play music better or do anything better. All dope can do for you is kill you - and kill you the long, slow, hard way."*
>
> Billie Holiday - (Blues Legend)
>
> *Comment: - Don't learn this the hard way!*

⬅ Your First Tunes ➡

Ok so now we'll put your practice into *practice* and start playing some real tunes.

You might find the first few tunes a bit *'naff'* but please practice them anyway as it's all for a purpose. And it's a good idea to start with something that you are actually capable of playing, which these will be.

If you've managed to do the initial 5 finger exercises, our first three pieces should prove no problem to you as they require no finger crossovers as in the scales. Even still you may need to learn these one hand at a time, bar by bar at a speed that suites your playing and reading ability. As always remember that speed is not important, but accuracy and fluency is!

In all cases I feel that it's important to be aware of which chords are being played; something that I was never taught initially. In our first piece *'The Jolly Farmer'* you may notice that the left-hand part forms the *'broken chords'* which are **C major (I)**, **F major (IV)** and **G7 (V7)**, (the **7th** being the **'F'** played in the right hand). Notice also that the right-hand melody follows these chords.

The Jolly Farmer

Copyright © Martin Woodward 2011 & 2017

This piece should be played *'joyfully'* and mainly staccato as indicated by the dots above / below many of the notes. Also, please notice the *'loop'* symbols seen in most of these pieces indicating that the sections effected should be repeated.

Now there's also a little story that goes with these first three pieces - just to make it a little more exciting!

The Jolly Farmer went into the jolly cowshed to check on his *'jolly udders'* and was met by the Jolly Milkmaid who asked the Jolly Farmer if he'd like *play* with her in the Jolly Haystack. The Jolly Farmer thought long and hard - for about a quarter of a second and decided that it might be *nice* to *play* with the Jolly Milkmaid in the Jolly Haystack so he agreed and off they jolly well went!

This brings us to our next piece the Jolly Milkmaid which should be played *'teasingly'* and with *'passion!'* You may notice that this piece only has 2 chords **C (I)** and **G7 (V7)** and is in **3/4** time.

Very importantly, also notice that the **left hand of this piece is in the treble clef!**

The Jolly Milkmaid

Now not long after the Jolly Farmer and the Jolly Milkmaid started *'playing'* in the Jolly Haystack who should come along but the Not So Jolly Farmer's Wife!

The Not So Jolly Farmer's Wife was not happy about the Jolly Farmer *'playing'* in the Jolly Haystack with the Jolly Milkmaid - I wonder why? Maybe she wanted to *'play'* too!

This brings us to our third piece *'The Not So Jolly Farmer's Wife'* which should be played slowly, angrily and heavily.

The theme in this piece is in fact exactly the same as *'The Jolly Farmer'* but the key has been changed to **C minor** (which remember is the relative minor to **E flat major**) introducing the **E flat** and the **A flat** which changes the chords used to **C *minor*** **(i)**, and **F *minor*** **(iv)** while retaining the **G7 (V7)**. These chords should be played heavily and in full, thereby creating a completely different feel from the broken chords used previously. You'll not fail to notice how changing to the minor key alters the piece dramatically, which is a technique regularly used in classical music.

The Not So Jolly Farmer's Wife

Also notice the *key signature* at the beginning of each line (**B flat**, **A flat** and **E flat**) indicating that all these notes should be flattened unless stated otherwise. *But* as the key is **C minor** and not **E flat major**, the '**B**'s' are *naturalised* - as indicated. This is because **'B natural'** is the leading note (**7th**) note of the **C minor** harmonic scale (see this scale in part 2).

Now back to the story. - Just before the Not So Jolly Farmer's Wife got to the Jolly Haystack (clutching her jolly rolling pin), Sam the Jolly Battering Ram came charging out (he was also playing in the Jolly Haystack) and *butted* the Not So Jolly Farmer's Wife down the Jolly Well. But don't worry she's alright - just a bit wet and even less jolly than before!

So briefly while the Not So Jolly Farmer's Wife was down the Jolly Well - all was *well* with the Jolly Farmer and the Jolly Milkmaid and Sam the Jolly Battering Ram (Heaven forbid) in the Jolly Haystack. That was until the Not So Jolly Farmer's Wife managed to climb out of the Jolly Well with the aid of her Jolly Broomstick. This was when the sharps and flats really started flying, but to be honest you're not quite ready for this yet, and neither am I, so we'll leave things as they are and move onto our next piece.

Our next two pieces are by Carl Czerny an Austrian composer who was famous for his technique studies. If you've successfully managed the first few 5 finger exercises *and* the **C major** scale you should have no difficulty in playing the first of these pieces.

Both of these pieces are in **C major** and very much based around the **C major** scale and therefore require finger crossovers as shown in the fingering. The left-hand chords are **C major**, **F major** and **G7 (I, IV & V7)** using various inversions. Make sure that you are aware of which chords (and inversions) that you are playing - and this will lead to a proper understanding.

Notice that both hands again use the *treble* clef in each of the Czerny pieces.

Although intended as a piano exercise, the left hand in the first piece is typical of what you would be doing with your left hand if using auto accompaniment - simply sustaining chords.

The second Czerny piece although still in **C major** and using the same three chords as before is more difficult than the first piece as the left hand is more active. However, when you look closely you will see that this consists of nothing but the broken chords in various inversions and is much easier to play when you understand *what* you are playing!

One downside to learning the piano is that it can make you *fat!*
With this in mind here's a great bit of nutritional advice from an acclaimed expert: -

"Never eat more than you can lift!"

Miss Piggy (the Muppets)

Copyright © Martin Woodward 2011 & 2017

Carl Czerny Piece 1

Carl Czerny Piece 2

Minuet - J.S Bach

This next piece in **G major** is perhaps a little more complicated but after some practice I'm sure you will find it very simple. Start by learning both hands separately - then piece it together with both hands bar by bar. Notice that the left hand is now using the bass clef.

Casio Privia PX-350

If you're looking for a low priced portable keyboard with a great piano feel, great sounds, auto accompaniment and built in speakers - this is hard to beat! In fact, for the price this is currently impossible to beat!

> *"Give Peace a Chance!"*
>
> John Lennon
>
> *Comment: - When will we learn the lesson?*

Greensleeves

We briefly featured this piece earlier in the *'Keys and Key Signature'* chapter which showed that this is in **E minor** (due to the **D#** and **C#**). Other chords used are **D major**, **B major** and **G major**. These can all easily be identified in the left hand. Notice how I've changed the left-hand chords to arpeggios from *bar 15*. And if you are aware of what the chords are, the piece (and every other piece) will be much easier to read and play!

I particularly like this piece as it's ideal for jazzing up and playing in many different ways.

Sustain Pedal

I haven't included any pedal references to any of these pieces herein, but now that you have started to gain a little experience, you may wish to use the sustain pedal sparingly as you see fit. The chord line above the staff gives a good clue as to when the pedal should be applied and released. *Generally,* the pedal can be applied / released at every chord change and not used at all when there are several chord changes in a bar. But for classical pieces, *always* follow the instructions in the notation.

Copyright © Martin Woodward 2011 & 2017

Silent Night

Personally, I'm not into hymns; I think that most are unbelievably boring. But out of all the hymns that I've heard, I think that Christmas Carols are by far the best. And for me the one that stands out above the rest is this one - a truly magnificent composition and so simple - still based around the same three chords (**I, IV** and **V7**). The music was written (originally for guitar) by Austrian headmaster Franz Xaver Gruber in 1818 to the words written by priest Joseph Mohr two years previously and was first performed on Christmas eve 1818 in the Church of ***St. Nicholas,*** Oberndorf, Austria. - *Thank you Wikipedia!*

This is in fact a very simple arrangement and playing it as written should give you some enjoyment. But it can also be embellished on easily by playing a repeat and using thirds or octaves in the right hand, although this will probably be a little too advanced for you at the moment.

At first glance, you may think that the left hand is incredibly complicated, but I assure you that it's not. It's just a series of broken chords / arpeggios as shown in the last chapter. And these are used again in my own tunes, *'Falora'* and *'Flo'* - shown shortly.

Even on pieces where the chords are not shown, they can easily be identified from the arpeggios, which is very useful to know.

> *"Yabba Dabba Doo!"*
>
> Fred Flintstone - (Early Rock Star)
>
> *Comment: - Shout this every morning when you wake up and you'll always be happy!*

Tales of the Riverbank

If you're an ancient old git like me you'll remember the 1960's TV series *'Tales of the Riverbank'* where real animals played the parts of Hammy the Hamster, Roderick the Rat and G.P. the Guinea Pig narrated by Johnny Morris - *the Hot Chestnut Man!*

If you're not quite as ancient you might remember the re-titled version *'Hammy Hamster'* in the 1970's in colour - *yeh, us old gits had to watch stuff in black and white!* Anyway, this is the title music which is correctly named **Andante in C major** by Italian guitarist / composer Mauro Giuliani (1781-1828).

Copyright © Martin Woodward 2011 & 2017

As the title suggests this is in **C major** and sounds best using a classical guitar sound, but ok with a piano sound as well. The piece is probably an absolute bitch to play on a guitar, but is relatively simple to play on the keyboard and very satisfying as it's a great little tune, especially if you're a *Hammy the Hamster* fan!

Without doubt the only tricky part is the short, syncopated bit in the last two bars, but don't let this put you off. As always practice one hand at a time and put it together bar by bar and you'll get it.

Yamaha CP4 Stage Piano

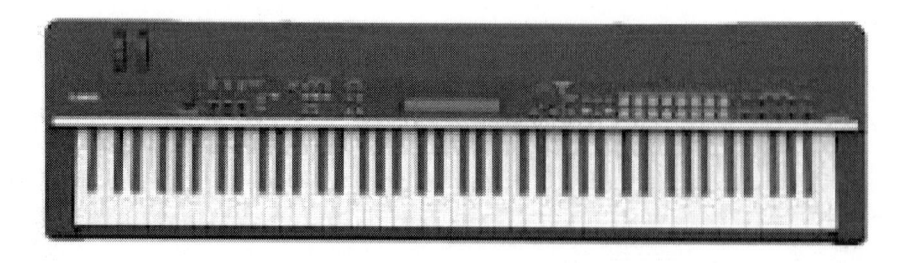

Clearly one of the best stage pianos available. The only reason I wouldn't have one of these is the lack of on board recording functions. But as a stage piano this is superb, lovely feel, lovely sounds - I love it!

> "It's a great thing about being a musician; you don't stop until the day you die, you can improve. So it's a wonderful thing to do."
>
> Marcus Miller (Jazz composer)

Copyright © Martin Woodward 2011 & 2017

Traditional Irish Melody in G major

Our next practice piece is a lovely little *'Traditional Irish melody'*. Unfortunately, I don't know what it's called (sorry) and to be honest I've written this arrangement just from memory, so it may not even be completely correct, but it's nice nonetheless.

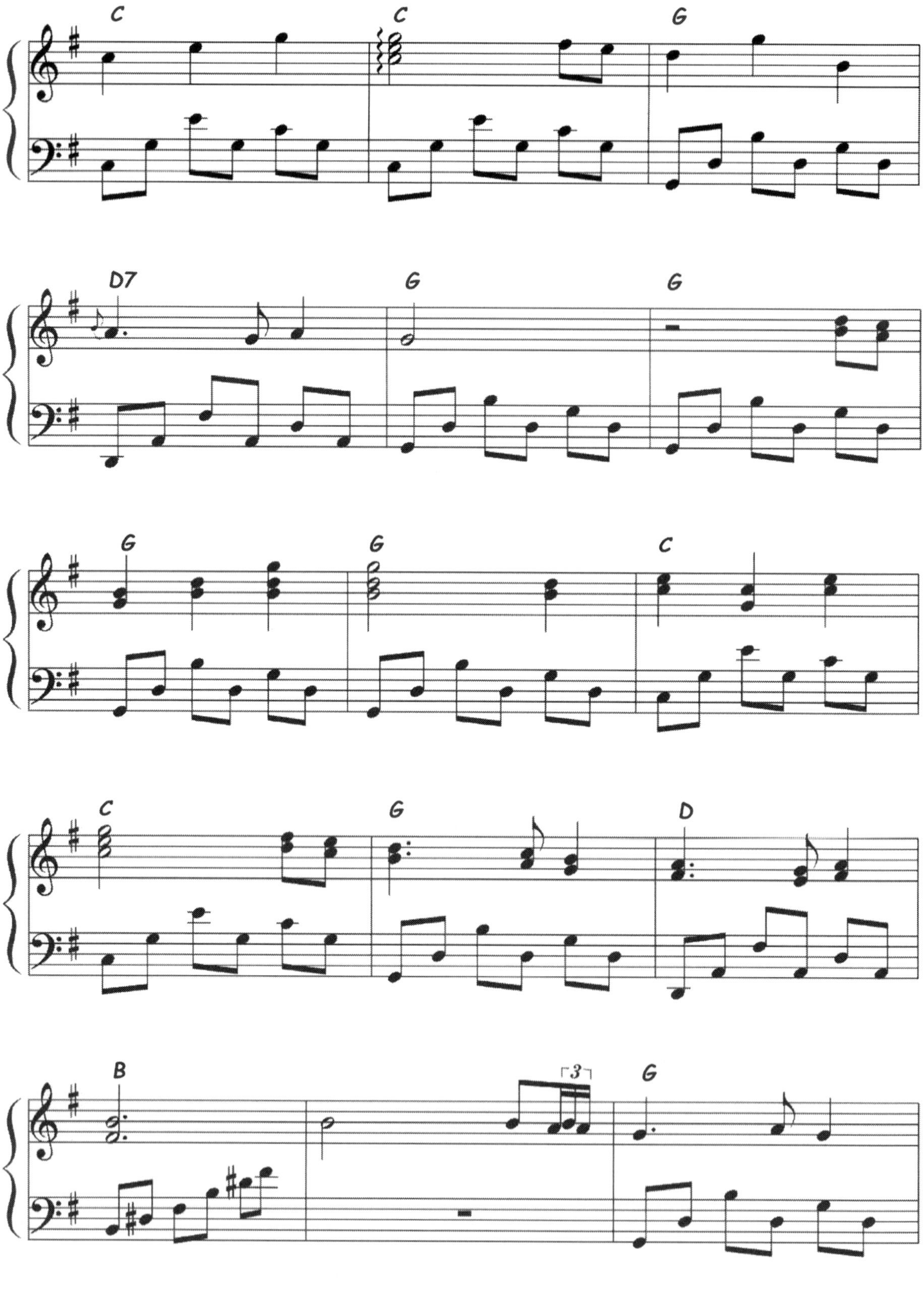
C
C
G
D7
G
G
G
G
C
C
G
D
B
3
G

This piece again uses mainly three chords (**G major**, **C major** and **D7**) although there is a **B major** in *bar 25* adding the accidental **D#** in the left hand. Remember that **D#** is the leading note (**7th**) in the **E minor** scales, the relative to **G major**.

The left hand uses exactly the same *'arpeggio'* arrangement as in *'Silent Night'*. And as with *'Silent Night'*, a repeat could be played using octaves in the main theme, but you may perhaps find this a little difficult at this stage.

Notice also that there are a couple of incidental *'grace notes'* in the right hand and also the *'arpeggio'* symbol (as shown in a previous chapter) is used a couple of times.

A Simple Arpeggio Composition

The next piece entitled *'Flo'* is a composition of mine comprised *entirely* of arpeggios (and *no* passing notes). Putting it another way, every single note in the piece is part of the chord itemised above the staff. Hopefully, this will demonstrate how very important and versatile arpeggios can be.

I've also said previously that most compositions are based around diatonic chords (found naturally in the scale) which is true, but this piece contains one *non*-diatonic chord - **B♭**. which is repeated regularly, demonstrating that non-diatonic chords *can* work very effectively even though theoretically perhaps they shouldn't. All the other chords are diatonic chords in the key of **A minor**.

And just a little fingering hint - in the left hand the 5th finger is used on all the lower *arpeggio* notes except the **B♭ s**, where the 3rd finger is used.

Following this piece is the final practice piece entitled *'Falora'* which I originally wrote for my sister in law Laura (hence the title), to help her get back into the piano after a long illness. I hope you like it!

And again, the left hand of both these pieces primarily uses the same pattern as the last two pieces.

The Audio link for this section is http://learn-keyboard.co.uk/first_tunes.html or click on the graphics.

Korg PA4X Arranger Keyboard (76 keys)

If you're not bothered about having a hammer action key bed, then this board is could be for you. Great sounds and great auto accompaniment with easy recording features.

I previously used one of the its predecessors the Korg PA2X.

"*Music is about the only thing left that people don't fight over.*"

Ray Charles

Flo

♩ = 90

Martin Woodward

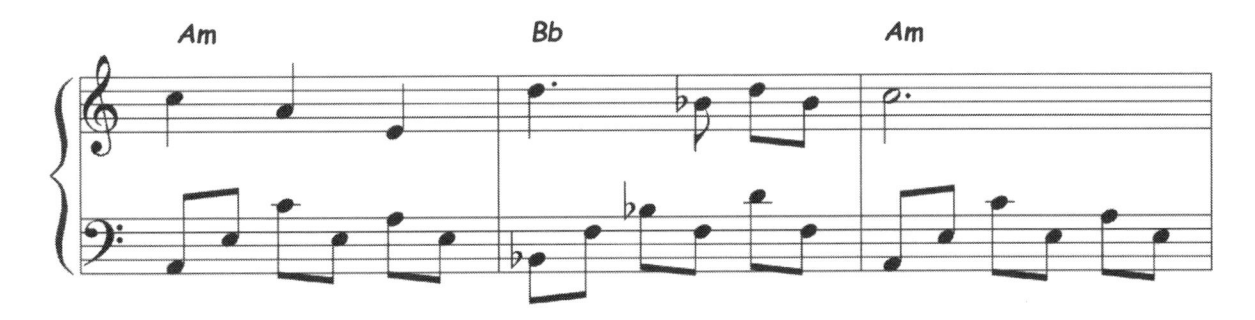

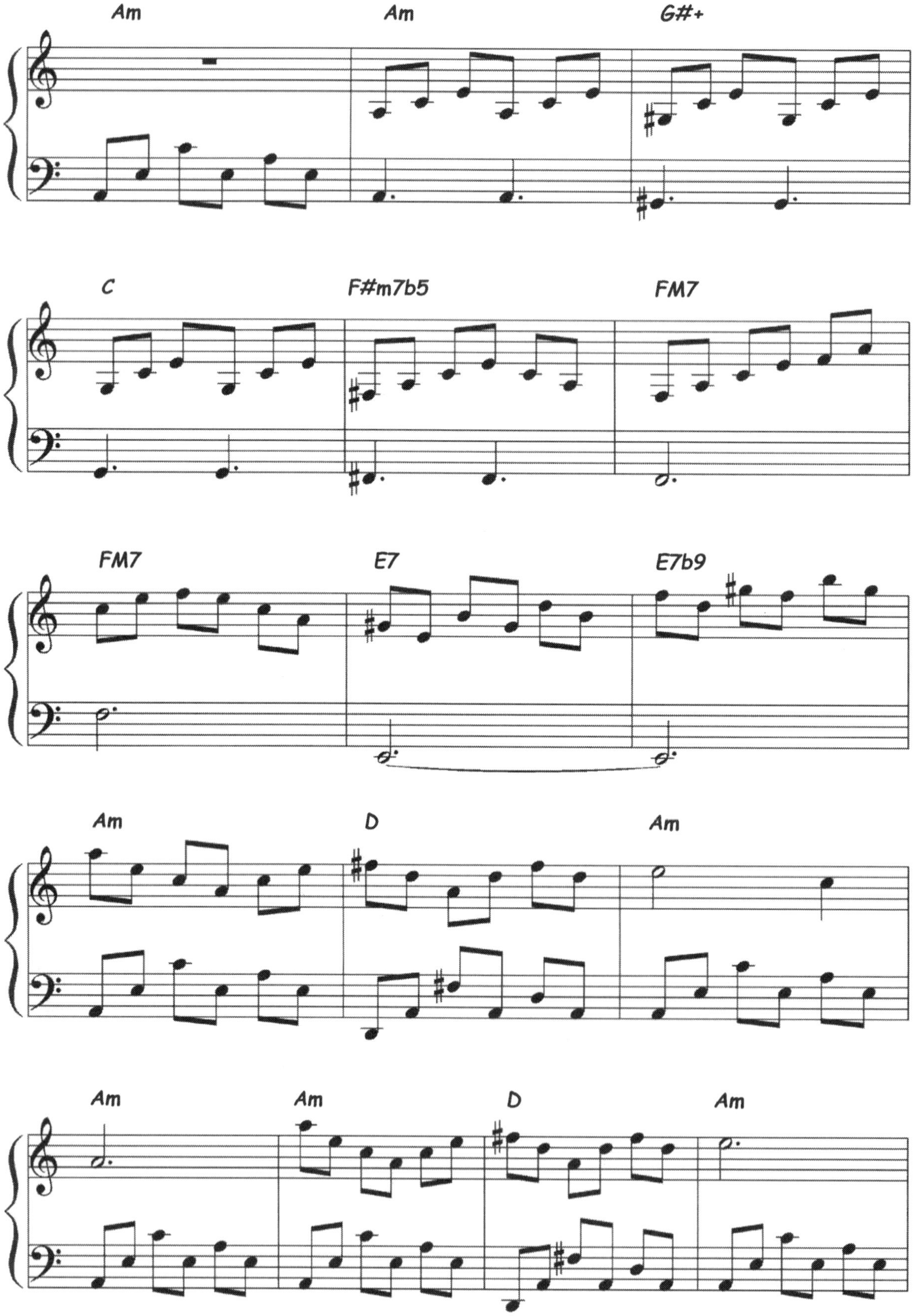
Am
Am
G#+
C
F#m7b5
FM7
FM7
E7
E7b9
Am
D
Am
Am
Am
D
Am

Audio link - http://learn-keyboard.co.uk/flo.mp3 or click on the graphics.

"After silence, that which comes nearest to expressing the inexpressible is music!"
Unknown

Falora

♩ = 75

Martin Woodward

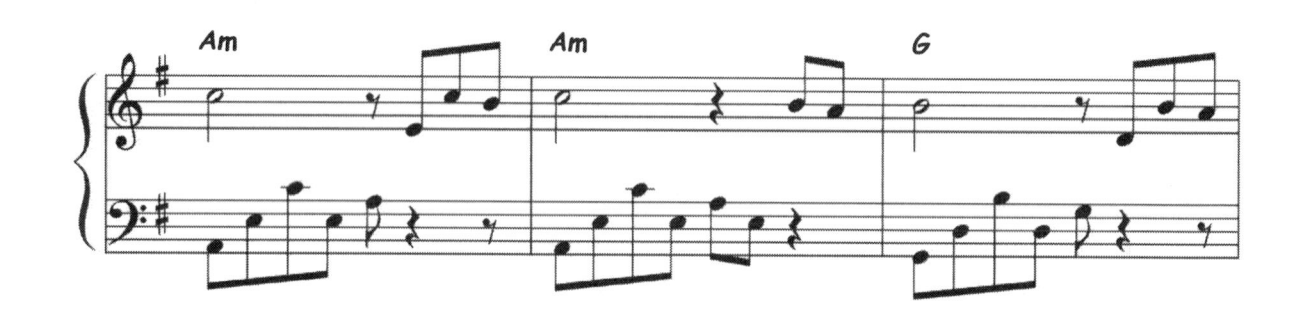

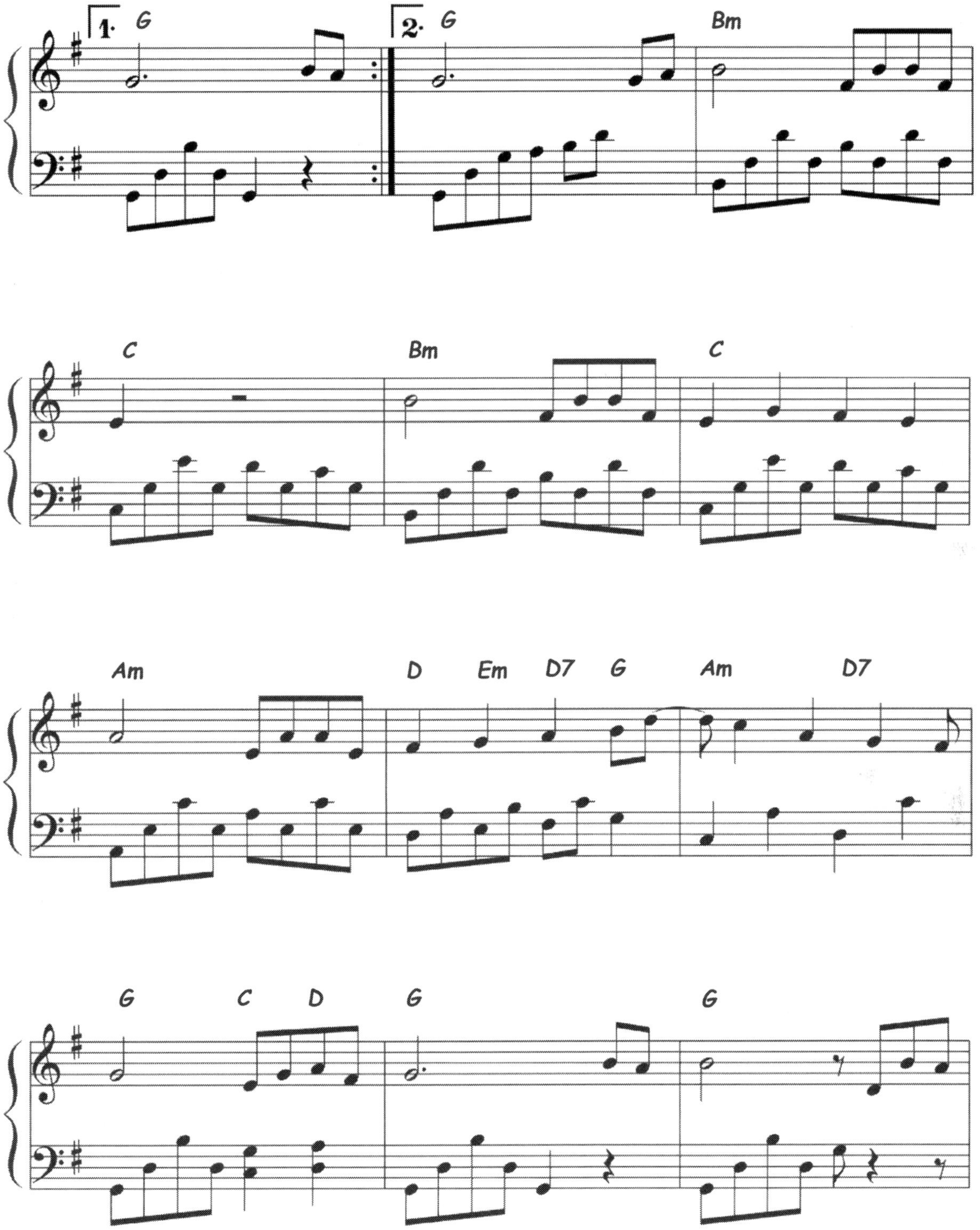
1. G
2. G
Bm
C
Bm
C
Am
D
Em
D7
G
Am
D7
G
C
D
G
G

Audio link - http://www.learn-keyboard.co.uk/falora.mp3

Playing from a Fake Book

Sheet music can be very expensive and even more so if you buy the full version including right / left hand notation. Often, I've bought books containing perhaps 20 pieces when there has been maybe only 3 or 4 that I've actually wanted.

Fake books typically consist of maybe 100 songs but only with top line (melody) notation and the appropriate chord symbols included. This is by far the most economical way of buying sheet music.

If playing from a fake book and using auto accompaniment simply choose the appropriate style and tempo, learn / play the melody with your right hand in the upper part of the keyboard and play the appropriate chords with your left hand in the lower section of the keyboard - easy peasy!

Alternatively, if you don't want to use the auto accompaniment, using the information from the chord symbols you could to play an arpeggio / broken chord type accompaniment as shown previously.

Here is a typical example of how one of the previous pieces featured would look in *'fake book'* format.

Traditional Irish Melody in G major - (top line)

Immediately you'll notice that printing the music in this format takes up less space and consequently is more economical to produce.

But if you intend playing classical music, I recommend that you obtain the full music notation and learn the pieces exactly as written. Also, if this is the route you want to take, you'd be advised to seek professional classical tuition at some point. Having said this, the information given here comes from a combination of classical tuition and professional *'pop'* experience and as such provides a good grounding for whichever direction you ultimately intend following.

What if There's No Chord Line?

With most fake books, there *will* be a chord line, but it's bound to happen at some point that you'll come across something that you want to play that doesn't have a chord line and you'll have to work out your own.

This is nowhere as difficult as you might imagine especially if you have learnt about chord construction as already dealt with.

As an example, we'll use the first few bars of UK national anthem.

The first thing always is to look at the key signature. In this case there is no key signature, so it has to be **C major** or **A minor**. To determine which of these it is, you need to look for any accidental sharps, particularly **F#** or **G#** which are included in the **A minor** scales.

Looking at the notation, you'll see that there are none of these, but there aren't any **G naturals** either, but because the phrase both starts and finishes on '**C**' it's clear to me that it's in **C major** and not **A minor**.

So, the first chord is probably **C major**, based on the fact that's it's clearly in the key of **C major** and the first note is '**C**'.

But '**C**' is also contained in other triads as follows:

- C is the tonic (root note) of **C major**;
- C is the tonic (root note) of **C minor**;
- C is the mediant (3rd) of **A minor**;
- C is the mediant (3rd) of **A♭ major**;
- C is the dominant (5th) of **F major**;
- C is the dominant (5th) of **F minor**.

So, you can see that there are a fair few possibilities, and this is before we start with suspended **4ths**, **7ths** and **9ths** etc.

But out of the six most likely contenders only three of these are *diatonic chords* in the key of **C major** (derived from the notes of the **C major** scale). And these are **C major**, **A minor** and **F major**. So, these are the most likely ones to fit easily, but that doesn't mean that the *non-diatonic* chords won't work, sometimes using these can add some colourful variations - as shown previously in my piece, **'Flo'**.

And the same method applies to the remaining notes.

So, with all this in mind a simple chord progression for this passage is as follows:

Or you could be a bit more inventive and add a few more chords as follows:

Notice that each chord contains the **1st**, **3rd** or **5th** note of the chosen chord as explained previously, with the exception of the **Dm7** where the **C** is the **7th**.

You may also note that there are quite a few **V - I** progressions as talked about earlier in the *'Circle of 5ths'* section. These are **Am - Dm - G7 - C**; **Am - Dm**; **Em7 - Am** and **Dm7 - G7 - C**. And as this progression is the strongest of all progressions it will also sound reasonably pleasing to the ear, although it has to be said that only Brian May can make this piece swing!

Now which of these is *'right'* or rather *'as written'* I really don't know and can't be bothered to find out, as both *work*, and that's all that matters.

Obviously if you were playing with other musicians, you'd all have to be playing the same arrangement, but if you're playing on your own you can do anything that works!

Acquiring Free Sheet Music

Very little *new* music is legally available free of charge due to copyright laws and I'm not suggesting that these laws should be violated. But 70 years after a composer has died his / her music becomes copyright free. And as many of the best composers have died over 70 years ago there's plenty to go at. All of the compositions that I've included in this book are copyright free, or my own, which is why I've chosen to use them.

So, don't waste a fortune buying classical, ragtime or even early blues pieces from music stores as they're virtually all available free of charge from internet sites such as http://www.sheetmusicfox.com and http://sheetmusic-free.com to name two. No doubt a simple *Google / Bing* search will reveal many more sources.

If selecting classical pieces, probably the hardest thing is being aware of which pieces are suitable for your ability. A good trick is to check out the Associated Board of Music's exam pieces which are graded **I - VIII**. Obviously start out with grade **I**.

If you intend gigging (or if you just want to be incredibly organised) it's a good idea to photocopy / scan the entire music notation that you need and collate it into one or two clear pocket folders in order to keep everything easy to find. Technically this is actually a breach of copyright, but if you do this just for your own use with music that you have legitimately purchased then I can't see anything unethical about it.

Additionally, you could store all the styles and settings for each piece into your keyboard, making it available for easy instant access.

Just about all of the modern *'pop'* music is available as sheet music for a price, but much of this is frankly unsuitable for piano as it's not been *written* for piano. Even the best pianist in the world isn't going to make a bit of *'Led Zeppelin'* sound descent on a piano!

I've personally scoured the music shops looking for music that sounds right on a piano and that I want to play. Often, I've bought a compilation of pieces which only contains one or two pieces that I actually want - very uneconomical!

The only book that I've ever bought where I can honestly say that I like every piece is called **'Tranquillity'** by Irish composer Phil Coulter. And all of these pieces sound great and can be played by *'mortals'*!

With this in mind I have written my own *sensibly priced* tune book: **'Original Piano / Keyboard Sheet Music (2nd Edition)'** which includes 16 great sounding original pieces available as either printable eBook or paperback. All of the pieces are fairly easy to play and suitable for solo piano or keyboard with accompaniment (with chord lines). These pieces can also be heard on my website - try before you buy at: http://learn-keyboard.co.uk/sheet_music.html .

Nord Electro 5 HP 73

This is a superb keyboard with all the top-notch sounds. Not quite as fully featured as the Stage 2, but not as complicated either. I love it!

Part 2

Practical Exercises

5 Finger Exercises

These exercises are a continuation of the *'tapping'* exercises shown earlier and should be practiced every day while you are reading and understanding the other information.

Even though the exercises are written in musical notation for both hands they really don't require any musical understanding to play them. All are played entirely on white notes and require no finger crossovers. Follow the patterns for ascending and descending as shown in the charts (7 bars ascending - 7 bars descending) and notice how they relate to the music notation.

Note that there is an interval of a third at the first measure of each bar which enables the exercises to ascend / descend up and down the scale.

They should be practiced with each hand separately and both hands together both staccato and legato at speeds that you are comfortable with.

These exercises are variations from the C L Hanon Virtuoso Pianist and are designed to create finger strength, speed, agility and independence in both hands - AND THEY WORK! There are no better exercises than these and they are simple and fun to play! Although these initial exercises will 'get you going', if your intentions are to progress classically, you'd be advised to seek out more of these exercises. The full set of Hanon's exercises takes about one hour a day to complete, but the rewards are phenomenal.

Section audio link: http://www.learn-keyboard.co.uk/5_finger_exercises_2.html

Quick link to Part 1

Casio CGP 700 Digital Piano

If you want a nice, low cost piano with auto-accompaniment, the Casio CGP 700 could be for you. This is not as programmable as the PX 560 but does have a great sound and feel!

Exercise 1

5 4 3 2 1 2 3 4 (5)
Left Hand Ascending

1 2 3 4 5 4 3 2 (1)
Right Hand Ascending

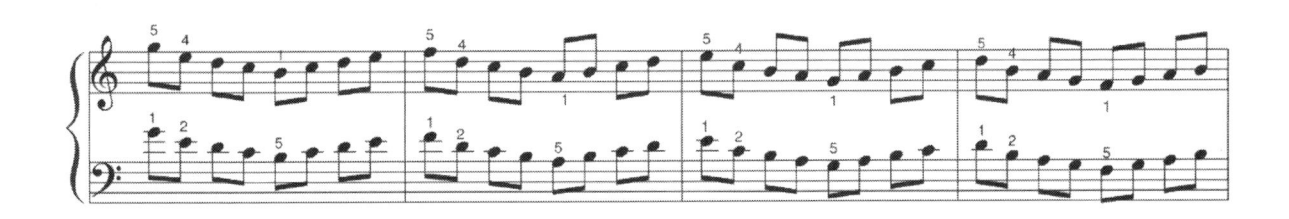

1 2 3 4 5 4 3 2 (1)
Left Hand Descending

5 4 3 2 1 2 3 4 (5)
Right Hand Descending

Exercise 2

5 1 2 1 3 2 4 3 (5)
Left Hand Ascending

1 5 4 5 3 4 2 3 (1)
Right Hand Ascending

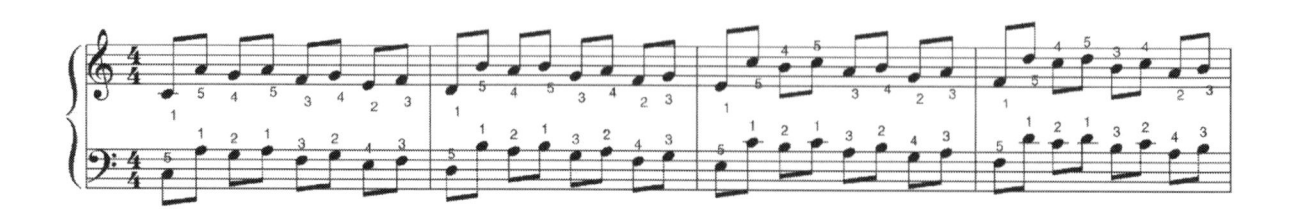

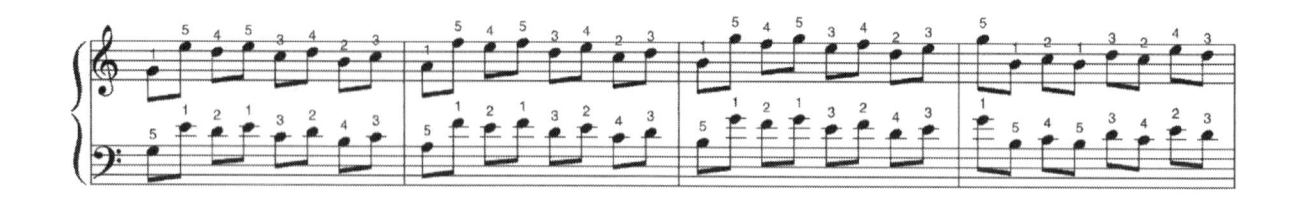

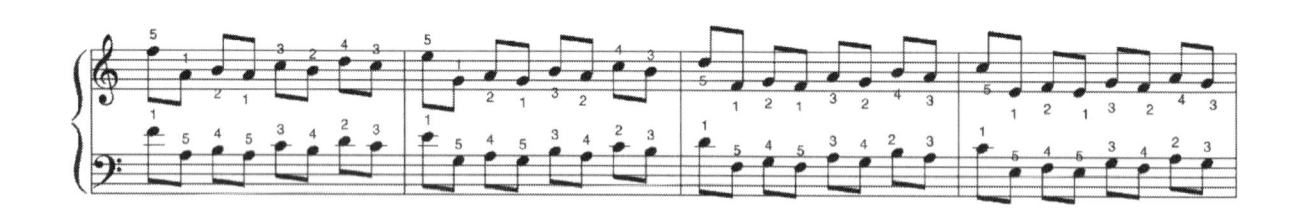

1 5 4 5 3 4 2 3 (1)
Left Hand Descending

5 1 2 1 3 2 4 3 (5)
Right Hand Descending

Exercise 3

5 1 2 1 3 1 4 1(5)
Left Hand Ascending

1 5 4 5 3 5 2 5 (1)
Right Hand Ascending

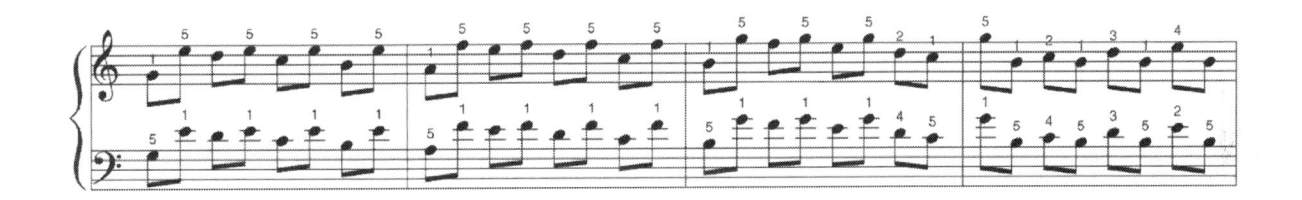

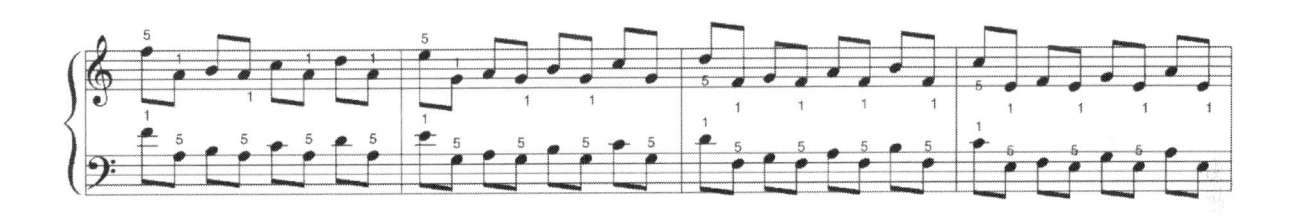

1 5 4 5 3 5 2 5 (1)
Left Hand Descending

5 1 2 1 3 1 4 1(5)
Right Hand Descending

Exercise 4

5 4 3 4 2 3 1 2 (5)
Left Hand Ascending

1 2 3 2 4 3 5 4 (1)
Right Hand Ascending

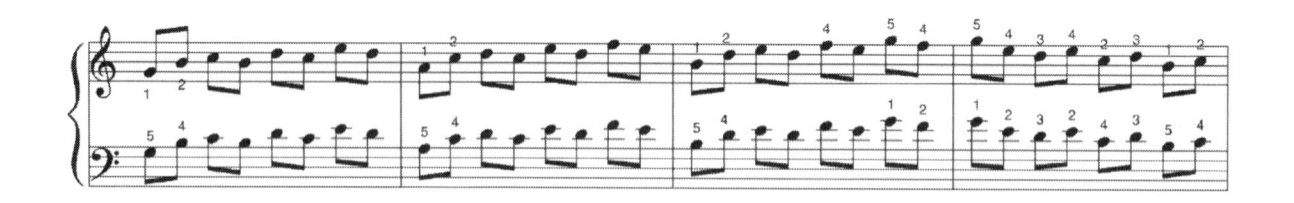

1 2 3 2 4 3 5 4 (1)
Left Hand Descending

5 4 3 4 2 3 1 2 (5)
Right Hand Descending

Exercise 5

5 3 4 2 3 1 2 4 (5)
Left Hand Ascending

1 3 2 4 3 5 4 2 (1)
Right Hand Ascending

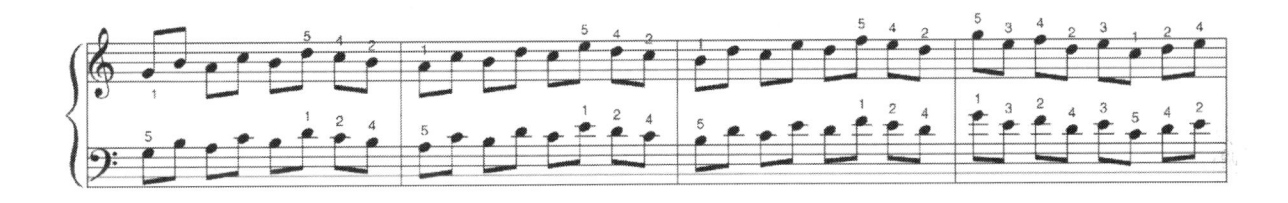

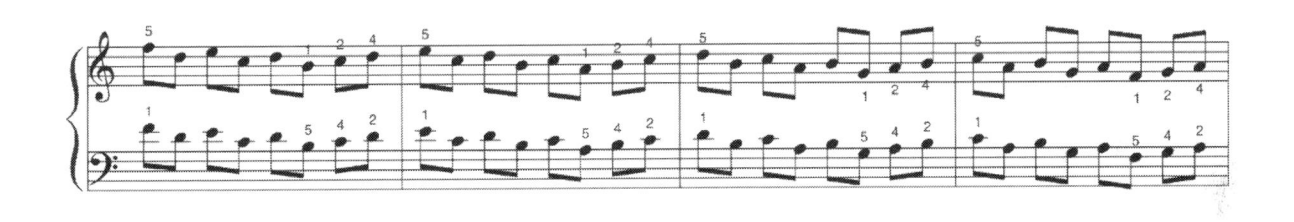

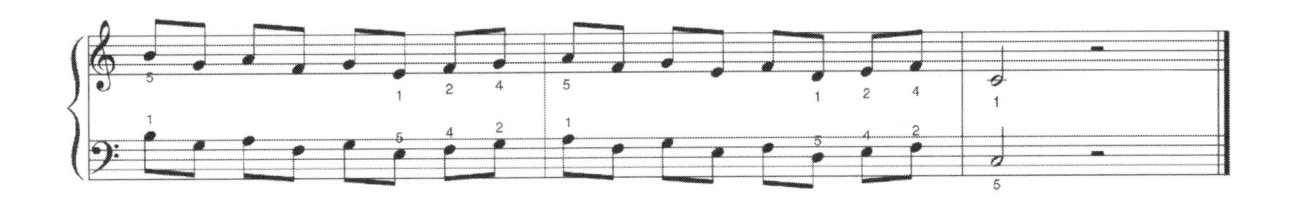

1 3 2 4 3 5 4 2 (1)
Left Hand Descending

5 3 4 2 3 1 2 4 (5)
Right Hand Descending

Scale Exercises (in full)

We discussed the importance of scales earlier; in this section, you have all the major and minor (natural / harmonic / melodic) scales in every key, and the pentatonic (major / minor) and blues scales in the most commonly used keys.

The next few pages show all the major and relative minor scales in the order in which they should be learnt. They are written here in two octaves, one octave apart, but can also be played for four octaves. Ideally these should be practiced with each hand separately and both hands together staccato and legato paying attention to accuracy and timing. Also make sure that each note is played with an equal pressure. Gradually increase the speed according to your ability. When you are familiar with them they can be practiced in any order.

If you have the eBook version, you can of course print out the pages that you require.

Scales don't have to be boring

I can't overestimate how important the scales are in order to improve technique, theoretical understanding and improvisation skills. This chapter should emphasise this.

Ideally every scale should be practised morning noon and night with both hands for four octaves ascending and descending at a speed that is comfortable. If you can't manage them all, do what you can.

However, I have to admit that scales practised in the normal way can be boring beyond belief and this fact no doubt puts people off practising them.

But let's look at why they are boring, using the **C major** scale as an example.

In case you haven't noticed, the scale begins on the first (strong) beat of the bar, but ends on an off-beat - it doesn't conclude very well - hence - boring! Even if we changed it to **3/4** timing it still wouldn't conclude nicely.

But look what happens when we add just one more note at the top.

Or one extra note at the bottom.

They finish on the first beat of a bar and consequently sound much better. And they're still just as good from the technique improvement / theoretical understanding point of view, but far better from the improvising point of view.

This can be taken a little further by:

    a) starting on a different note;

    b) changing direction at any time;

    c) incorporating arpeggios;

    d) adding incidental / passing notes / slurs;

    e) changing from major / minor to pentatonic / blues or

    f) a combination of all of them.

All of a sudden, the possibilities are endless and infinity takes on a new meaning! The whole thing becomes pleasurable and more inventive and in fact leads automatically to improvisation - and fun!

Following are a few more examples, all of which are excellent finger exercises. But remember these are just examples - see what you can come up with and make sure you use all of your fingers, particularly the fourth and fifth.

The first example below is very similar to one of the 5 finger exercises (Ex. 4).

Casio PX 360

This is the PX 560's little brother, and has the same basic sounds and recording facilities, but it's not quite so programable.

The next exercise is clearly in **A minor** and consists of portions of the **C major** scale starting on **A** and finishing with a broken **A minor** chord / arpeggio.

Although this example is written in **4/4** triplets it could have also been written as straight quavers in **12/8** timing to achieve the same result.

The next example is a variation of the 5-finger exercise (Ex. 2) ending with the **C major** scale descending starting on **C**, **G** and **D** and a **CM7** arpeggio.

Have fun by creating your own similar patterns and guess what? - You'll be improvising!

Look what **Vivaldi** did using the same technique in **E major**. Analyse this and you'll see that it's an extremely good example of what I'm talking about.

Notice that the **E major** scale in bar 5 starts and finishes on **G sharp**.

Millions of compositions of all types have been produced by just messing with scales and arpeggios either consciously or unconsciously.

Ideally learn all of the scales in the following pages by memory. After only a short while you should only need to refer to the music notation in order to learn the fingering. Make sure that you learn each scale thoroughly before proceeding to the next one and obviously progress at a rate that suits your ability and time scale.

The first scale listed in full is the *'chromatic'* which although shown here beginning and ending on **C**, should be learnt starting (and ending) on any key for two or more octaves with each hand separately and also together.

If you look at the fingering below you may notice that in both hands the 3rd finger is used on all the black notes and the 1st on all the white notes *except* **F** and **C** in the right hand and **B** and **E** on the left hand where the 2nd finger is used. Remembering this little trick makes learning this scale simple!

Chromatic Scale 2 Octaves on C

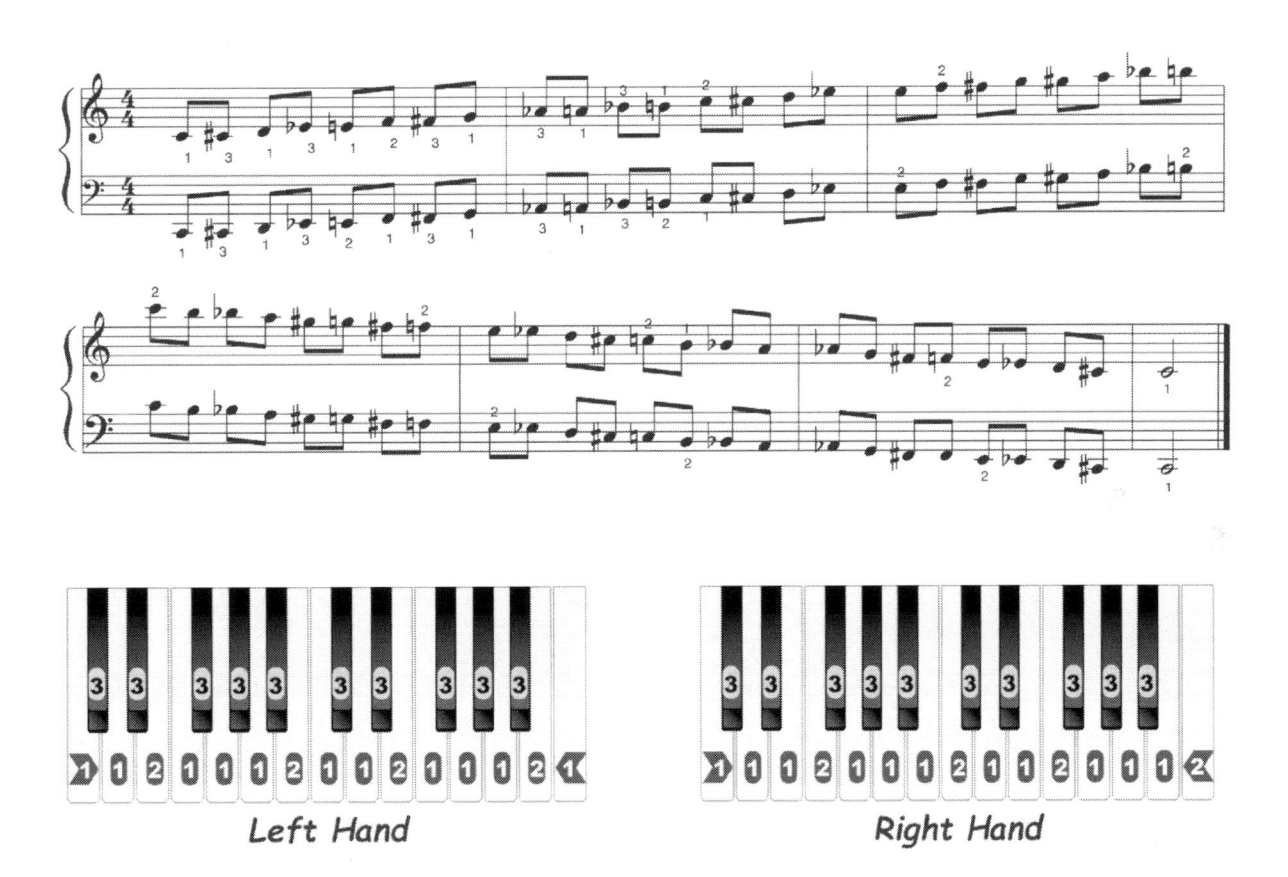

Note that on the following pages the *'natural minor scales'*, are only shown in keyboard view. But remember these are exactly the same as the melodic minor scale descending, or the relative major starting on the submediant (**6th**).

The audio link for this section is: http://learn-keyboard.co.uk/scales_full.html

Quick link back to Part 1

C major Scale

A Harmonic Minor Scale

A Melodic Minor Scale

C Major

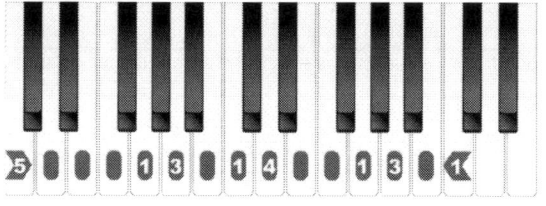

Left Hand 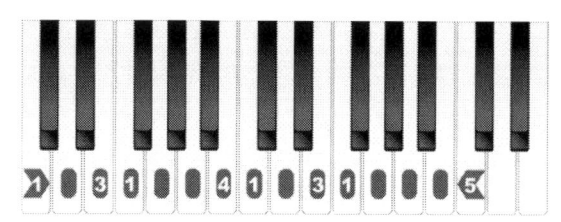 — *Right Hand*

A Natural Minor

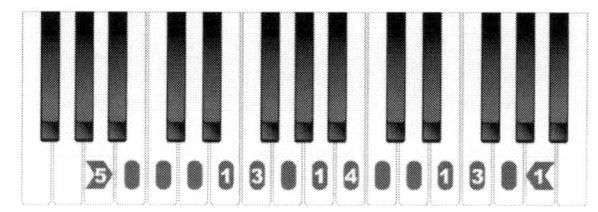

Left Hand 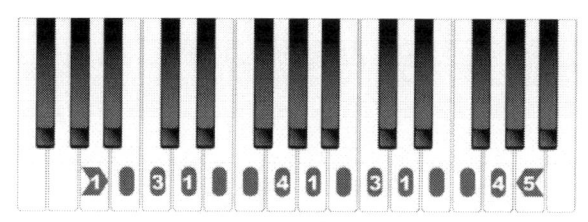 — *Right Hand*

A Harmonic Minor

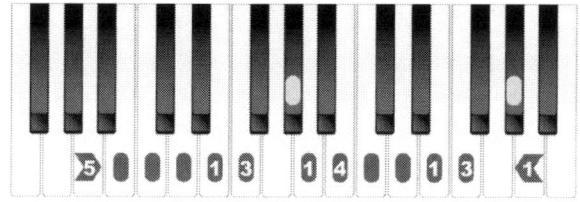

Left Hand 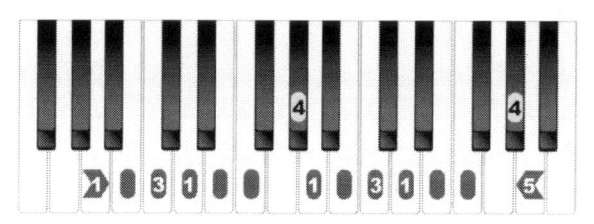 — *Right Hand*

A Melodic Minor (Ascending)

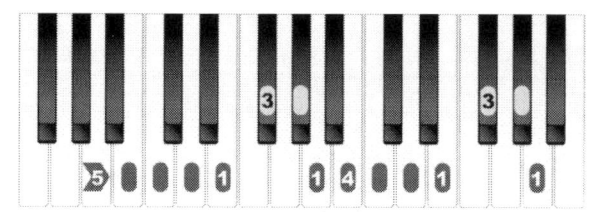

Left Hand 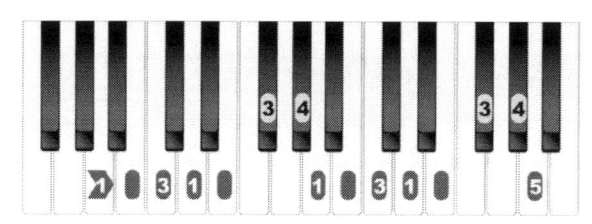 — *Right Hand*

A Melodic Minor (Descending)

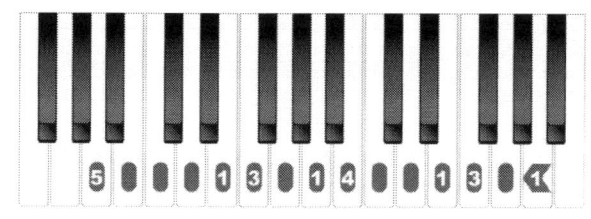

Left Hand 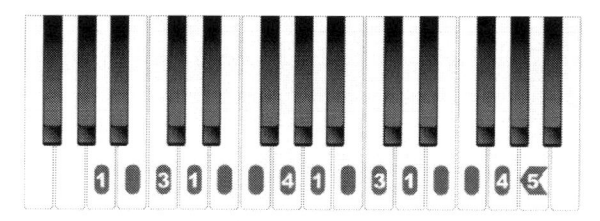 — *Right Hand*

Copyright © Martin Woodward 2011 & 2017

F major Scale

D Harmonic Minor Scale

D Melodic Minor Scale

F Major

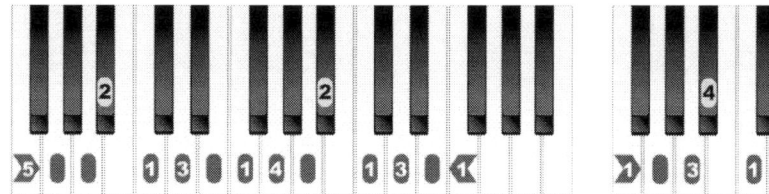

Left Hand 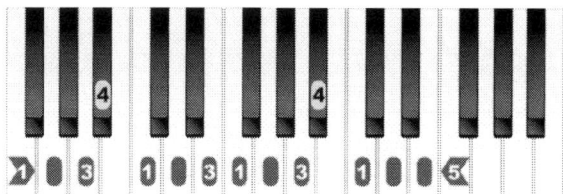 — *Right Hand*

D Natural Minor

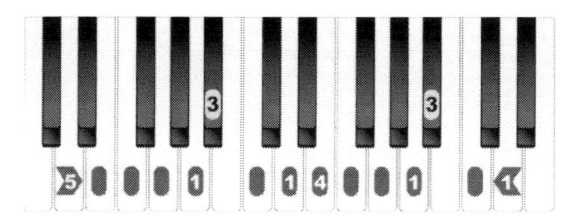

Left Hand 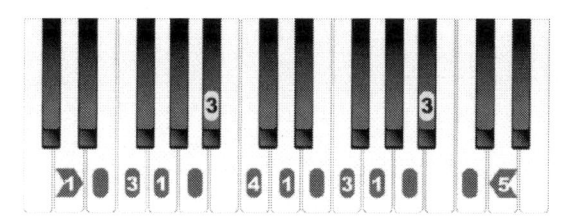 — *Right Hand*

D Harmonic Minor

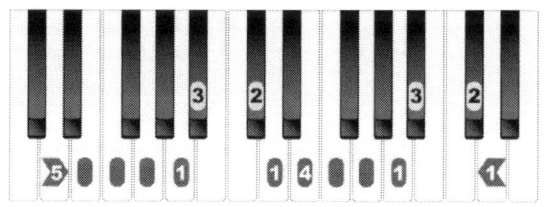

Left Hand 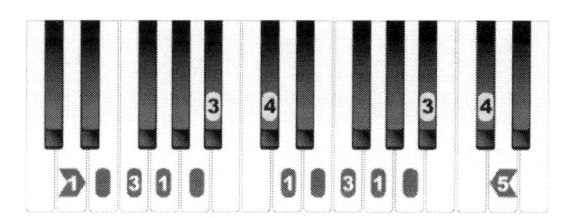 — *Right Hand*

D Melodic Minor (Ascending)

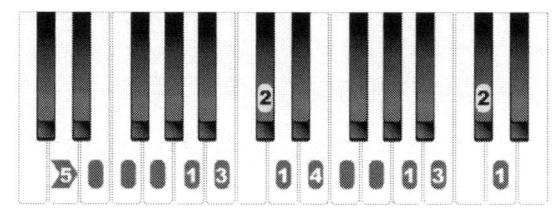

Left Hand 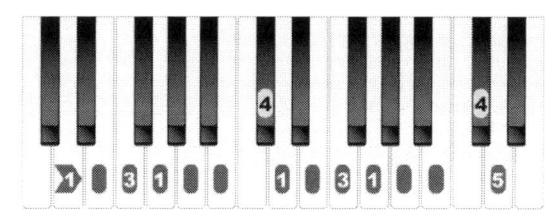 — *Right Hand*

D Melodic Minor (Descending)

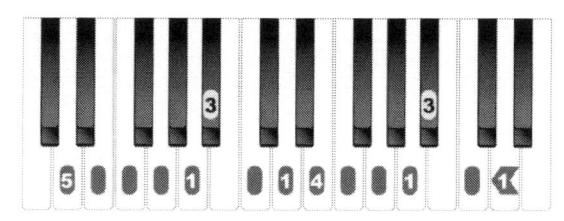

Left Hand 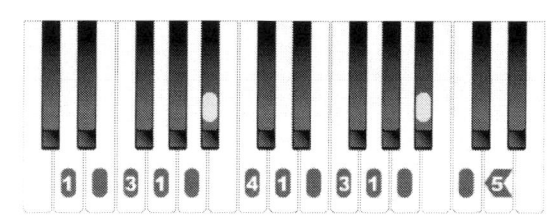 — *Right Hand*

Copyright © Martin Woodward 2011 & 2017

G major Scale

E Harmonic Minor Scale

E Melodic Minor Scale

G Major

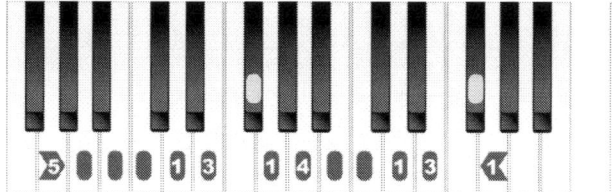

Left Hand 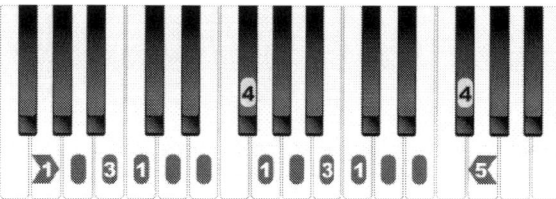 · Right Hand

E Natural Minor

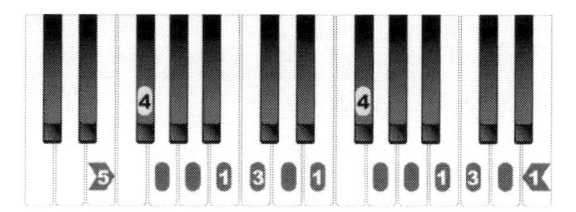

Left Hand 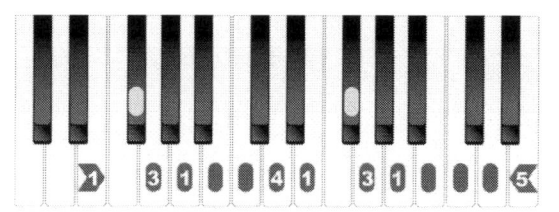 · Right Hand

E Harmonic Minor

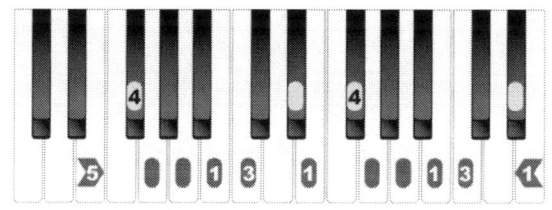

Left Hand 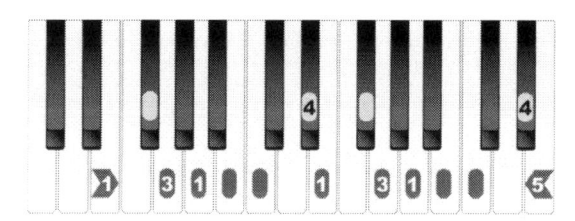 · Right Hand

E Melodic Minor (Ascending)

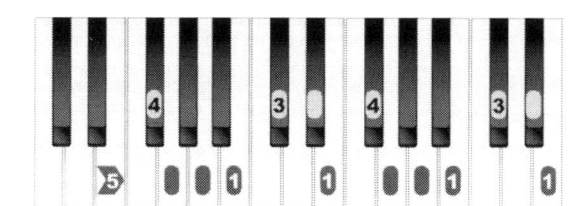

Left Hand 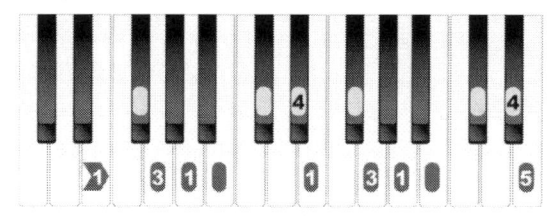 · Right Hand

E Melodic Minor (Descending)

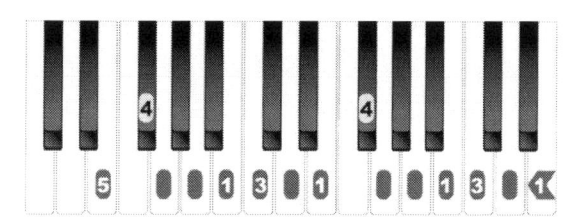

Left Hand 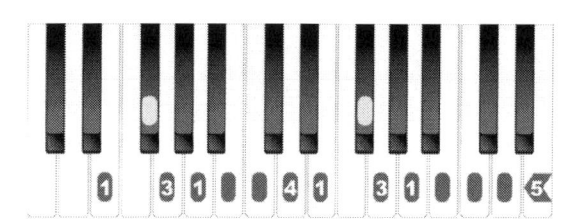 · Right Hand

D Major Scale

B Harmonic Minor Scale

B Melodic Minor Scale

D Major

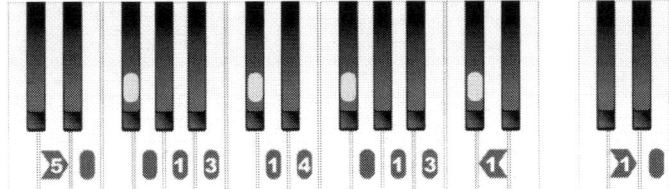

Left Hand 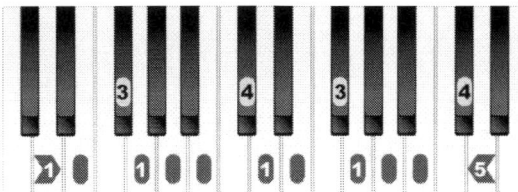   *Right Hand*

B Natural Minor

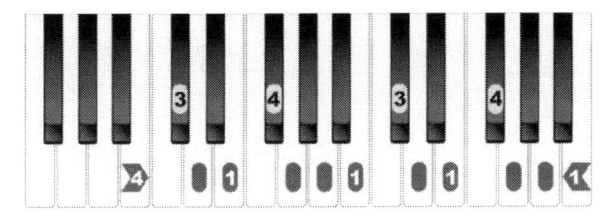

Left Hand 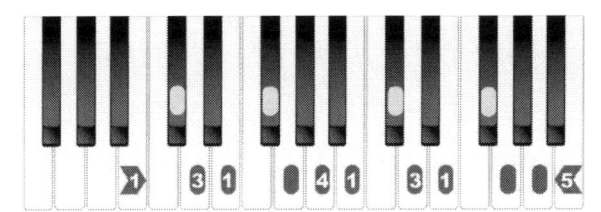   *Right Hand*

B Harmonic Minor

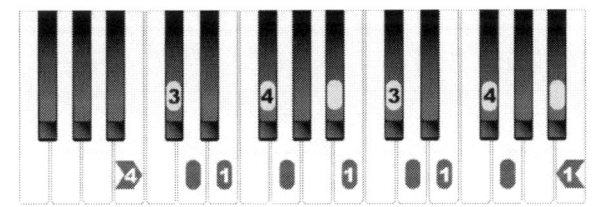

Left Hand 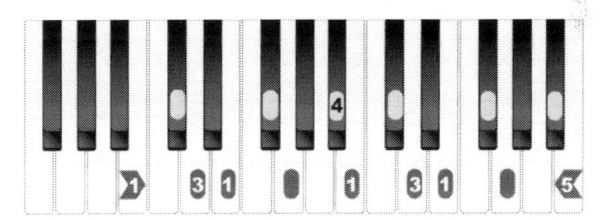   *Right Hand*

B Melodic Minor (Ascending)

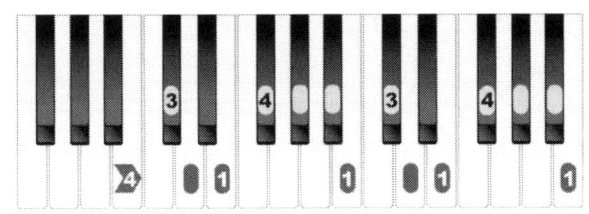

Left Hand 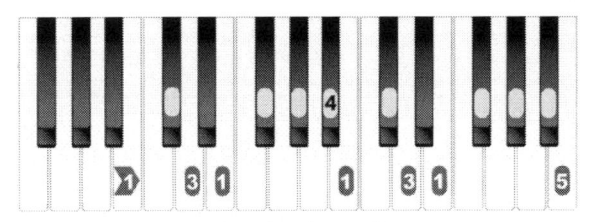   *Right Hand*

B Melodic Minor (Descending)

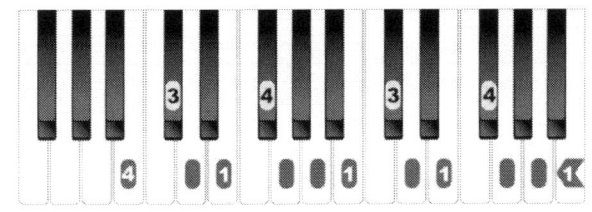

Left Hand 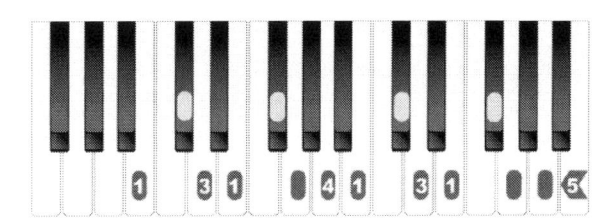   *Right Hand*

B♭ Major Scales

G Harmonic Minor Scale

G Melodic Minor Scale

B♭ Major

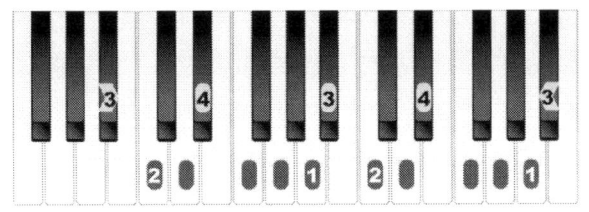

Left Hand 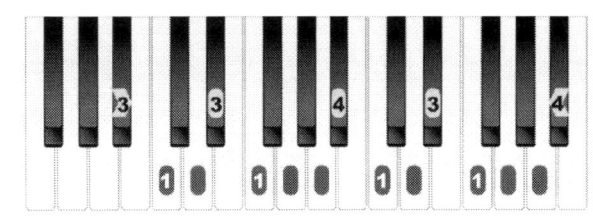   Right Hand

G Natural Minor

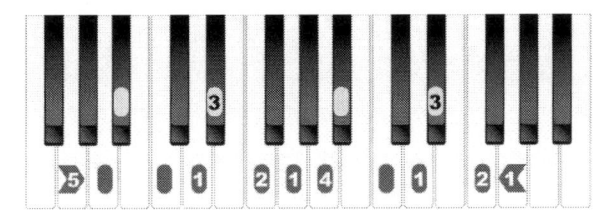

Left Hand 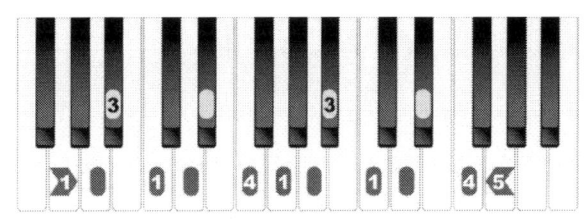   Right Hand

G Harmonic Minor

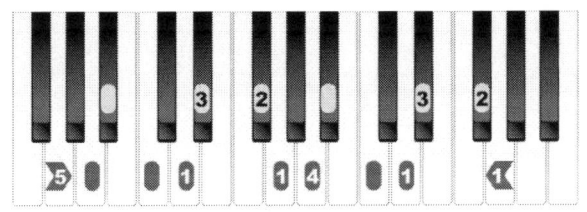

Left Hand 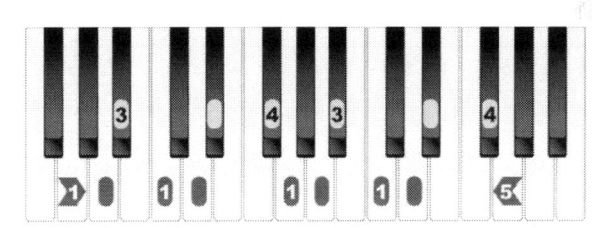   Right Hand

G Melodic Minor (Ascending)

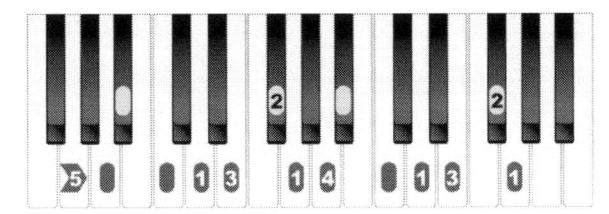

Left Hand 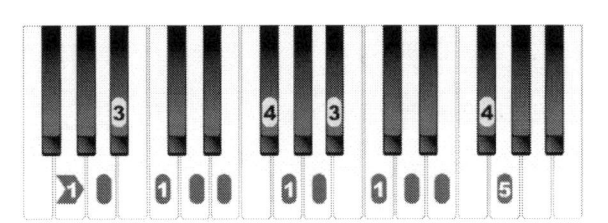   Right Hand

G Melodic Minor (Descending)

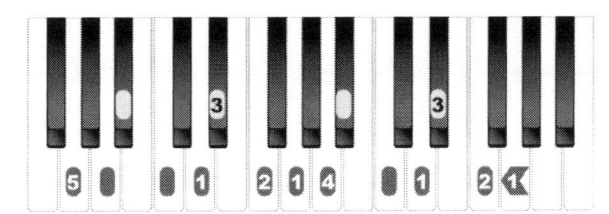

Left Hand 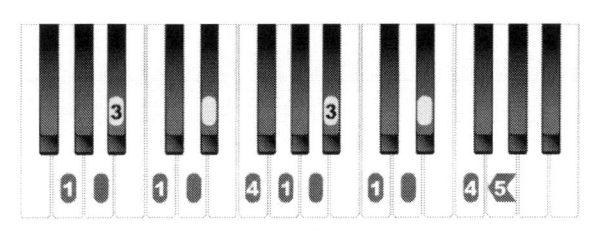   Right Hand

Copyright © Martin Woodward 2011 & 2017

E♭ Major Scales

C Harmonic Minor Scale

C Melodic Minor Scale

E♭ Major

Left Hand   *Right Hand*

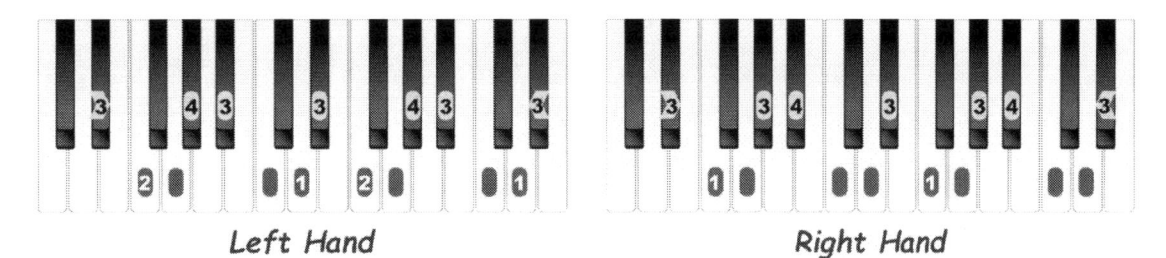

C Natural Minor

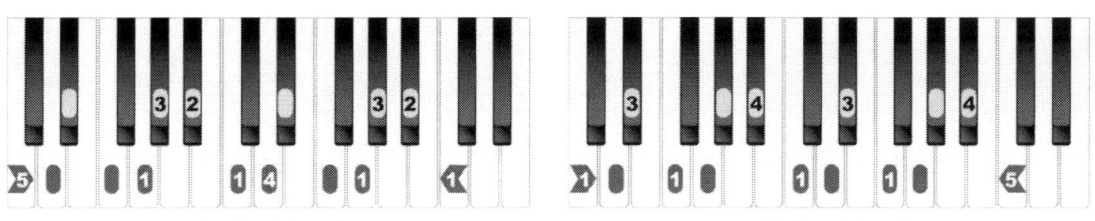

Left Hand   *Right Hand*

C Harmonic Minor

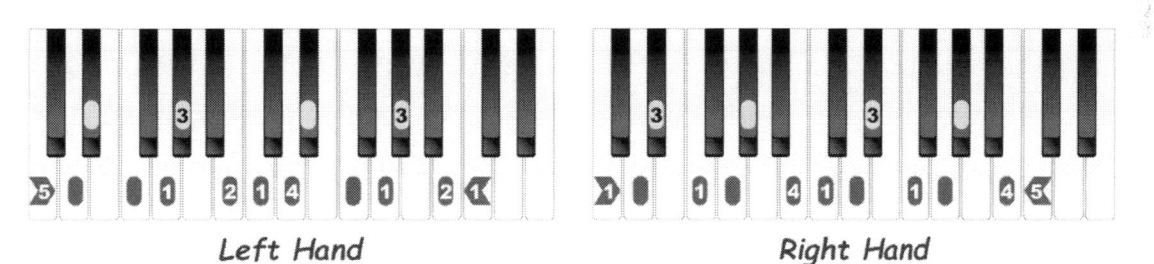

Left Hand   *Right Hand*

C Melodic Minor (Ascending)

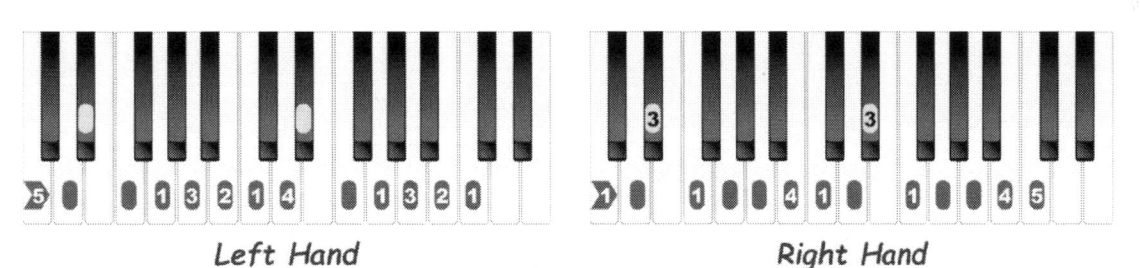

Left Hand   *Right Hand*

C Melodic Minor (Descending)

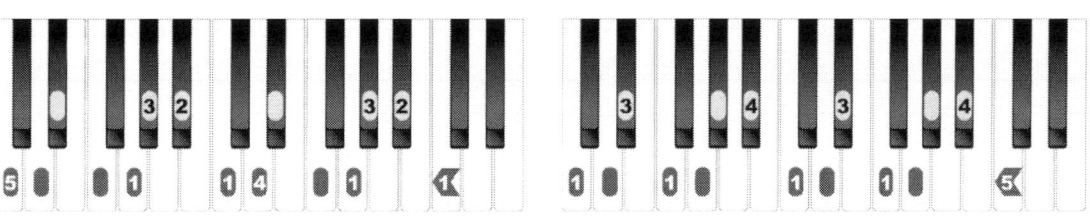

Left Hand   *Right Hand*

Copyright © Martin Woodward 2011 & 2017

A Major Scales

F# Harmonic Minor Scale

F# Melodic Minor Scale

A Major

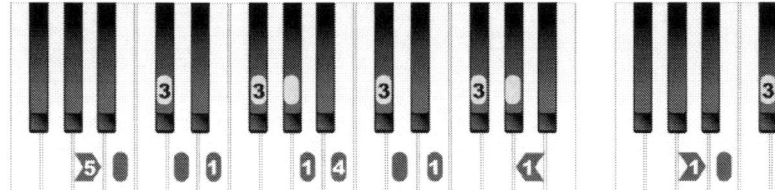

Left Hand 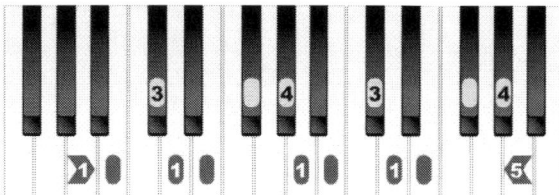   *Right Hand*

F# Natural Minor

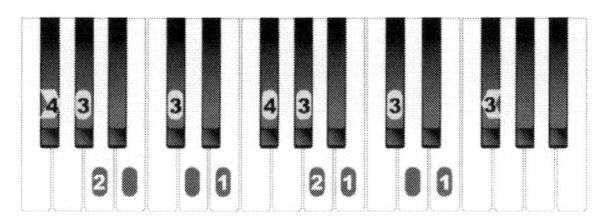

Left Hand 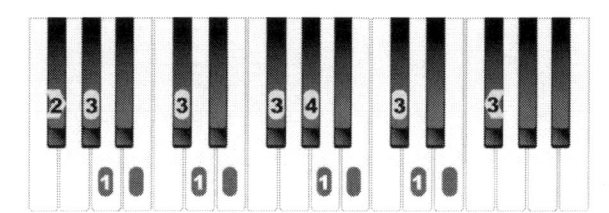   *Right Hand*

F# Harmonic Minor

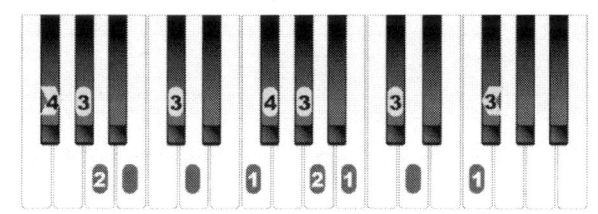

Left Hand 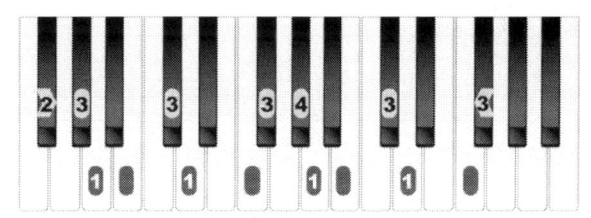   *Right Hand*

F# Melodic Minor (Ascending)

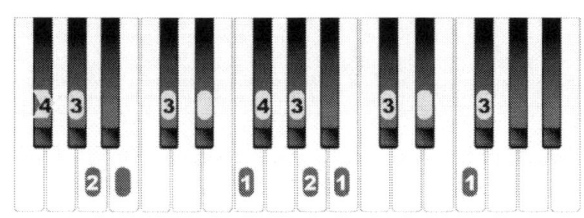

Left Hand 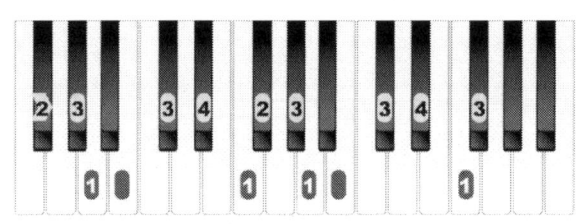   *Right Hand*

F# Melodic Minor (Descending)

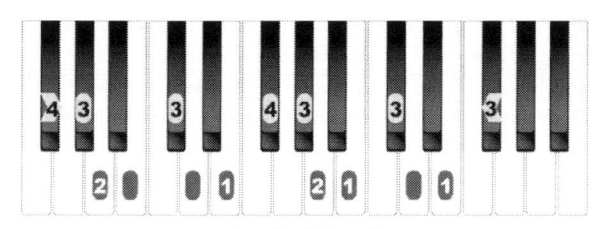

Left Hand 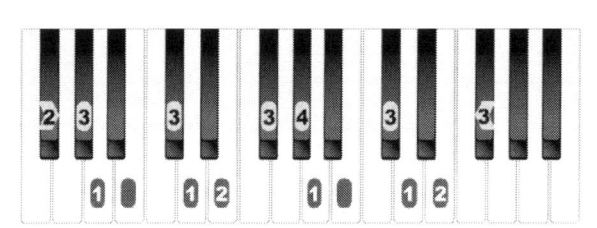   *Right Hand*

Copyright © Martin Woodward 2011 & 2017

E Major Scales

C# Harmonic Minor Scale

C# Melodic Minor Scale

E Major

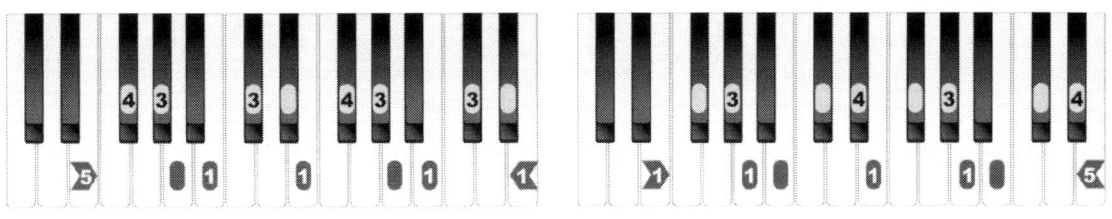

Left Hand   *Right Hand*

C# Natural Minor

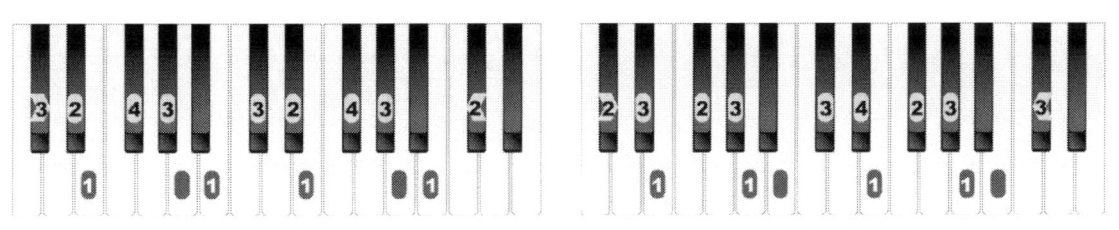

Left Hand   *Right Hand*

C# Harmonic Minor

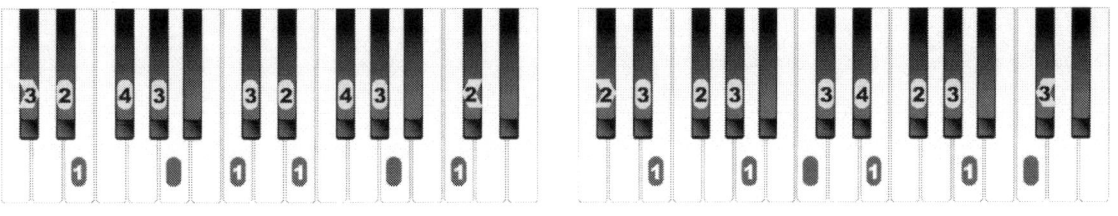

Left Hand   *Right Hand*

C# Melodic Minor (Ascending)

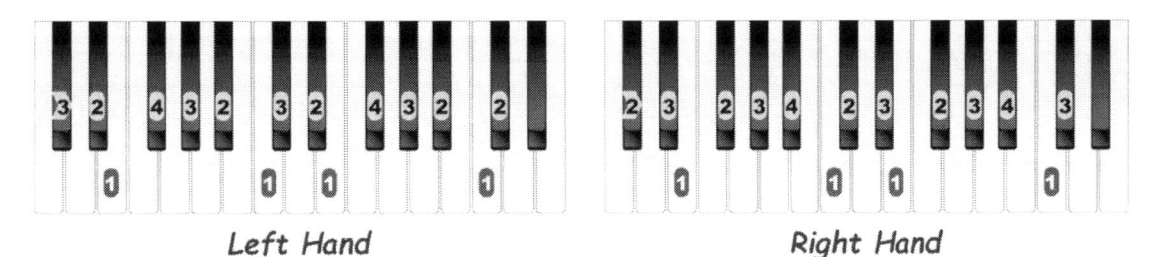

Left Hand   *Right Hand*

C# Melodic Minor (Descending)

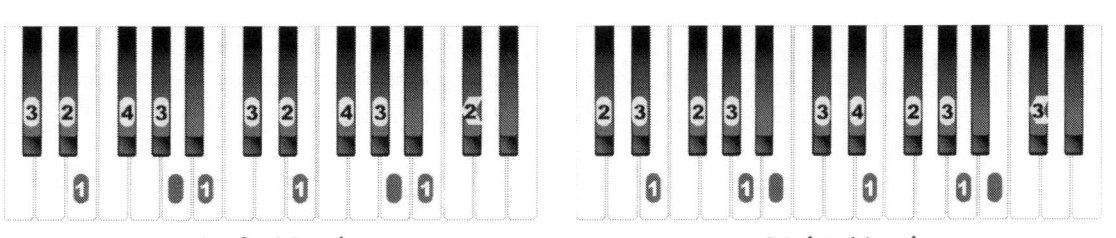

Left Hand   *Right Hand*

Copyright © Martin Woodward 2011 & 2017

A♭ Major Scales

F Harmonic Minor Scale

F Melodic Minor Scale

A♭ Major

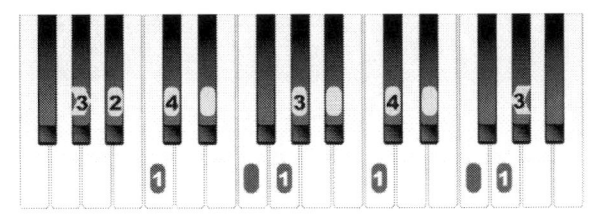

Left Hand 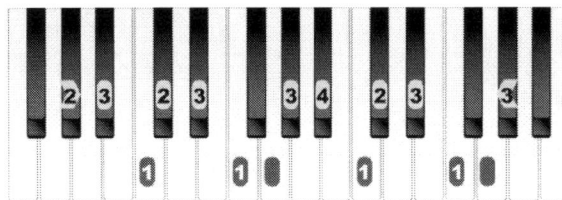 *Right Hand*

F Natural Minor

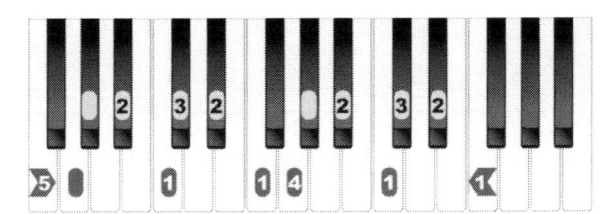

Left Hand 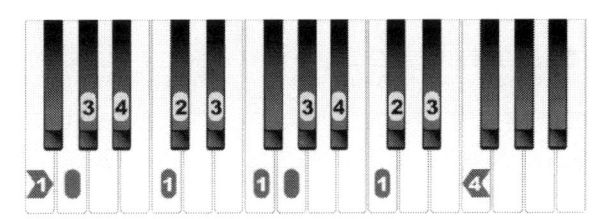 *Right Hand*

F Harmonic Minor

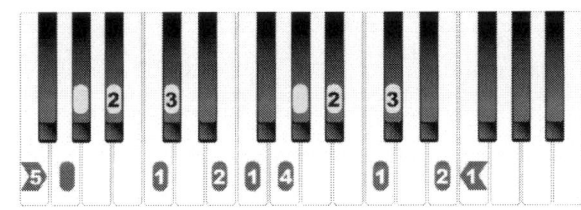

Left Hand 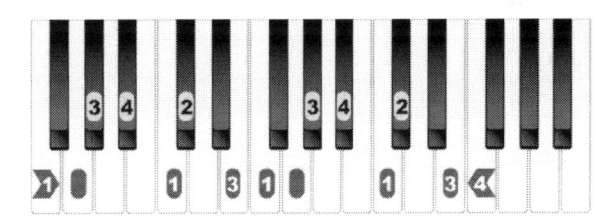 *Right Hand*

F Melodic Minor (Ascending)

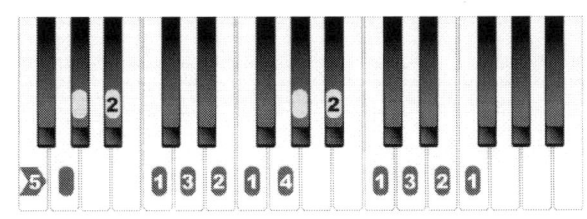

Left Hand 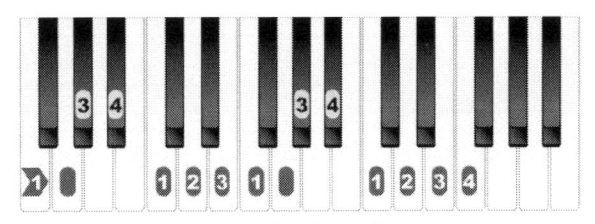 *Right Hand*

F Melodic Minor (Descending)

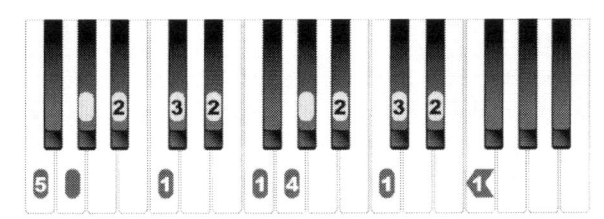

Left Hand 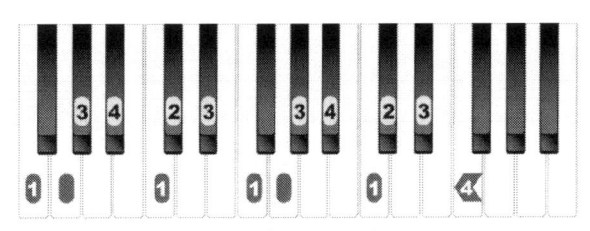 *Right Hand*

B Major Scales

G# Harmonic Minor Scale

G# Melodic Minor Scale

B Major

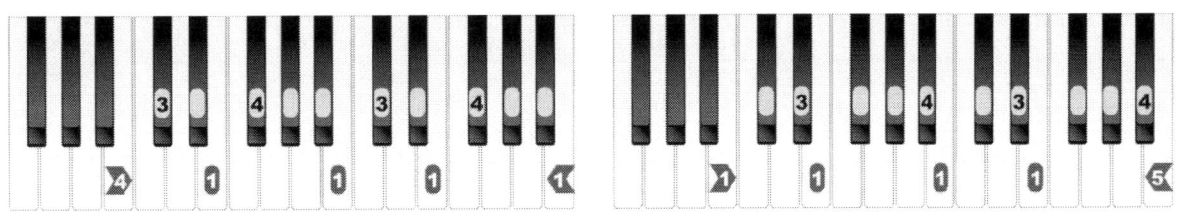

Left Hand   *Right Hand*

G# Natural Minor

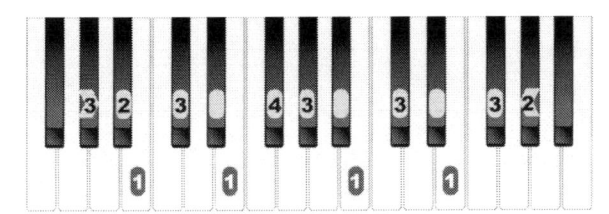

Left Hand 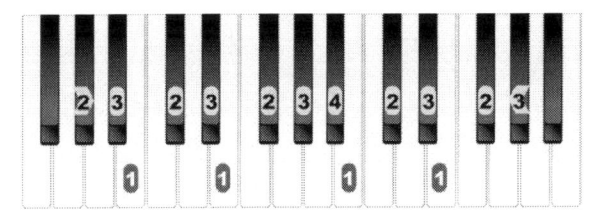   *Right Hand*

G# Harmonic Minor

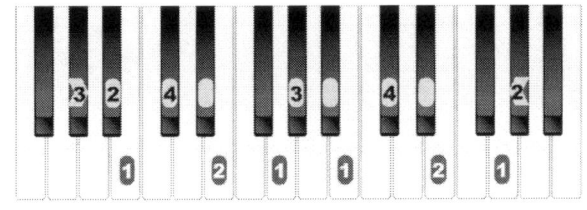

Left Hand 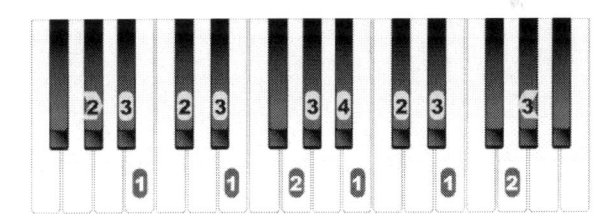   *Right Hand*

G# Melodic Minor (Ascending)

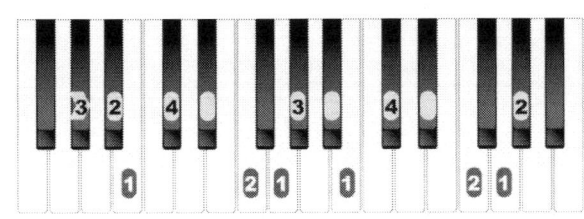

Left Hand 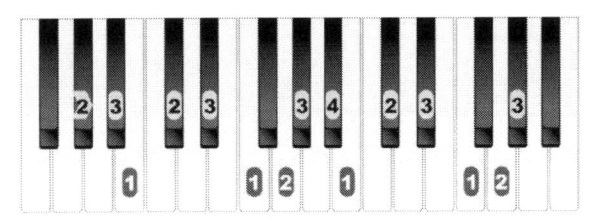   *Right Hand*

G# Melodic Minor (Descending)

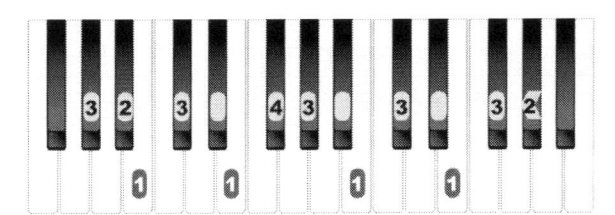

Left Hand 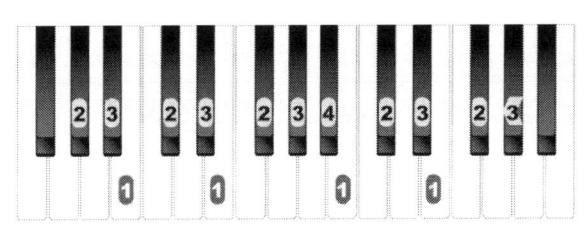   *Right Hand*

Copyright © Martin Woodward 2011 & 2017

D♭ Major Scales

B♭ Harmonic Minor Scale

B♭ Melodic Minor Scale

D♭ Major

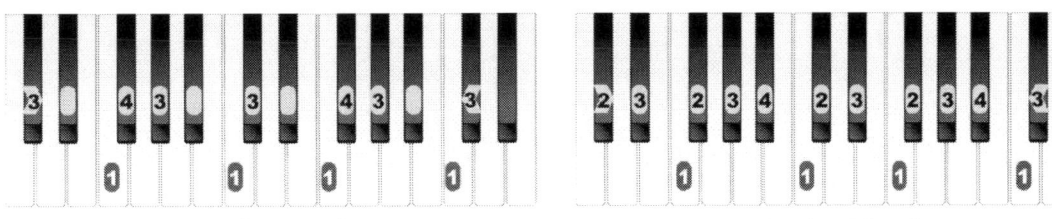

Left Hand   *Right Hand*

B♭ Natural Minor

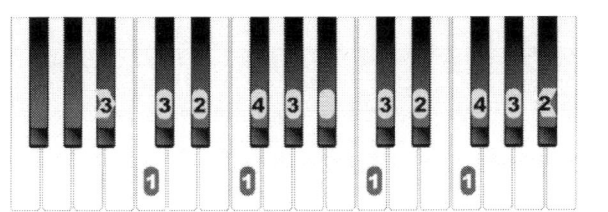

Left Hand 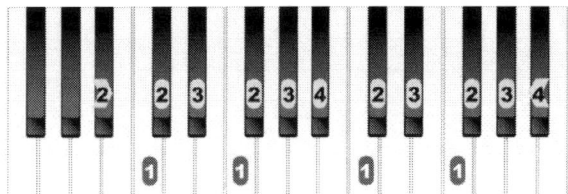   *Right Hand*

B♭ Harmonic Minor

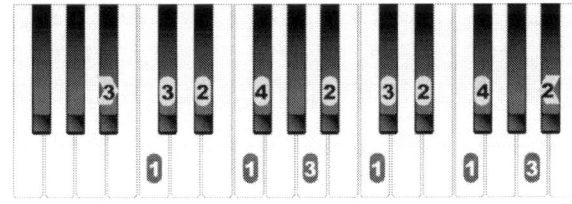

Left Hand 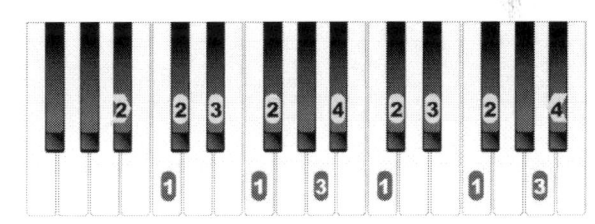   *Right Hand*

B♭ Melodic Minor (Ascending)

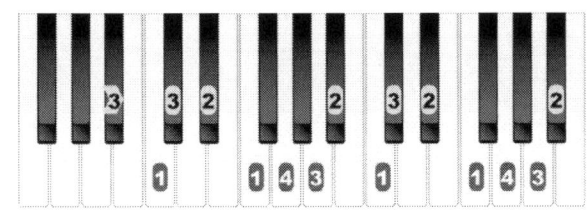

Left Hand 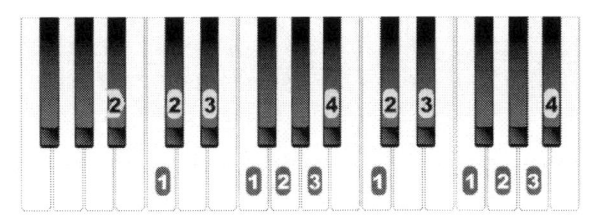   *Right Hand*

B♭ Melodic Minor (Descending)

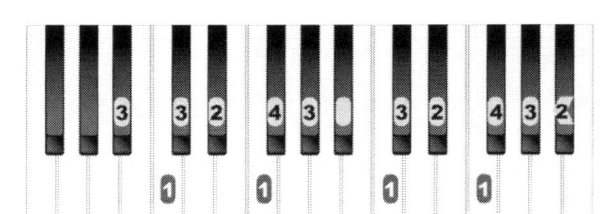

Left Hand 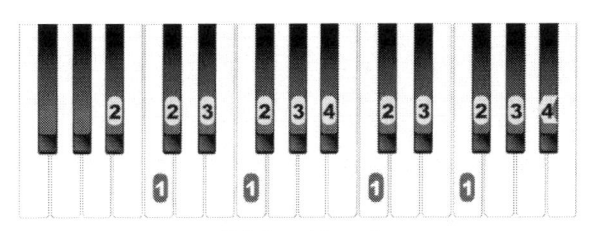   *Right Hand*

G♭ Major Scales

E♭ Harmonic Minor Scale

E♭ Melodic Minor Scale

G♭ Major

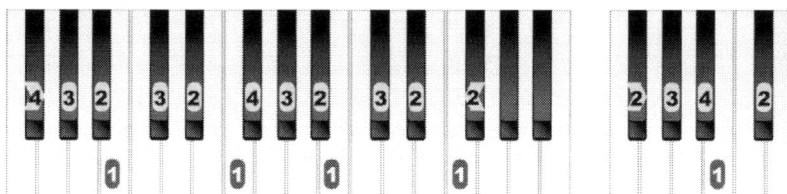

Left Hand 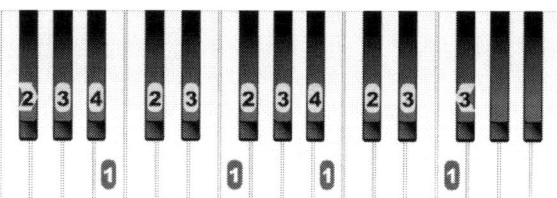   *Right Hand*

E♭ Natural Minor

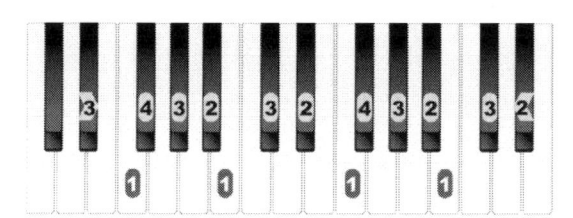

Left Hand 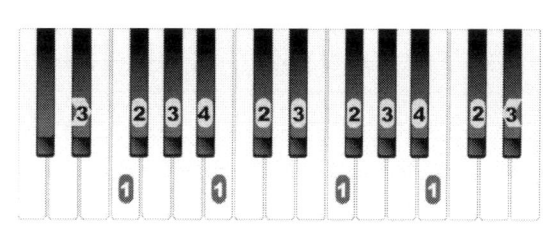   *Right Hand*

E♭ Harmonic Minor

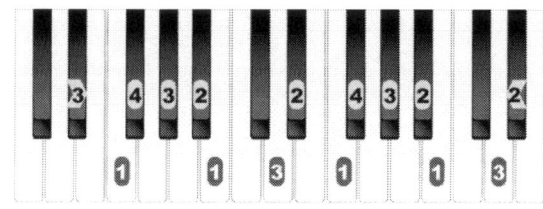

Left Hand 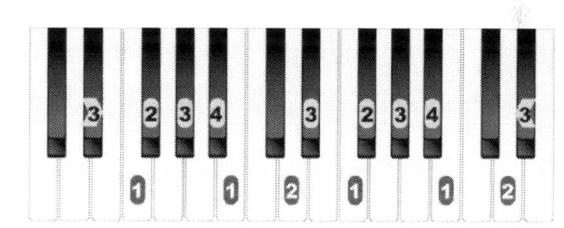   *Right Hand*

E♭ Melodic Minor (Ascending)

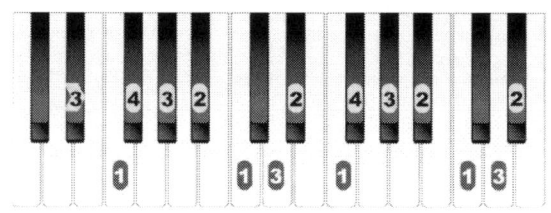

Left Hand 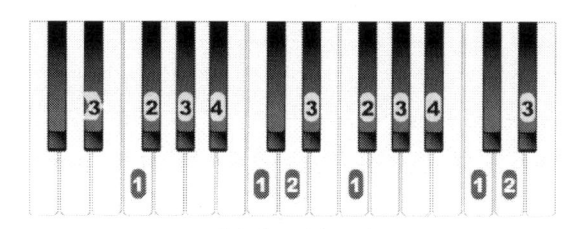   *Right Hand*

E♭ Melodic Minor (Descending)

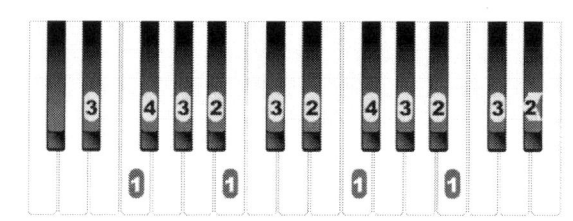

Left Hand 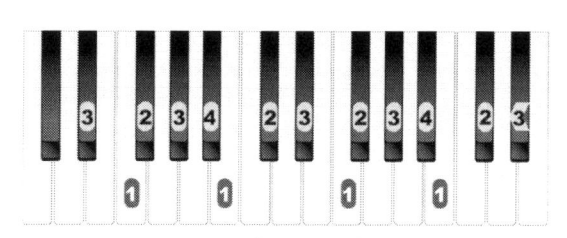   *Right Hand*

← Pentatonic & Blues Scales in the most used keys →

These scales are used extensively in jazz, blues and pop improvisation. The fingering given here is for a guide only as there are many possible alternatives - if it works it's correct!

Note that the major pentatonic scales are always the same as the relative minor, but start on different notes. The major pentatonic being based around the **major 6/9** chord and the minor based round the **minor 7sus4** chord - which are the same chords. Know these chords and you will automatically know these scales!

Note also that the blues scale is almost identical to the minor pentatonic - the only difference being the added flattened fifth. The blues scales listed here are all written in the same key as the pentatonic scales, but note that the blues scale is neither major nor minor (or both).

Using variations on these scales alone can produce some really inventive improvisations. But add broken chords, arpeggios and the major scales starting on various notes (modes) and you will have it all!

In all cases in this section the major pentatonic scale is listed first, then the minor pentatonic and finally the blues scale that relates closest to the minor pentatonic.

And notice that the treble clef is occasionally used in the left hand.

The audio for this section is: http://learn-keyboard.co.uk/scales_full.html, or click on the graphics where applicable.

Quick link to Part 1

Korg Kronos 2 Workstation (76 keys) - very Hi Tech

This is probably the ultimate recording keyboard / workstation. Totally amazing in every respect, but very expensive and certainly not for beginners.
My advice is - learn to play before taking the time to learn the intricacies of synths and workstations.

C Major Pentatonic Scale

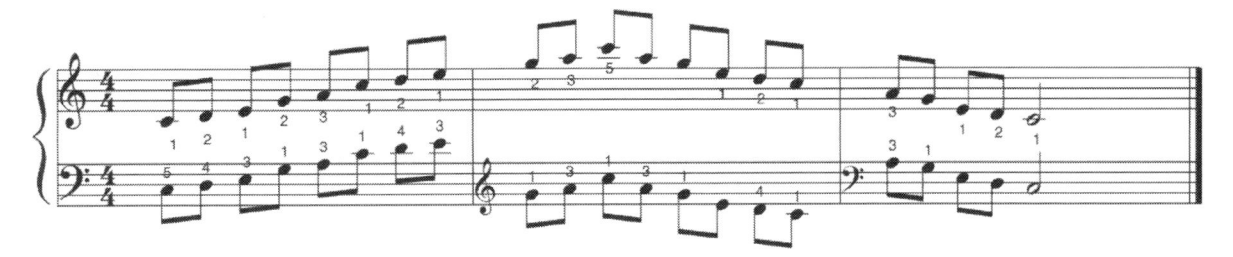

A minor Pentatonic Scale

A Blues Scale

Keyboard View (Right Hand Fingering Only)

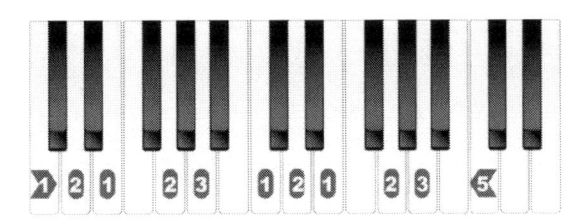

C Major Pentatonic

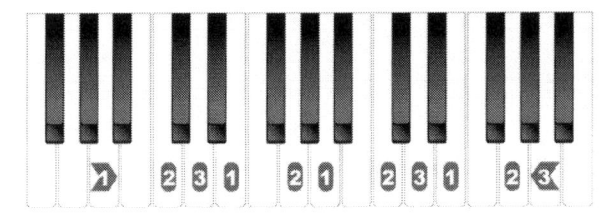

A Minor Pentatonic

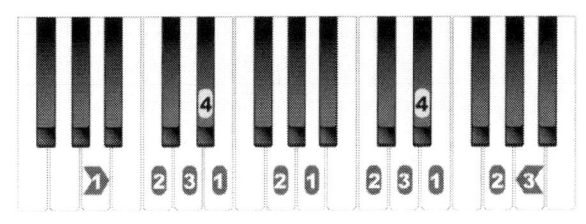

A Blues Scale

Copyright © Martin Woodward 2011 & 2017

G Major Pentatonic Scale

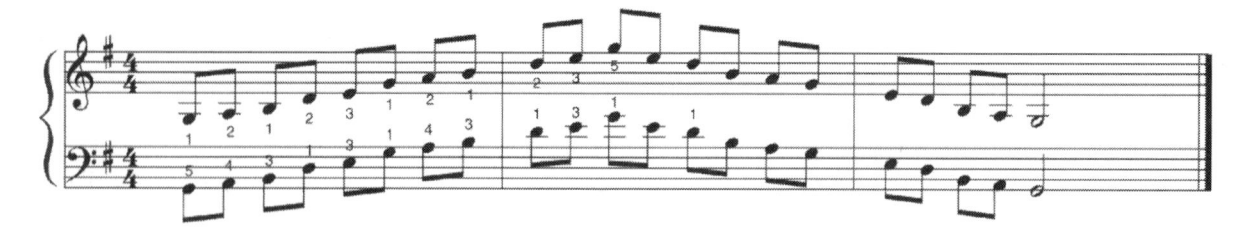

E minor Pentatonic Scale

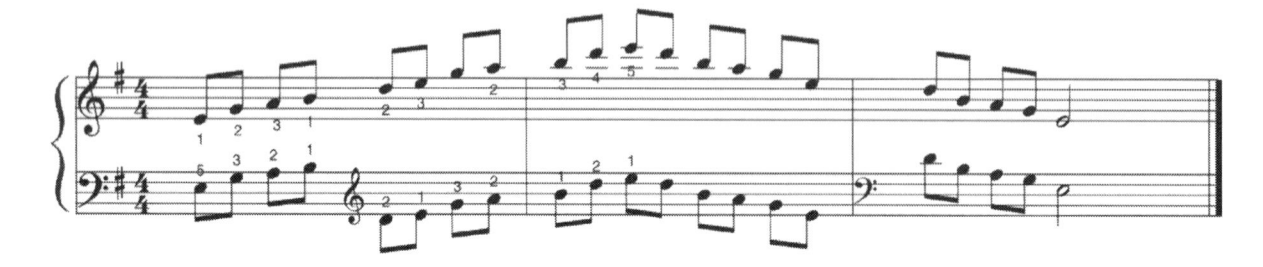

E Blues Scale

Keyboard View (Right Hand Fingering Only)

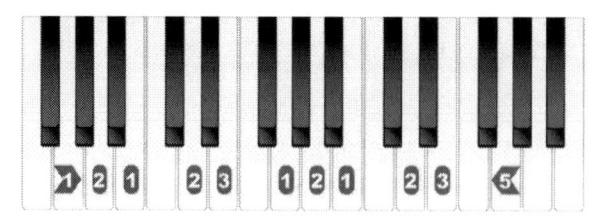

G Major Pentatonic

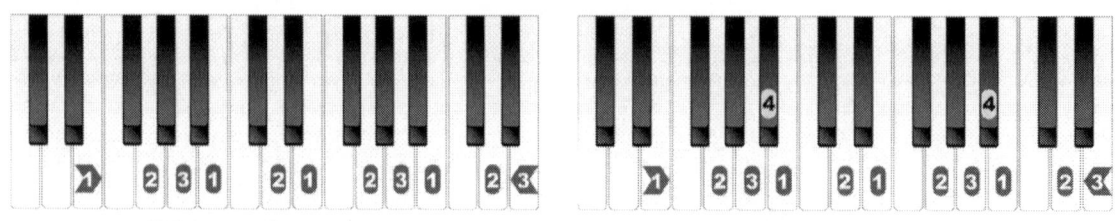

E Minor Pentatonic

E Blues Scale

F Major Pentatonic Scale

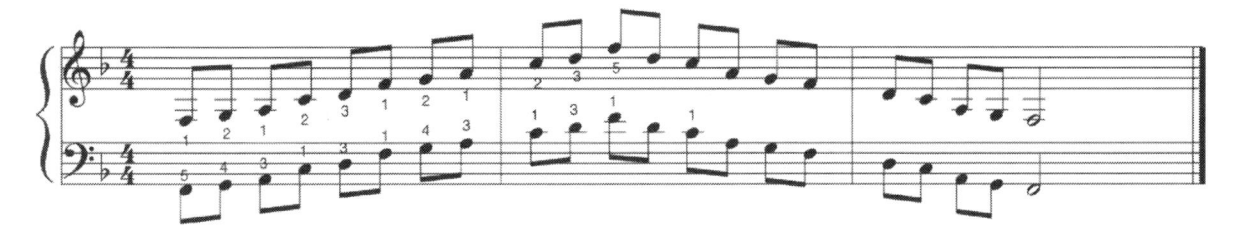

D minor Pentatonic Scale

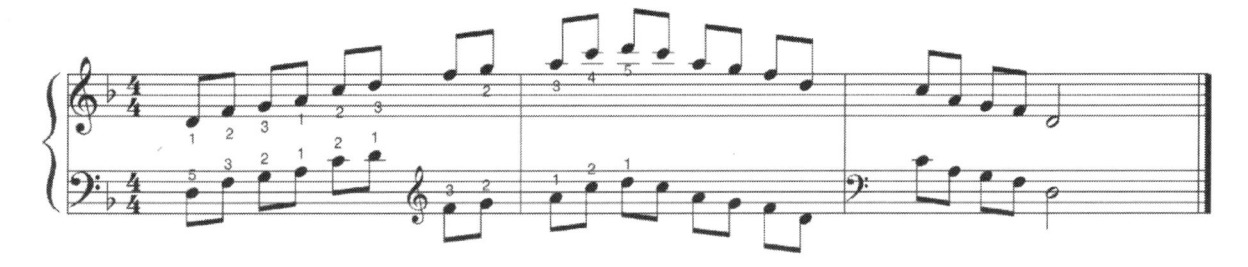

D Blues Scale

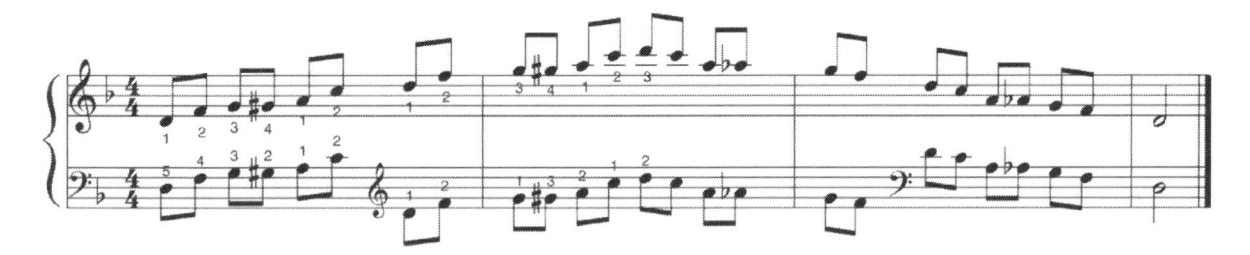

Keyboard View (Right Hand Fingering Only)

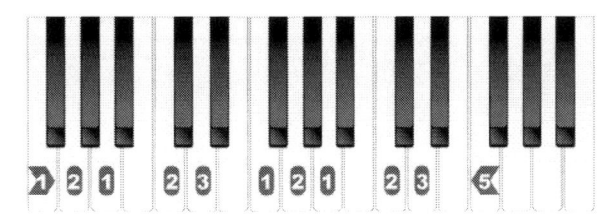

F Major Pentatonic

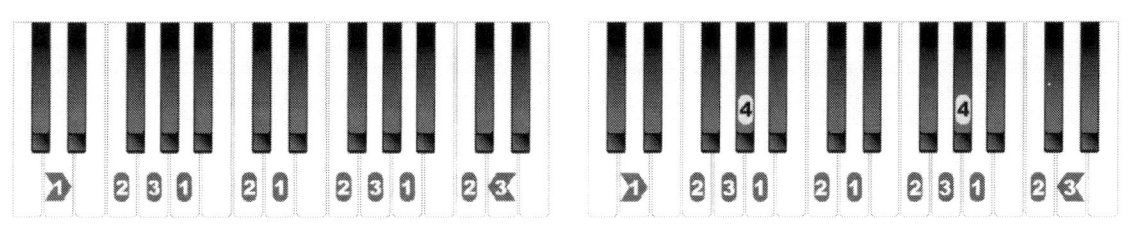

D Minor Pentatonic

D Blues Scale

Copyright © Martin Woodward 2011 & 2017

D Major Pentatonic Scale

B minor Pentatonic Scale

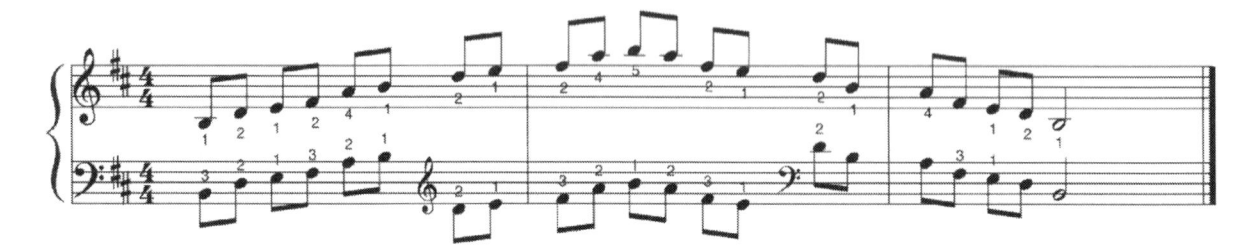

B Blues Scale

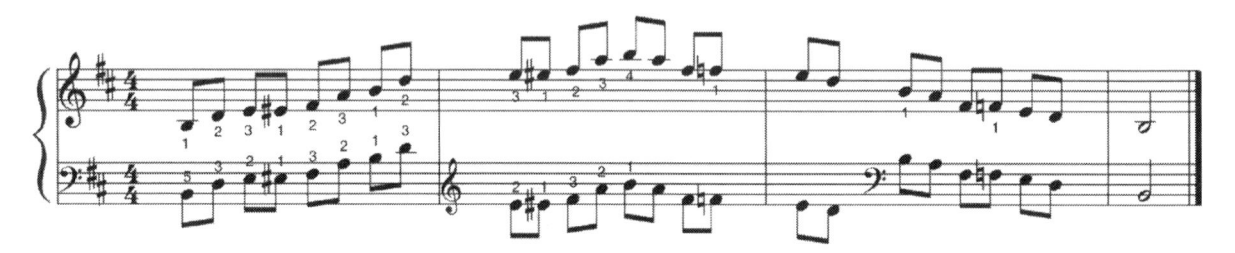

Keyboard View (Right Hand Fingering Only)

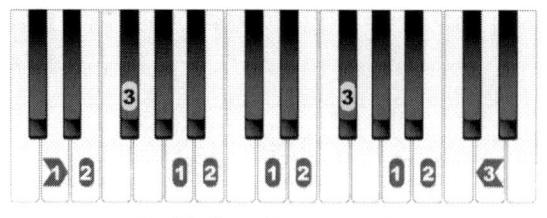

D Major Pentatonic

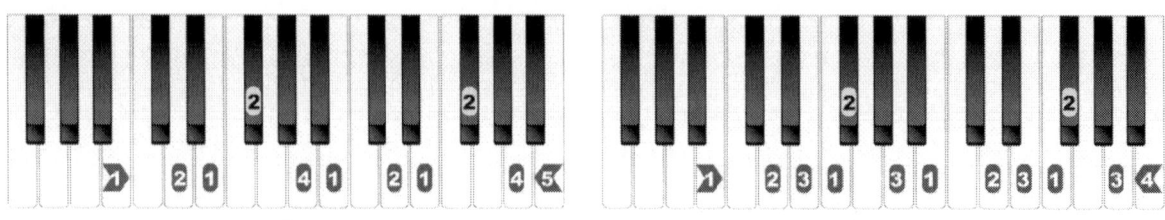

B Minor Pentatonic

B Blues Scale

Copyright © Martin Woodward 2011 & 2017

B♭ Major Pentatonic Scale

G minor Pentatonic Scale

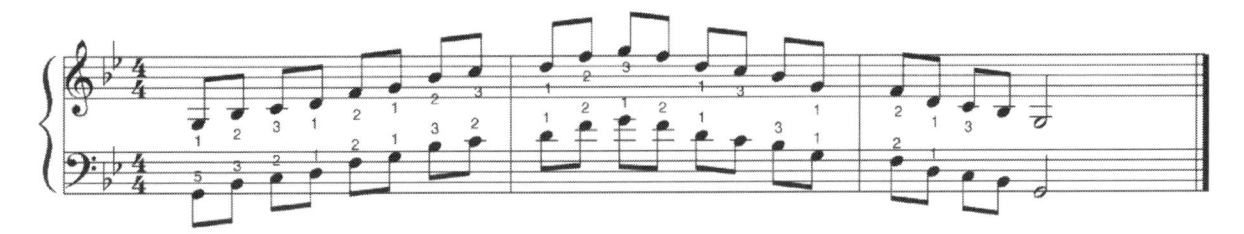

G Blues Scale

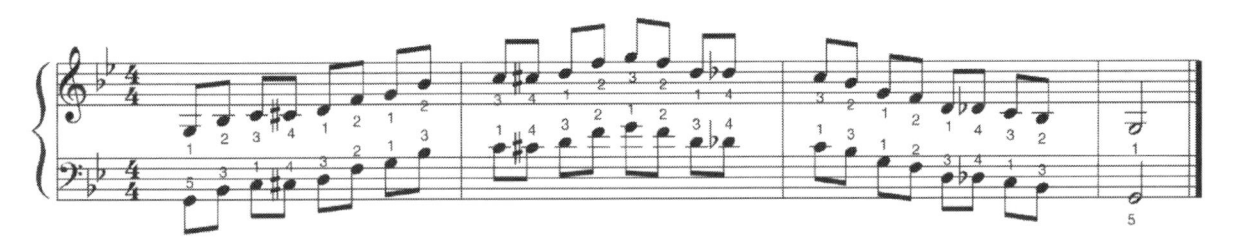

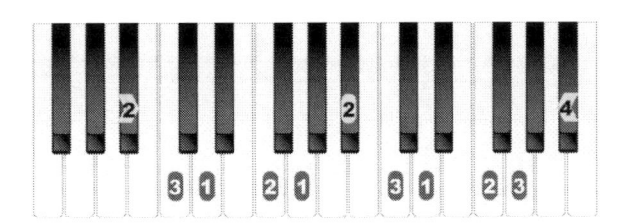

Keyboard View (Right Hand Fingering Only)

Bb Major Pentatonic

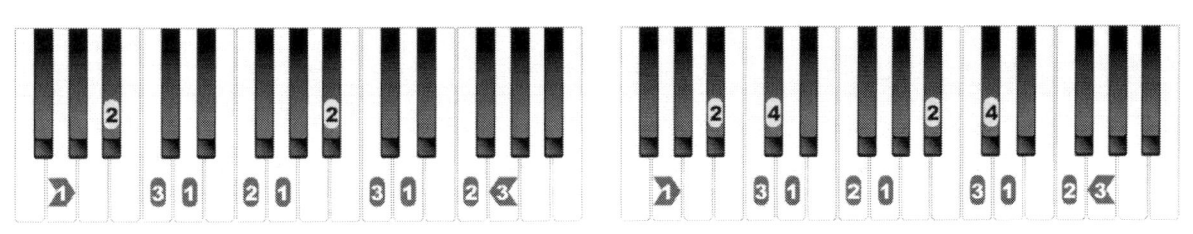

G Minor Pentatonic

G Blues Scale

A Major Pentatonic Scale

F# minor Pentatonic Scale

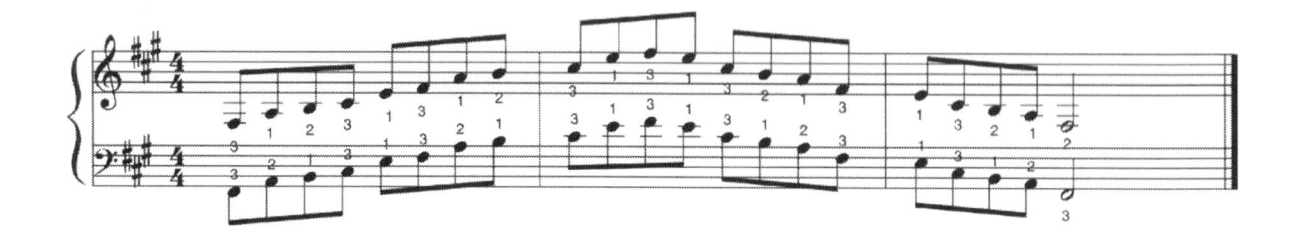

F# Blues Scale

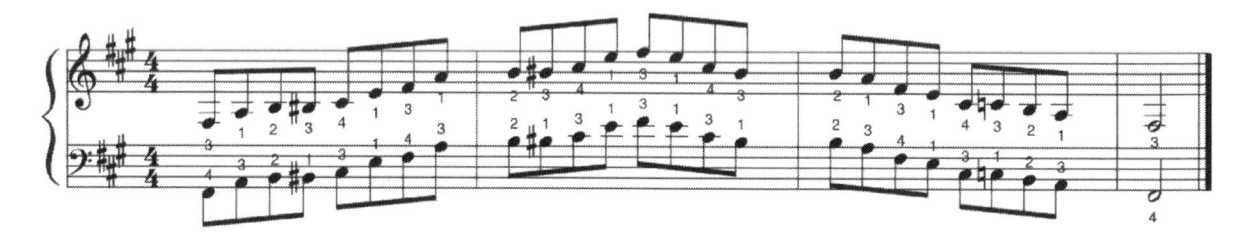

Keyboard View (Right Hand Fingering Only)

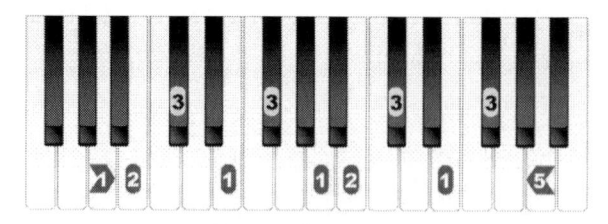

A Major Pentatonic

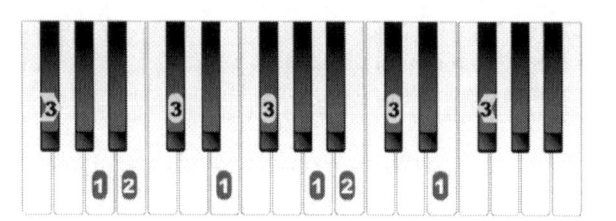

F# Minor Pentatonic

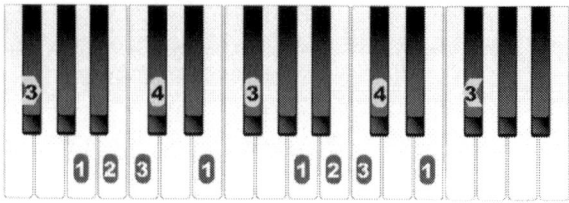

F# Blues Scale

E♭ Major Pentatonic Scale

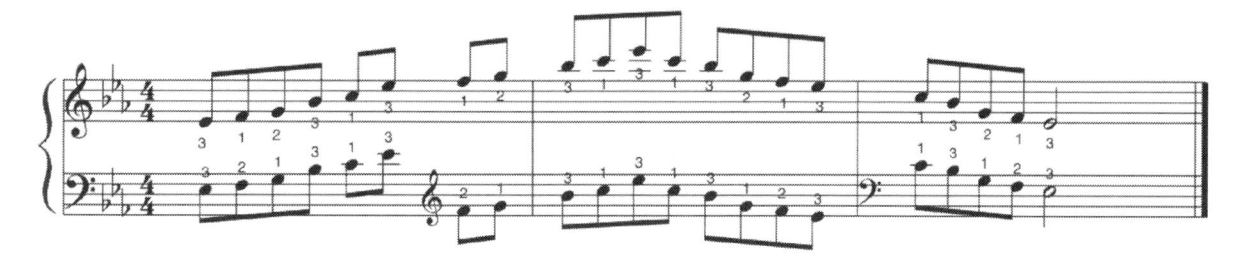

C minor Pentatonic Scale

C Blues Scale

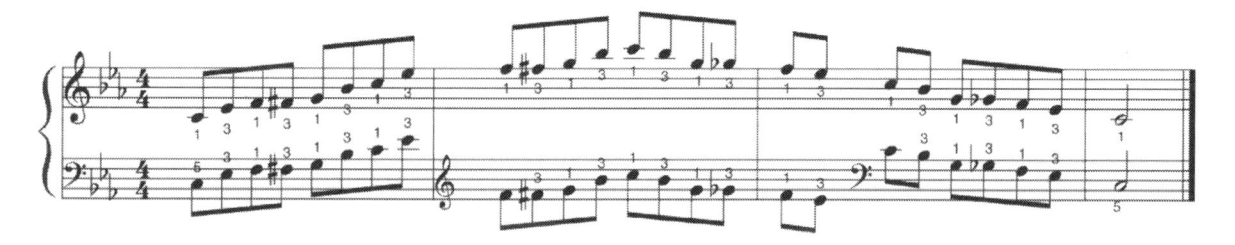

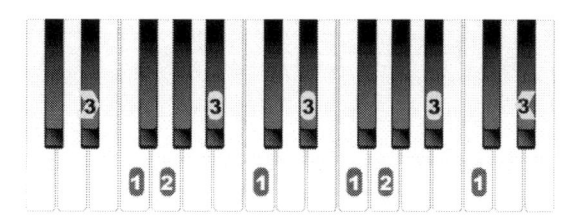

Keyboard View (Right Hand Fingering Only)

Eb Major Pentatonic

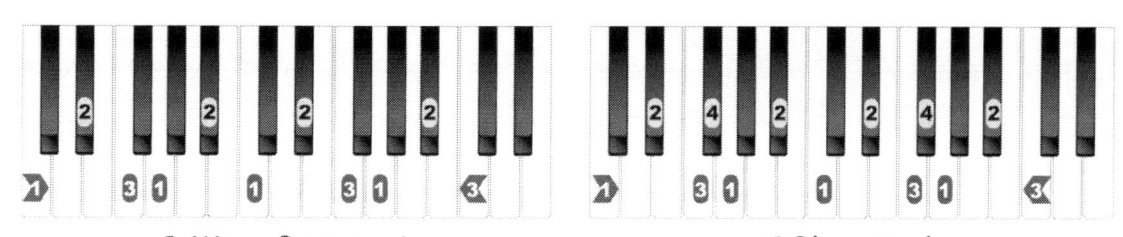

C Minor Pentatonic

C Blues Scale

A♭ Major Pentatonic Scale

F minor Pentatonic Scale

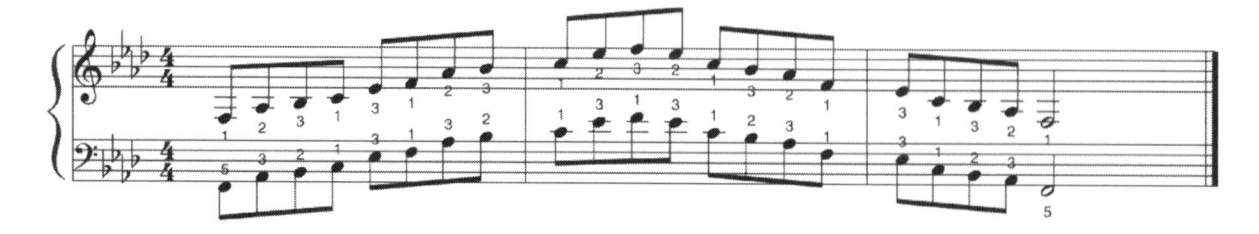

F Blues Scale

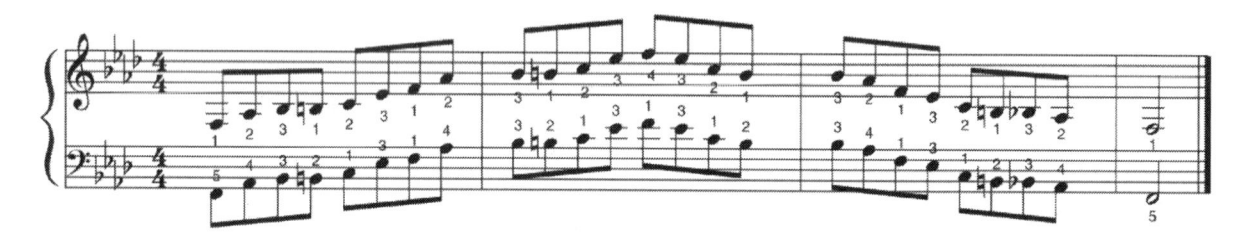

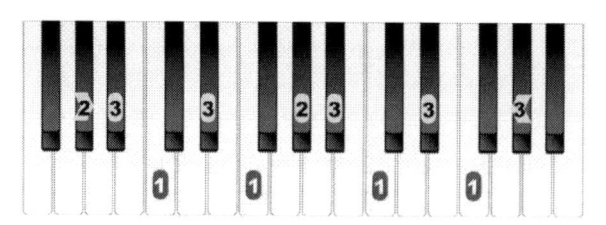

Keyboard View (Right Hand Fingering Only)

Ab Major Pentatonic

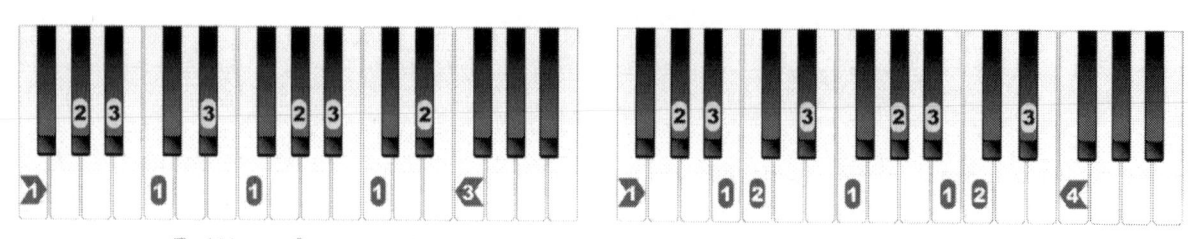

F Minor Pentatonic

F Blues Scale

Copyright © Martin Woodward 2011 & 2017

Diatonic Chords

The next few pages show the diatonic chords in the most used keys.

I know I've said this before, but to make it perfectly clear: - diatonic chords are chords which are derived from the notes of the relevant scale and as such all diatonic chords are related - think of them as *'families'* of chords.

Due to the *relationship*, it's likely that many compositions will use *only* diatonic chords, but this is not necessarily the case!

Here I have listed the major and relative minor chords on the same page.

Note that there are more diatonic chords in the minor keys due to the ascending / descending difference in the melodic scale. They are listed here in the order in which they are recommended to be practised / understood.

Only the basic, **Major 7th**, **Dominant 7th**, **diminished** and **augmented** chords are listed (as well as the **6ths** and **6/9ths**) progressing up the scale to show how they come into being. But please note that more complicated chords can also be created by adding further extensions. For instance, all of the notes of the **C major** scale can be rearranged to form **G13th** and as such this is also a diatonic chord in the key of **C major**.

The following pages also form a good starting base for composition, i.e. knowing which chords are most likely to fit together - but remember there are always exceptions and anything is ok if it sounds ok!

As this section is simply for reference, no audio links are included.

All of these chords can be seen in keyboard view further on.

Quick link to Part 1

Kawai MP7 Stage Piano

This machine has nothing but great reviews, but I did a 7-hour round trip to try one and I was disappointed - just didn't feel right for me at all. But I was blown away by the Yamaha CP4 which was right next to it!

C Major Diatonic Chords

I	C	CM7	C6
ii	Dm	Dm7	Dm6
iii	Em	Em7	
IV	F	FM7	F6
V	G	G7	G6
vi	Am	Am7	
vii	Bdim	Bm7b5	

C major has no sharps or flats

A Minor Diatonic Chords

i	Am	Am7	Am6	AmM7
ii	Bdim	Bm7b5	Bm	Bm7
III	C	CM7	C6	C+
IV	D	D7	D6	
iv	Dm	Dm7	Dm6	
iv	Ddim	Ddim7	Dm7b5	
v / V	Em	Em7	E	E7
VI	F	FM7	F6	
vi	Fm	Fm7	Fm6	
vi	Fdim	Fdim7	F#dim	F#m7b5
VII	G	G7	G6	GM7
vii	G#dim	G#dim7		

A Natural minor has no sharps or flats - A Harmonic minor has one sharp which is G# - A Melodic minor has F# and G# ascending, but no sharps or flats descending which creates many more diatonic chords.

F Major Diatonic Chords

I	F	FM7	F6
ii	Gm	Gm7	Gm6
iii	Am	Am7	
IV	Bb	BbM7	Bb6
V	C	C7	C6
vi	Dm	Dm7	
vii	Edim	Em7b5	

F major has 1 flat which is Bb

D Minor Diatonic Chords

i	Dm	Dm7	Dm6	DmM7
ii	Edim	Em7b5	Em	Em7
III	F	FM7	F6	F+
IV	G	G7	G6	
iv	Gm	Gm7	Gm6	
iv	Gdim	Gdim7	Gm7b5	
v / V	Am	Am7	A	A7
VI	Bb	BbM7	Bb6	
vi	Bbm	Bbm7	Bbm6	
vi	Bbdim	Bbdim7	Bdim	Bm7b5
VII	C	C7	C6	CM7
vii	C#dim	C#dim7		

D Natural minor has 1 flat which is Bb - D Harmonic minor has Bb and C# - D Melodic minor has, B natural and C# ascending, but Bb, C natural descending which creates many more diatonic chords.

G Major Diatonic Chords

I	G	GM7	G6
ii	Am	Am7	Am6
iii	Bm	Bm7	
IV	C	CM7	C6
V	D	D7	D6
vi	Em	Em7	
vii	F#dim	F#m7b5	

G major has 1 sharp which is F#

E Minor Diatonic Chords

i	Em	Em7	Em6	EmM7
ii	F#dim	F#m7b5	F#m	F#m7
III	G	GM7	G6	G+
IV	A	A7	A6	
iv	Am	Am7	Am6	
iv	Adim	Adim7	Am7b5	
v / V	Bm	Bm7	B	B7
VI	C	CM7	C6	
vi	Cm	Cm7	Cm6	
vi	Cdim	Cdim7	C#dim	C#m7b5
VII	D	D7	D6	DM7
vii	D#dim	D#dim7		

E Natural minor has 1 sharp which is F# - E Harmonic minor has F# and D# - E Melodic minor has F#, D# and C# ascending, but F#, D natural and C natural descending which creates many more diatonic chords.

B♭ Major Diatonic Chords

I	Bb	BbM7	Bb6
ii	Cm	Cm7	Cm6
iii	Dm	Dm7	
IV	Eb	EbM7	Eb6
V	F	F7	F6
vi	Gm	Gm7	
vii	Adim	Am7b5	

Bb major has 2 flats: Bb and Eb

G Minor Diatonic Chords

i	Gm	Gm7	Gm6	GmM7
ii	Adim	Am7b5	Am	Am7
III	Bb	BbM7	Bb6	Bb+
IV	C	C7	C6	
iv	Cm	Cm7	Cm6	
iv	Cdim	Cdim7	Cm7b5	
v / V	Dm	Dm7	D	D7
VI	Eb	EbM7	Eb6	
vi	Ebm	Ebm7	Ebm6	
vi	Ebdim	Ebdim7	Edim	Em7b5
VII	F	F7	F6	FM7
vii	Gbdim	Gbdim7		

G Natural minor has 2 flats: Bb and Eb - G Harmonic minor has Bb, Eb and F# - G Melodic minor has Bb, E natural and F# ascending, but Bb, Eb, Ab and F natural descending which creates many more diatonic chords.

D Major Diatonic Chords

I	D	DM7	D6
ii	Em	Em7	Em6
iii	F#m	F#m7	
IV	G	GM7	G6
V	A	A7	A6
vi	Bm	Bm7	
vii	C#dim	C#m7b5	

D major has 2 sharps: F# and C#

B Minor Diatonic Chords

i	Bm	Bm7	Bm6	BmM7
ii	C#dim	C#m7b5	C#m	C#m7
III	D	DM7	D6	D+
IV	E	E7	E6	
iv	Em	Em7	Em6	
iv	Edim	Edim7	Em7b5	
v / V	F#m	F#m7	F#	F#7
VI	G	GM7	G6	
vi	Gm	Gm7	Gm6	
vi	Gdim	Gdim7	G#dim	G#m7b5
VII	A	A7	A6	AM7
vii	A#dim	A#dim7		

B Natural minor has 2 sharps: F# and C# - B Harmonic minor has F#, C# and A# - B Melodic minor has F#, C#, G# and A# ascending, but F#, C#, G natural and A natural descending which creates many more diatonic chords.

E♭ Major Diatonic Chords

I	Eb	EbM7	Eb6
ii	Fm	Fm7	Fm6
iii	Gm	Gm7	
IV	Ab	AbM7	Ab6
V	Bb	Bb7	Bb6
vi	Cm	Cm7	
vii	Ddim	Dm7b5	

Eb major has 3 flats: Bb, Eb and Ab.

C Minor Diatonic Chords

i	Cm	Cm7	Cm6	CmM7
ii	Ddim	Dm7b5	Dm	Dm7
III	Eb	EbM7	Eb6	Eb+
IV	F	F7	F6	
iv	Fm	Fm7	Fm6	
iv	Fdim	Fdim7	Fm7b5	
v / V	Gm	Gm7	G	G7
VI	Ab	AbM7	Ab6	
vi	Abm	Abm7	Abm6	
vi	Abdim	Abdim7	Adim	Am7b5
VII	Bb	Bb7	Bb6	BbM7
vii	Bdim	Bdim7		

C Natural minor has 3 flats: Bb, Eb and Ab - C Harmonic minor has Eb and Ab - C Melodic minor has Eb, B natural and A natural ascending, but Eb, Ab and Bb descending which creates many more diatonic chords.

A Major Diatonic Chords

I	A	AM7	A6
ii	Bm	Bm7	Bm6
iii	C#m	C#m7	
IV	D	DM7	D6
V	E	E7	E6
vi	F#m	F#m7	
vii	G#dim	G#m7b5	

A major has 3 sharps: F#, C# and G#

F# Minor Diatonic Chords

i	F#m	F#m7	F#m6	F#mM7
ii	G#dim	G#m7b5	G#m	G#m7
III	A	AM7	A6	A+
IV	B	B7	B6	
iv	Bm	Bm7	Bm6	
iv	Bdim	Bdim7	Bm7b5	
v / V	C#m	C#m7	C#	C#7
VI	D	DM7	D6	
vi	Dm	Dm7	Dm6	
vi	Ddim	Ddim7	D#dim	D#m7b5
VII	E	E7	E6	EM7
vii	Fdim	Fdim7		

F# Natural minor has 3 sharps: F#, C# and G# - F# Harmonic minor has F#, C#, G# and E# (F) - F# Melodic minor has F#, C#, G#, D# and E# (F) ascending, but E natural and D natural descending which creates many more diatonic chords.

A♭ Major Diatonic Chords

I	Ab	AbM7	Ab6
ii	Bbm	Bbm7	Bbm6
iii	Cm	Cm7	
IV	Db	DbM7	Db6
V	Eb	Eb7	Eb6
vi	Fm	Fm7	
vii	Gdim	Gm7b5	

Ab major has 4 flats: Bb, Eb, Ab and Db

F Minor Diatonic Chords

i	Fm	Fm7	Fm6	FmM7
ii	Gdim	Gm7b5	Gm	Gm7
III	Ab	AbM7	Ab6	Ab+
IV	Bb	Bb7	Bb6	
iv	Bbm	Bbm7	Bbm6	
iv	Bbdim	Bbdim7	Bbm7b5	
v / V	Cm	Cm7	C	C7
VI	Db	DbM7	Db6	
vi	Dbm	Dbm7	Dbm6	
vi	Dbdim	Dbdim7	Ddim	Dm7b5
VII	Eb	Eb7	Eb6	EbM7
vii	Edim	Edim7		

F Natural minor has 4 flats: Bb, Eb, Ab and Db - F Harmonic minor has Bb, Ab Db and E natural - F Melodic minor has Bb and Ab but D natural and E natural ascending, then Bb, Eb, Ab and Db descending which creates many more diatonic chords.

E Major Diatonic Chords

I	E	EM7	Eb
ii	F#m	F#m7	Fm6
iii	G#m	G#m7	
IV	A	AM7	A6
V	B	B7	B6
vi	C#m	C#m7	
vii	D#dim	D#m7b5	

E major has 4 sharps: F#, C#, G# and D#

C# Minor Diatonic Chords

i	C#m	C#m7	C#m6	C#mM7
ii	Ddim	Dm7b5	Dm	Dm7
III	E	EM7	E6	E+
IV	F#	F#7	F#6	
iv	F#m	F#m7	F#m6	
iv	F#dim	F#dim7	F#m7b5	
v / V	G#m	G#m7	G#	G#7
VI	A	AM7	A6	
vi	Am	Am7	Am6	
vi	Adim	Adim7	G#dim	G#m7b5
VII	B	B7	B6	BM7
vii	Cdim	Cdim7		

C# Natural minor has 4 sharps: F#, C#, G# and D# - C# Harmonic minor has: F#, C#, G#, D# and B# (C) - C# Melodic minor has F#, C#, G#, D#, A# and B# (C) ascending, then A natural and B natural descending which creates many more diatonic chords.

Chords in Keyboard View

The next few pages show the following chords in keyboard view in each of the twelve keys:

- **Major** (including **6th**, **7th** and **M7th**);
- **Minor** (including **6th**, **7th**, **mM7th** and **m7♭5th**);
- **Diminished** (including **7th**);
- **Augmented** (including **7th**);
- **Suspended 4th** (also called just **'sus'**);
- **Suspended 9th (2nd)**.

These form a good starting point and all of them should be recognised by auto accompaniment features. So, if you intend using these features, knowing all these chords will be extremely useful.

More complicated extensions such as **9ths**, **11ths** and **13ths** etc. are often not correctly recognised by auto accompaniment and these are shown in the next section.

Why do I need to learn chords?

As I've said before, all music is based around chords, so you will be playing them in a roundabout way whether you like it or not. But if you *understand* which chords you are playing, it makes the whole process easier. Furthermore, if you intend using auto accompaniment or playing from a fake book, they are essential.

When I first took classical lessons, I was never taught anything about chords, even though I was playing them, - maybe I was too young. But I actually learnt much more about chords as a *'pop'* musician.

As this chapter is for reference only, there are no hyperlinks.

Quick link back to Part 1.

> "When I am completely myself, entirely alone... or during the night when I cannot sleep, it is on such occasions that my ideas flow best and most abundantly. Whence and how these ideas come I know not nor can I force them."
>
> Mozart

C Chords

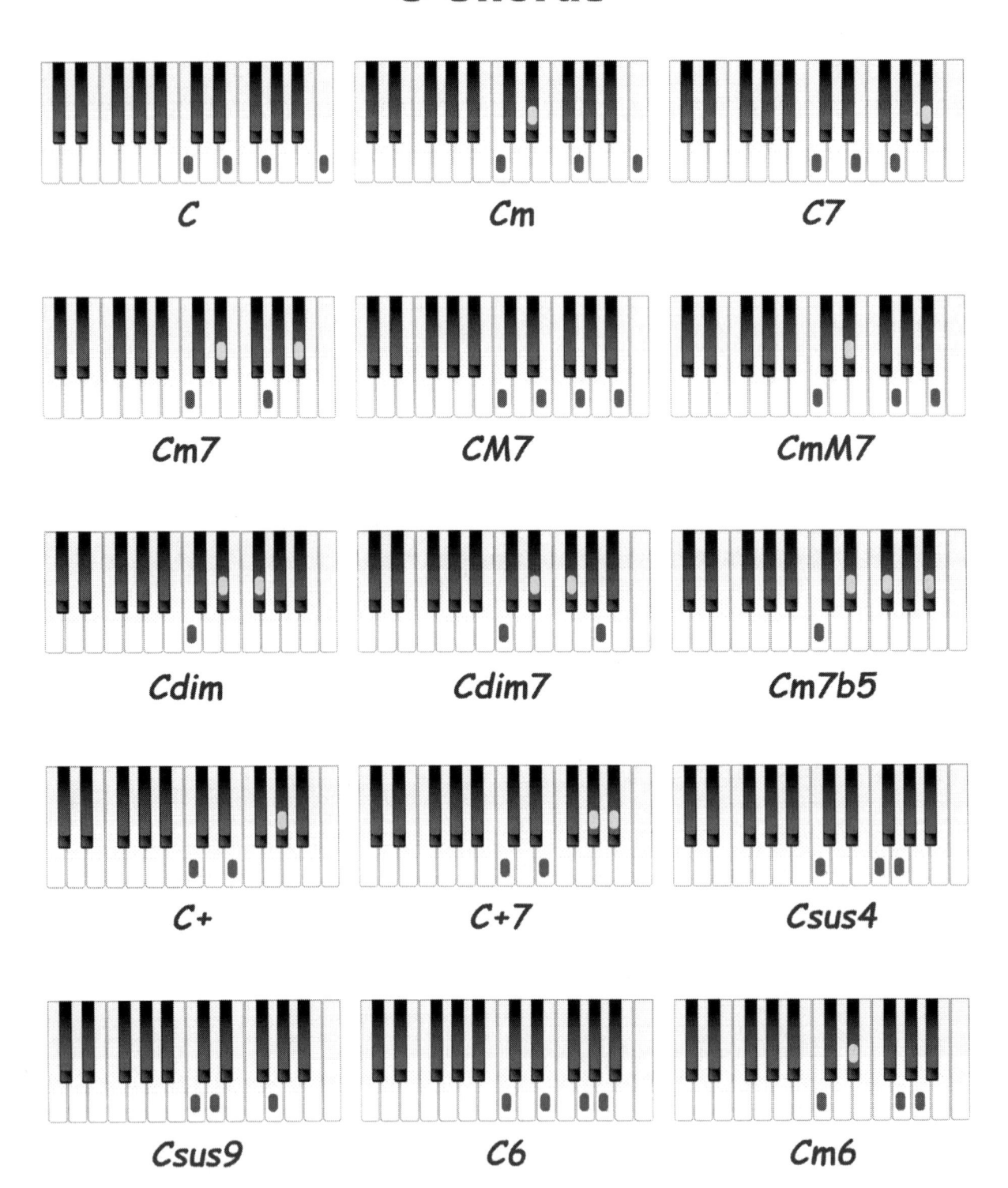

C	Cm	C7
Cm7	CM7	CmM7
Cdim	Cdim7	Cm7b5
C+	C+7	Csus4
Csus9	C6	Cm6

All chords shown are in Root position only. To find the 1st inversions simply move the bottom note of each chord to the top. Repeat for the 2nd and (where applicable) 3rd inversions.

C# Chords

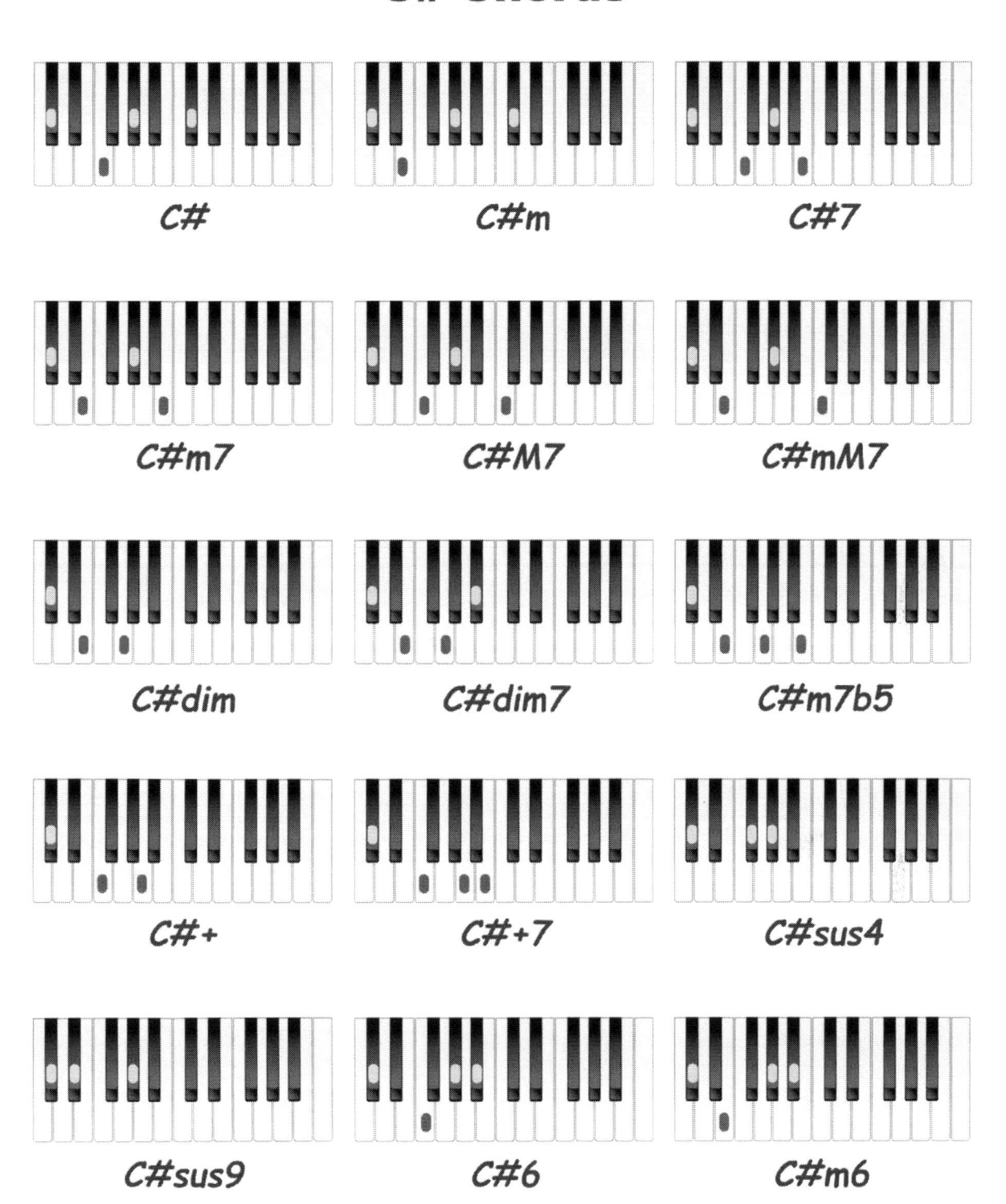

C#	C#m	C#7

C#m7	C#M7	C#mM7

C#dim	C#dim7	C#m7b5

C#+	C#+7	C#sus4

C#sus9	C#6	C#m6

All chords shown are in Root position only. To find the 1st inversions simply move the bottom note of each chord to the top. Repeat for the 2nd and (where applicable) 3rd inversions.

Copyright © Martin Woodward 2011 & 2017

D Chords

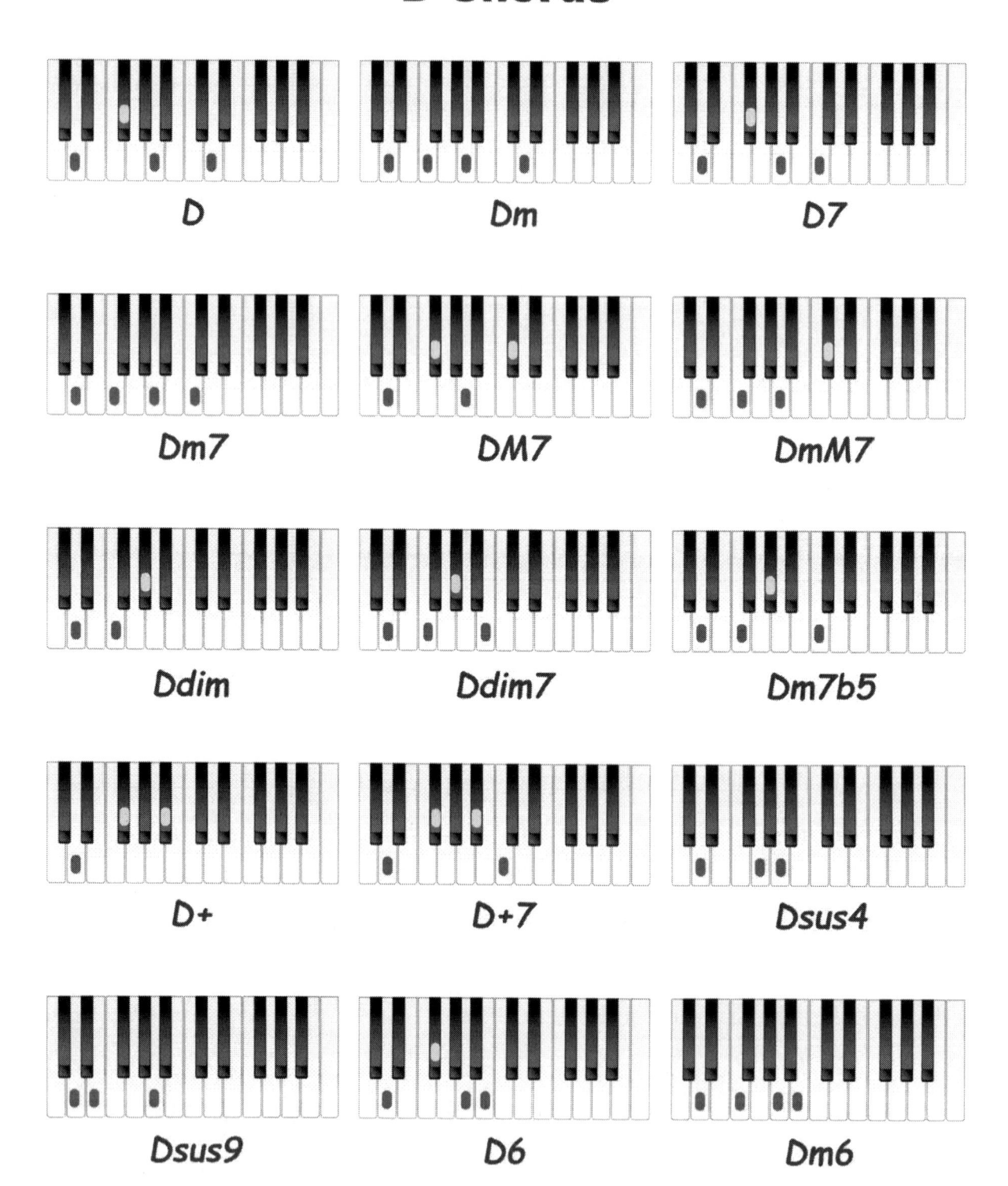

| D | Dm | D7 |

| Dm7 | DM7 | DmM7 |

| Ddim | Ddim7 | Dm7b5 |

| D+ | D+7 | Dsus4 |

| Dsus9 | D6 | Dm6 |

All chords shown are in Root position only. To find the 1st inversions simply move the bottom note of each chord to the top. Repeat for the 2nd and (where applicable) 3rd inversions.

Copyright © Martin Woodward 2011 & 2017

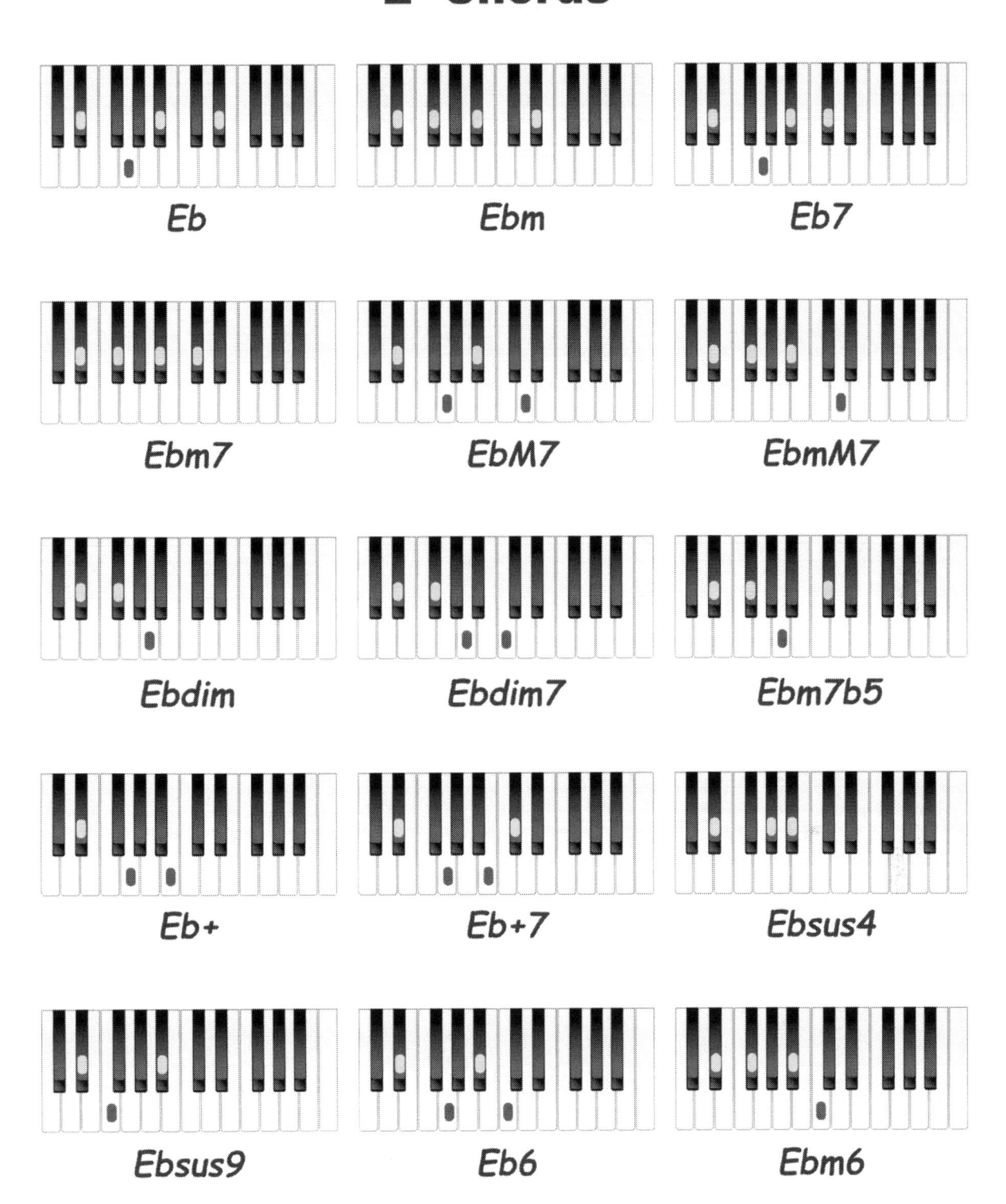

E♭ Chords

Eb	Ebm	Eb7
Ebm7	EbM7	EbmM7
Ebdim	Ebdim7	Ebm7b5
Eb+	Eb+7	Ebsus4
Ebsus9	Eb6	Ebm6

All chords shown are in Root position only. To find the 1st inversions simply move the bottom note of each chord to the top. Repeat for the 2nd and (where applicable) 3rd inversions.

Copyright © Martin Woodward 2011 & 2017

E Chords

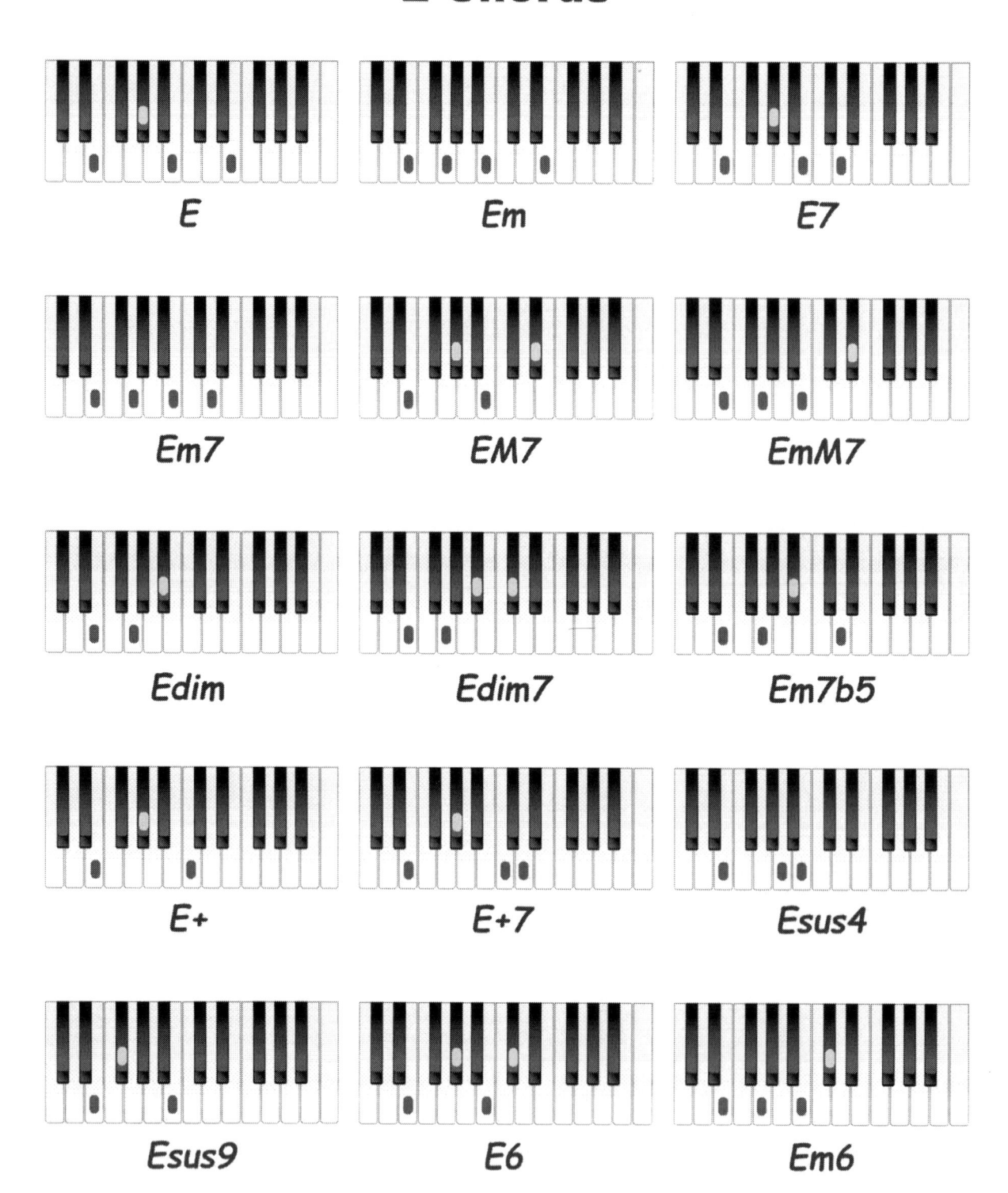

E	Em	E7

Em7	EM7	EmM7

Edim	Edim7	Em7b5

E+	E+7	Esus4

Esus9	E6	Em6

All chords shown are in Root position only. To find the 1st inversions simply move the bottom note of each chord to the top. Repeat for the 2nd and (where applicable) 3rd inversions.

F Chords

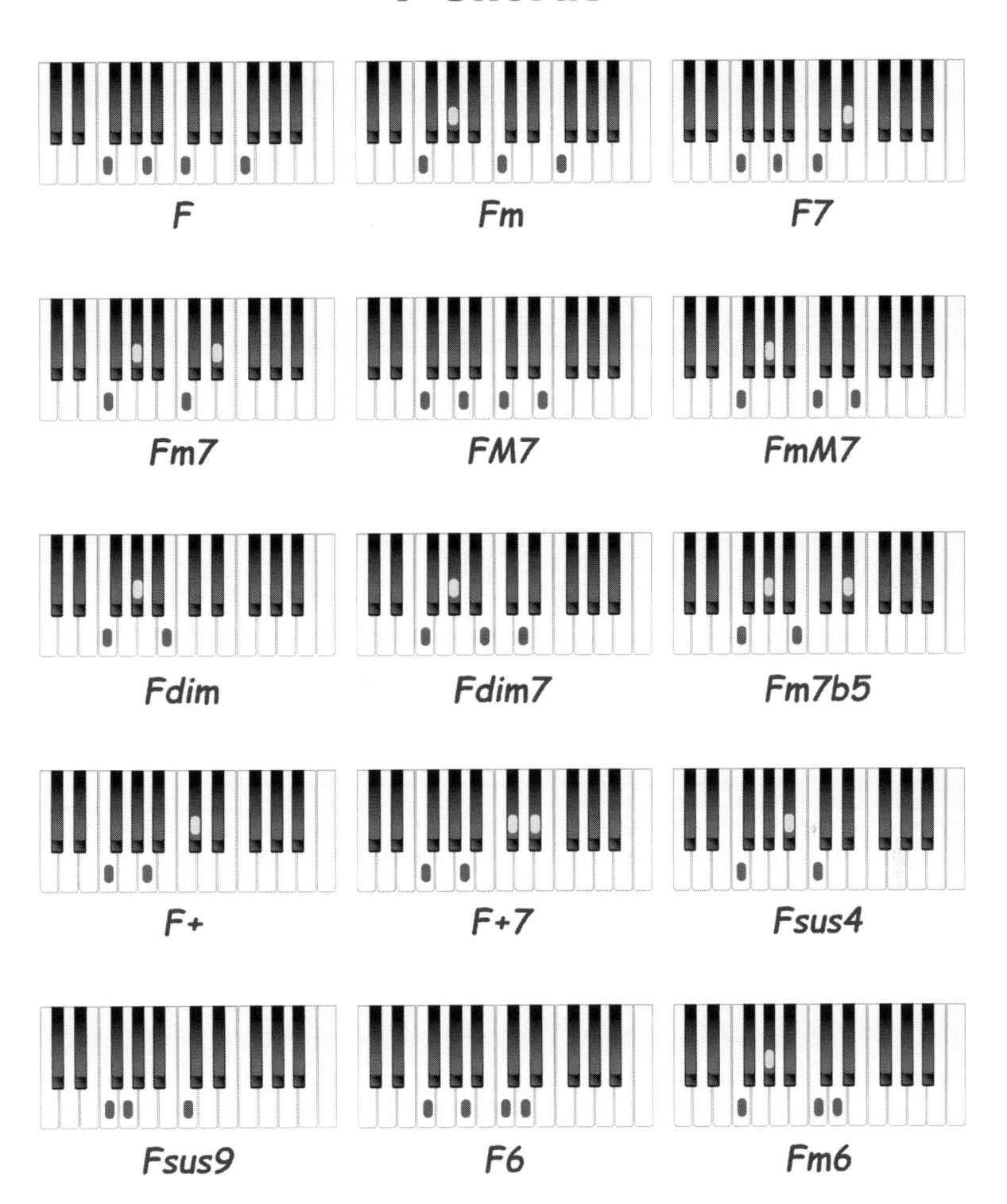

| F | Fm | F7 |

| Fm7 | FM7 | FmM7 |

| Fdim | Fdim7 | Fm7b5 |

| F+ | F+7 | Fsus4 |

| Fsus9 | F6 | Fm6 |

All chords shown are in Root position only. To find the 1st inversions simply move the bottom note of each chord to the top. Repeat for the 2nd and (where applicable) 3rd inversions.

Copyright © Martin Woodward 2011 & 2017

F# Chords

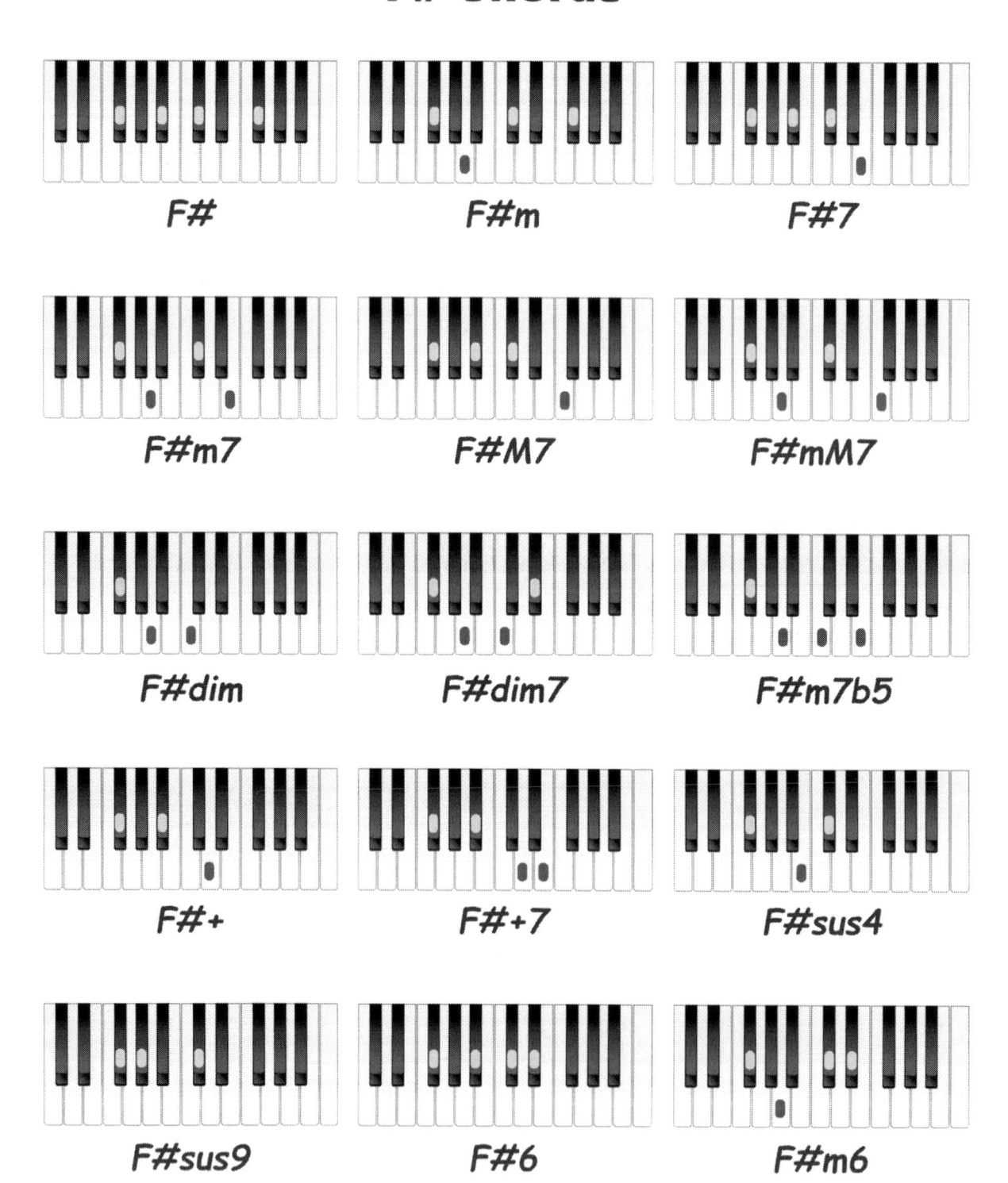

F#	F#m	F#7
F#m7	F#M7	F#mM7
F#dim	F#dim7	F#m7b5
F#+	F#+7	F#sus4
F#sus9	F#6	F#m6

All chords shown are in Root position only. To find the 1st inversions simply move the bottom note of each chord to the top. Repeat for the 2nd and (where applicable) 3rd inversions.

G Chords

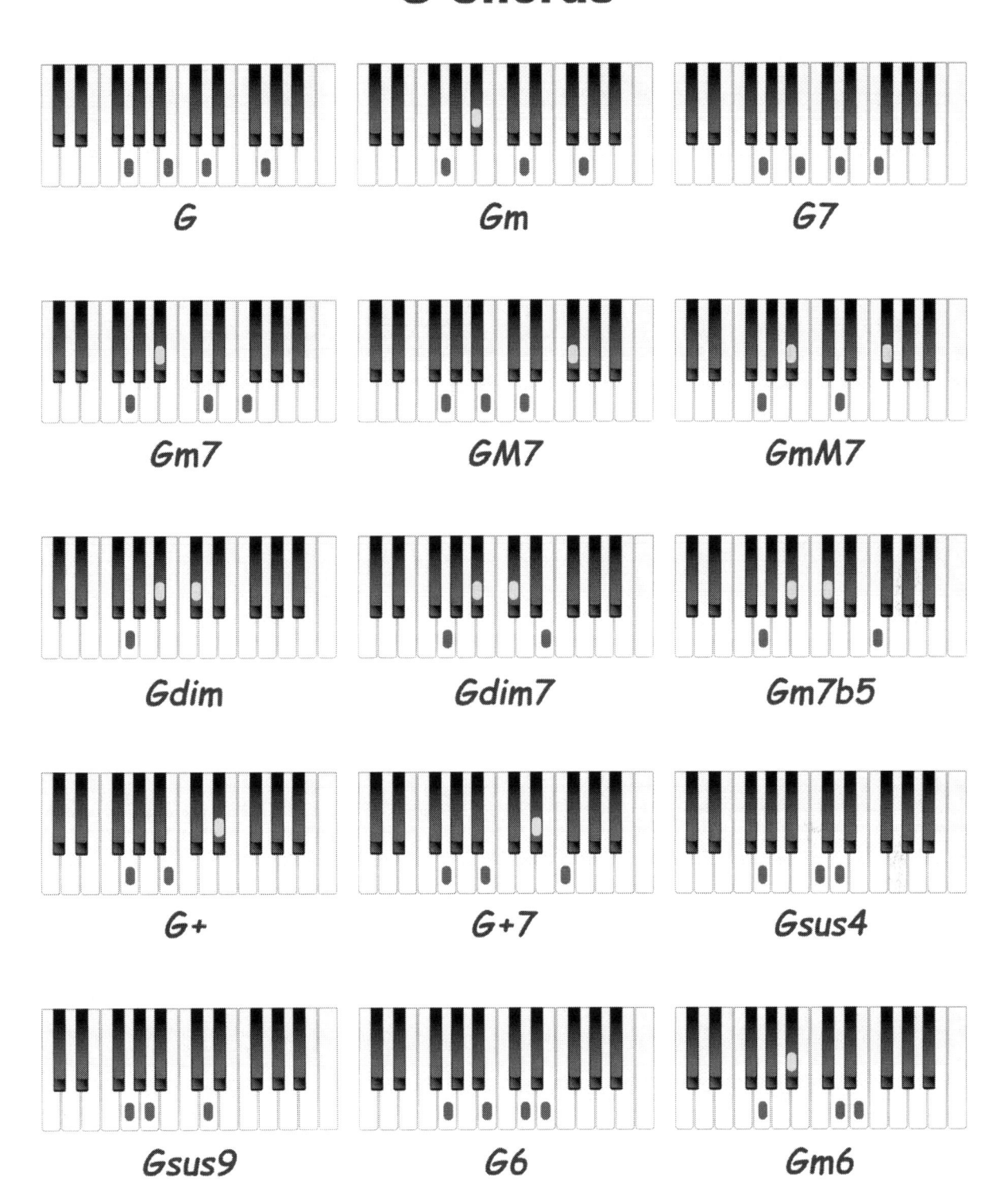

G	Gm	G7
Gm7	GM7	GmM7
Gdim	Gdim7	Gm7b5
G+	G+7	Gsus4
Gsus9	G6	Gm6

All chords shown are in Root position only. To find the 1st inversions simply move the bottom note of each chord to the top. Repeat for the 2nd and (where applicable) 3rd inversions.

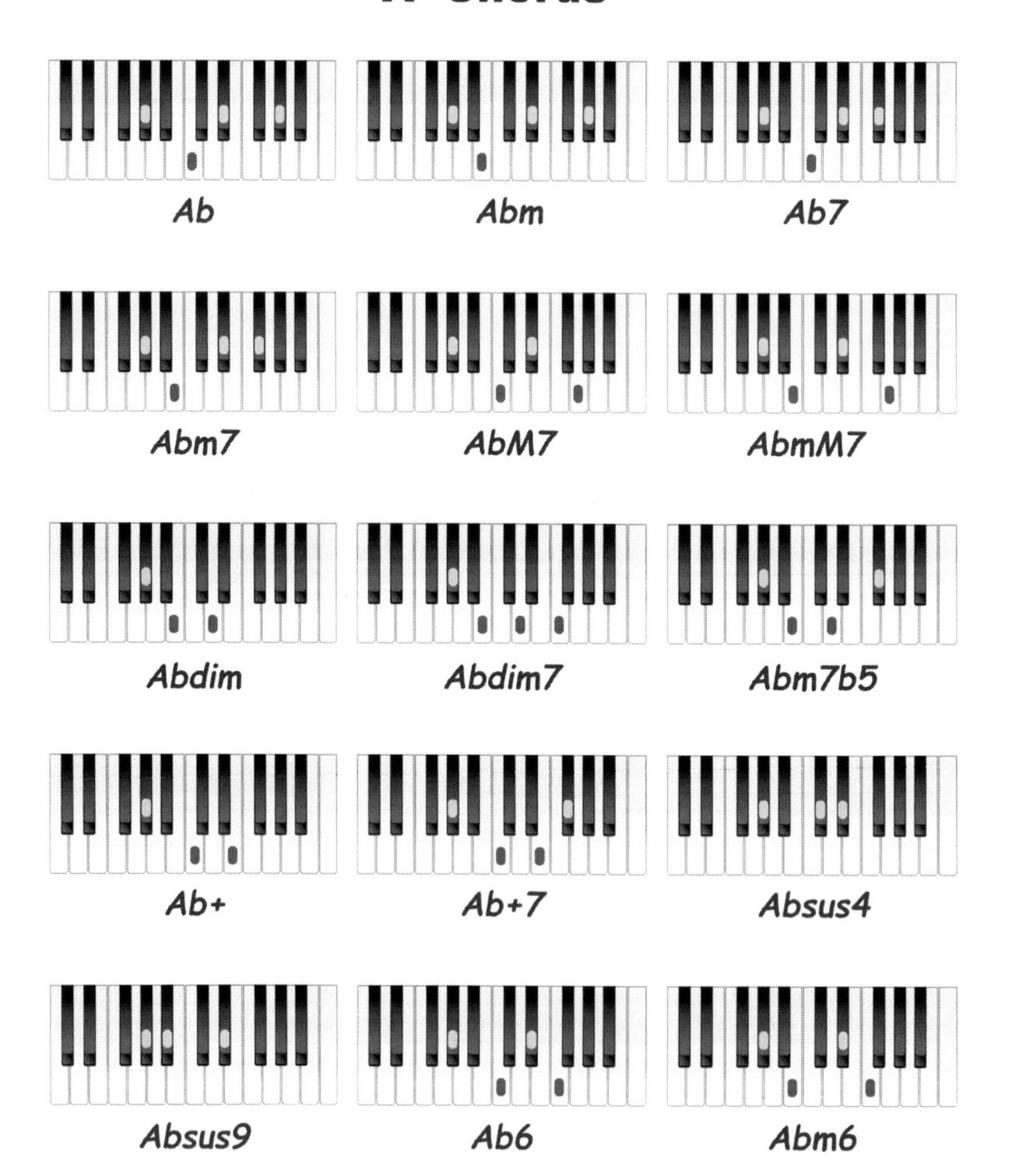

A♭ Chords

Ab	Abm	Ab7
Abm7	AbM7	AbmM7
Abdim	Abdim7	Abm7b5
Ab+	Ab+7	Absus4
Absus9	Ab6	Abm6

All chords shown are in Root position only. To find the 1st inversions simply move the bottom note of each chord to the top. Repeat for the 2nd and (where applicable) 3rd inversions.

A Chords

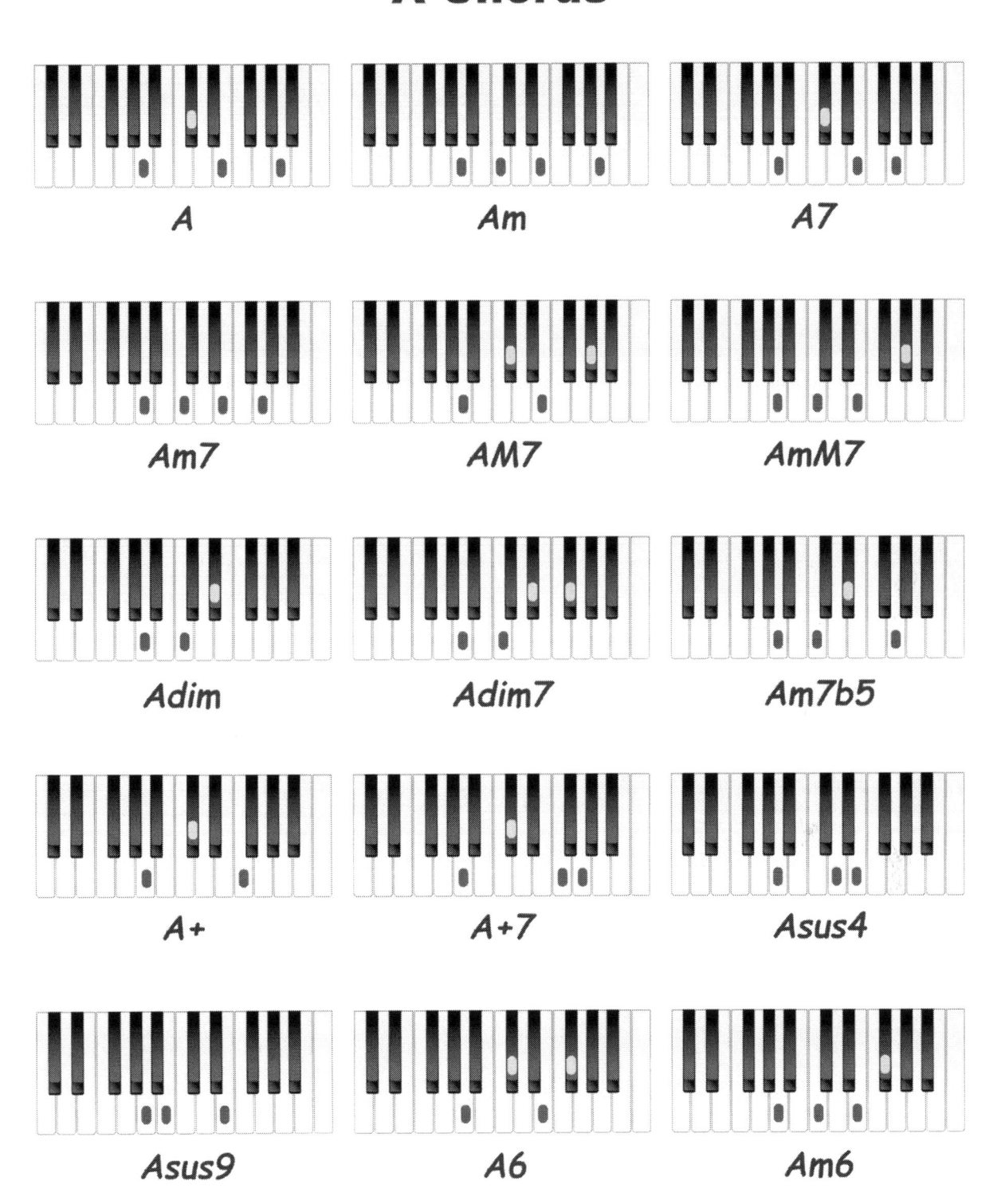

A	Am	A7
Am7	AM7	AmM7
Adim	Adim7	Am7b5
A+	A+7	Asus4
Asus9	A6	Am6

All chords shown are in Root position only. To find the 1st inversions simply move the bottom note of each chord to the top. Repeat for the 2nd and (where applicable) 3rd inversions.

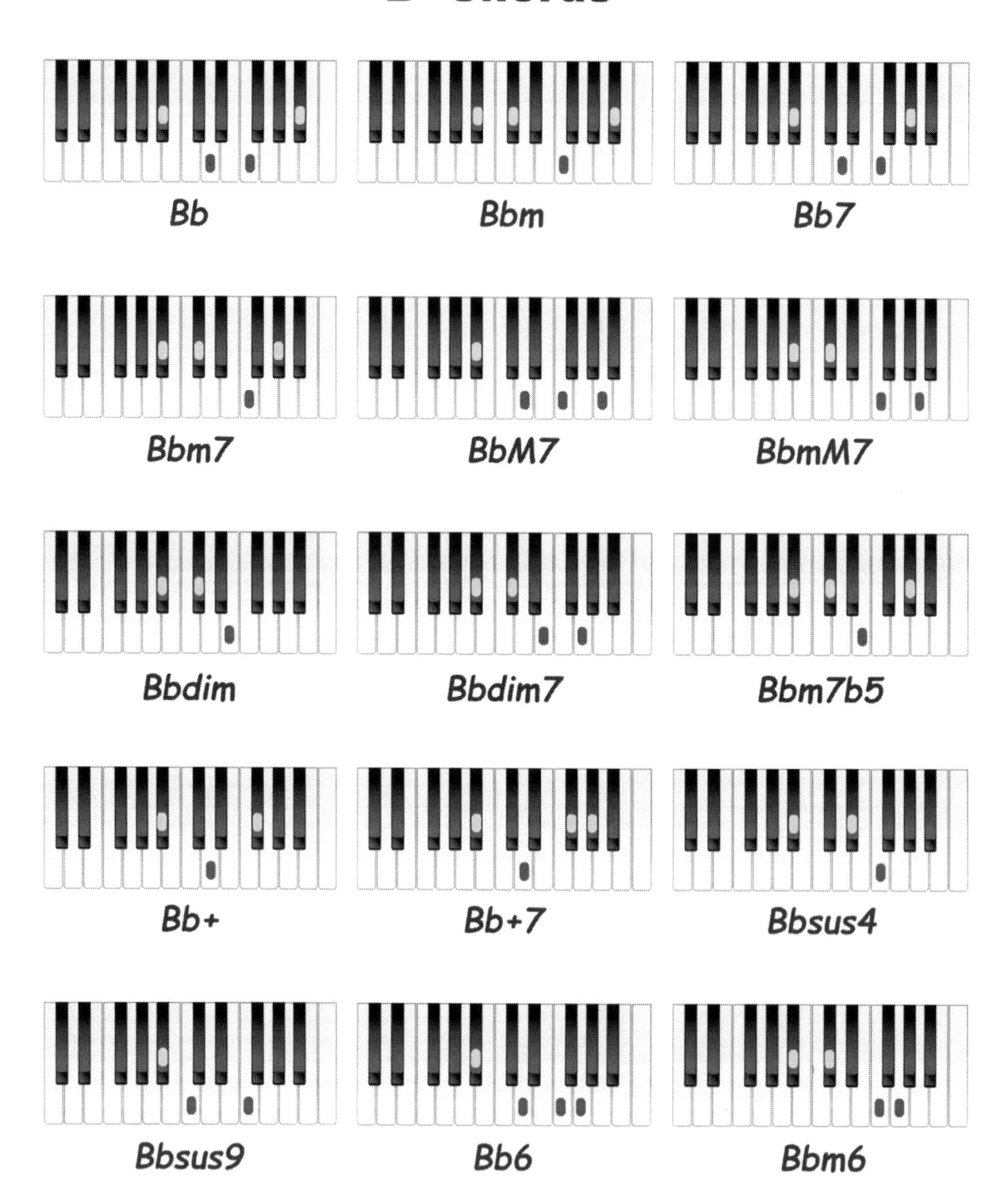

B♭ Chords

Bb	Bbm	Bb7
Bbm7	BbM7	BbmM7
Bbdim	Bbdim7	Bbm7b5
Bb+	Bb+7	Bbsus4
Bbsus9	Bb6	Bbm6

All chords shown are in Root position only. To find the 1st inversions simply move the bottom note of each chord to the top. Repeat for the 2nd and (where applicable) 3rd inversions.

B Chords

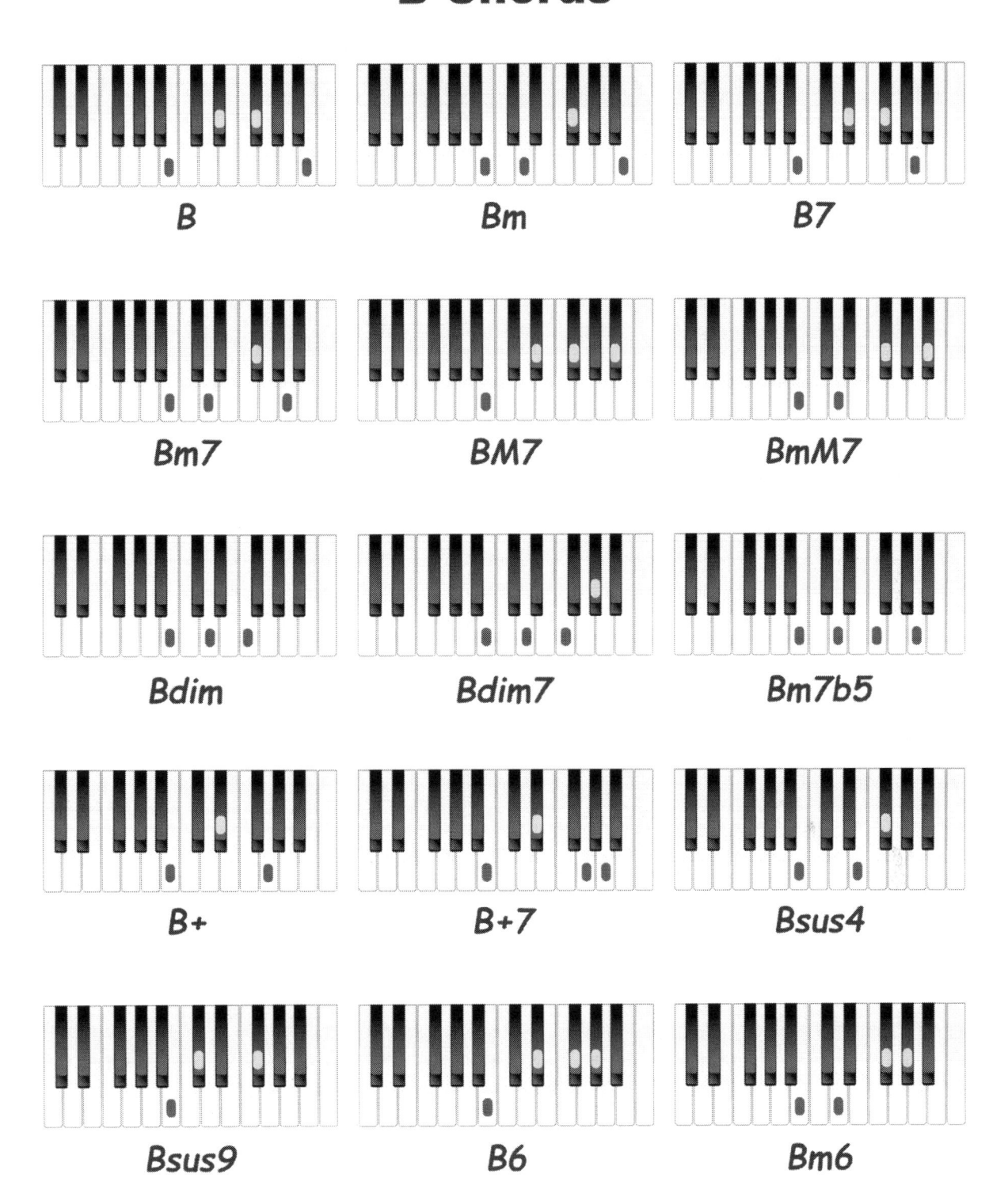

B	Bm	B7
Bm7	BM7	BmM7
Bdim	Bdim7	Bm7b5
B+	B+7	Bsus4
Bsus9	B6	Bm6

All chords shown are in Root position only. To find the 1st inversions simply move the bottom note of each chord to the top. Repeat for the 2nd and (where applicable) 3rd inversions.

⬅ Extended Chords ➡

The next twelve pages show the following chords in keyboard view in each of the twelve keys:

- **6/9th, m6/9th, m7sus4th;**
- **9th, m9th, M9th & 7♭9th;**
- **11th & m11th;**
- **13th, ♭13th & 13♭9th;**
- **♭10th.**

With the exception of the first three chords of each page, the two lowest notes (the root and 5th) are to be played with the left hand.

Note that if playing the short (right hand) version of these chords, it's doubtful, that they would be recognised by auto accompaniment. In this event, just play the relevant major (or minor if applicable) chord with your left hand and the more complicated extension (as shown) with your right hand. It will work - try it! But also note that the chords shown are my suggestions which have served me well, but there are of course others - the possibilities are endless! As you get to understand how chords are constructed, you will be able to figure out different inversions.

If playing with a band, you may only *need* to play the right-hand parts, omitting the tonic and 5th which will be dealt with by the bass player.

As this chapter is for reference only, there are no hyperlinks.

Quick link back to Part 1.

Roland RD 800 Stage Piano (88 keys)

This is a great stage piano with superb sounds and a lovely keybed.
It also has a rhythm function to play along with and audio recording features.
Intuitive and easy to use - well enough 'bells and whistles' for me!
I love it! - It's so difficult to pick which is best!

C Extended Chords

C6/9   Cm6/9   Cm7sus4

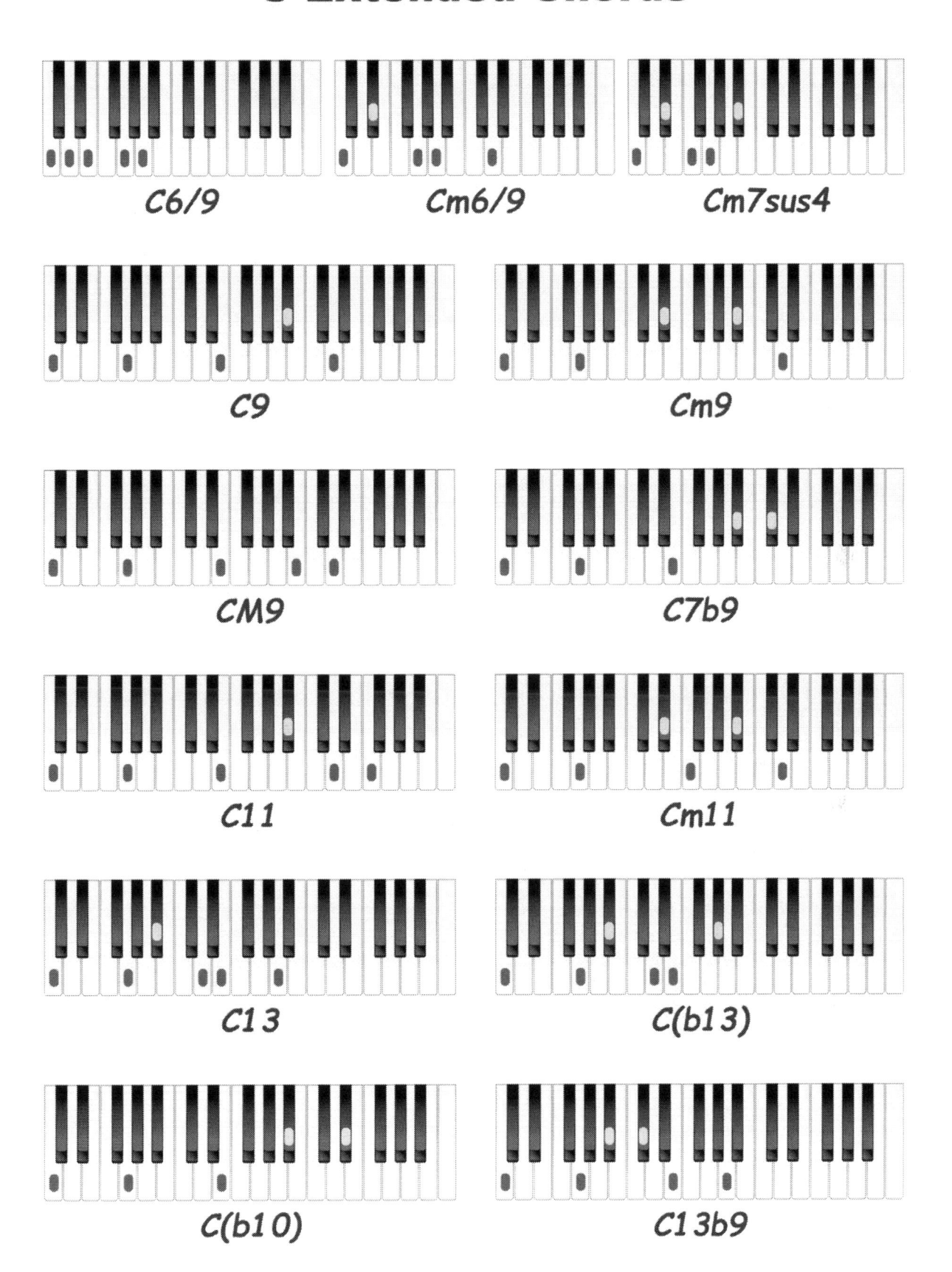

C9   Cm9

CM9   C7b9

C11   Cm11

C13   C(b13)

C(b10)   C13b9

C# Extended Chords

C#6/9   C#m6/9   C#m7sus4

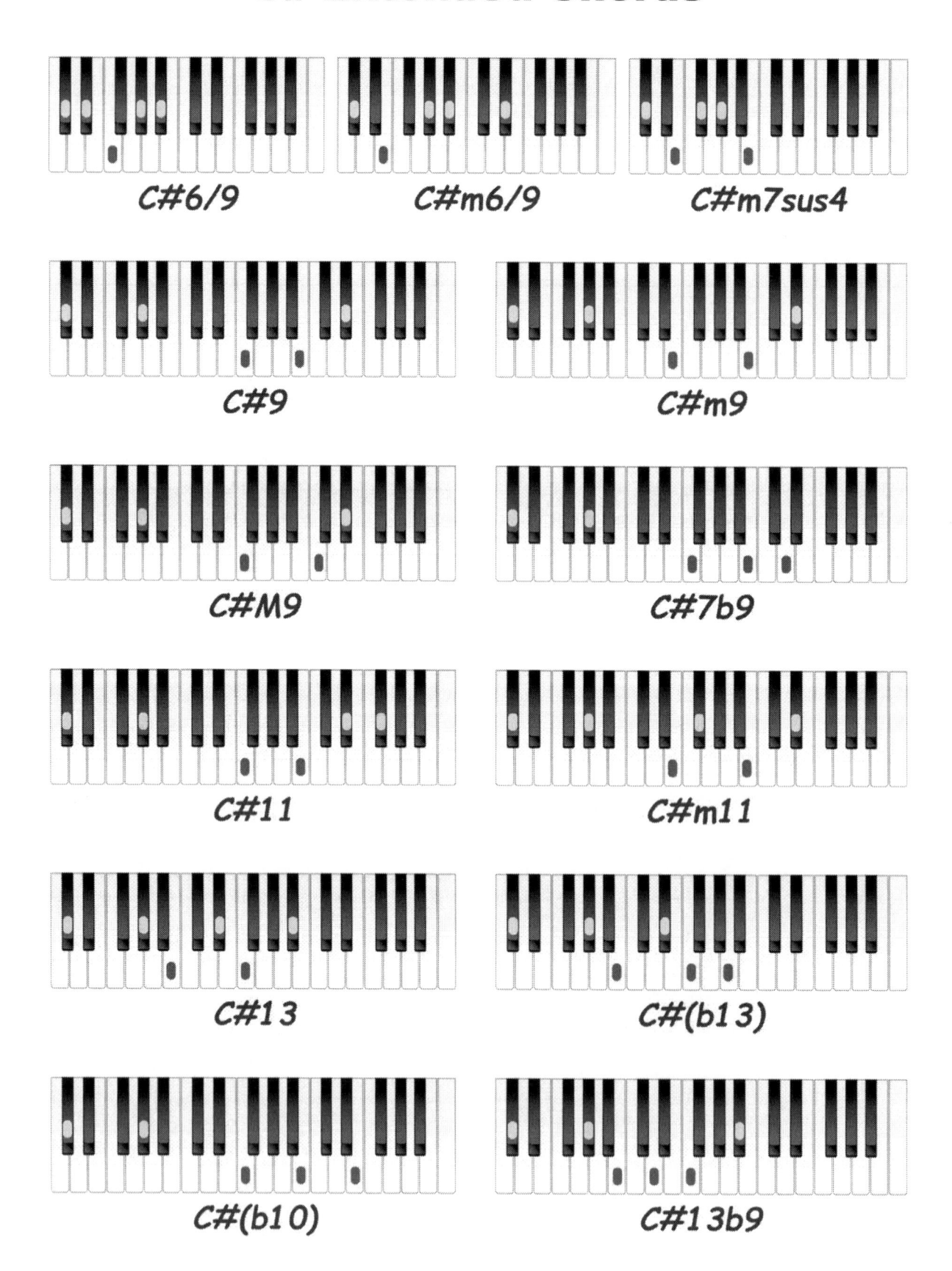

C#9   C#m9

C#M9   C#7b9

C#11   C#m11

C#13   C#(b13)

C#(b10)   C#13b9

D Extended Chords

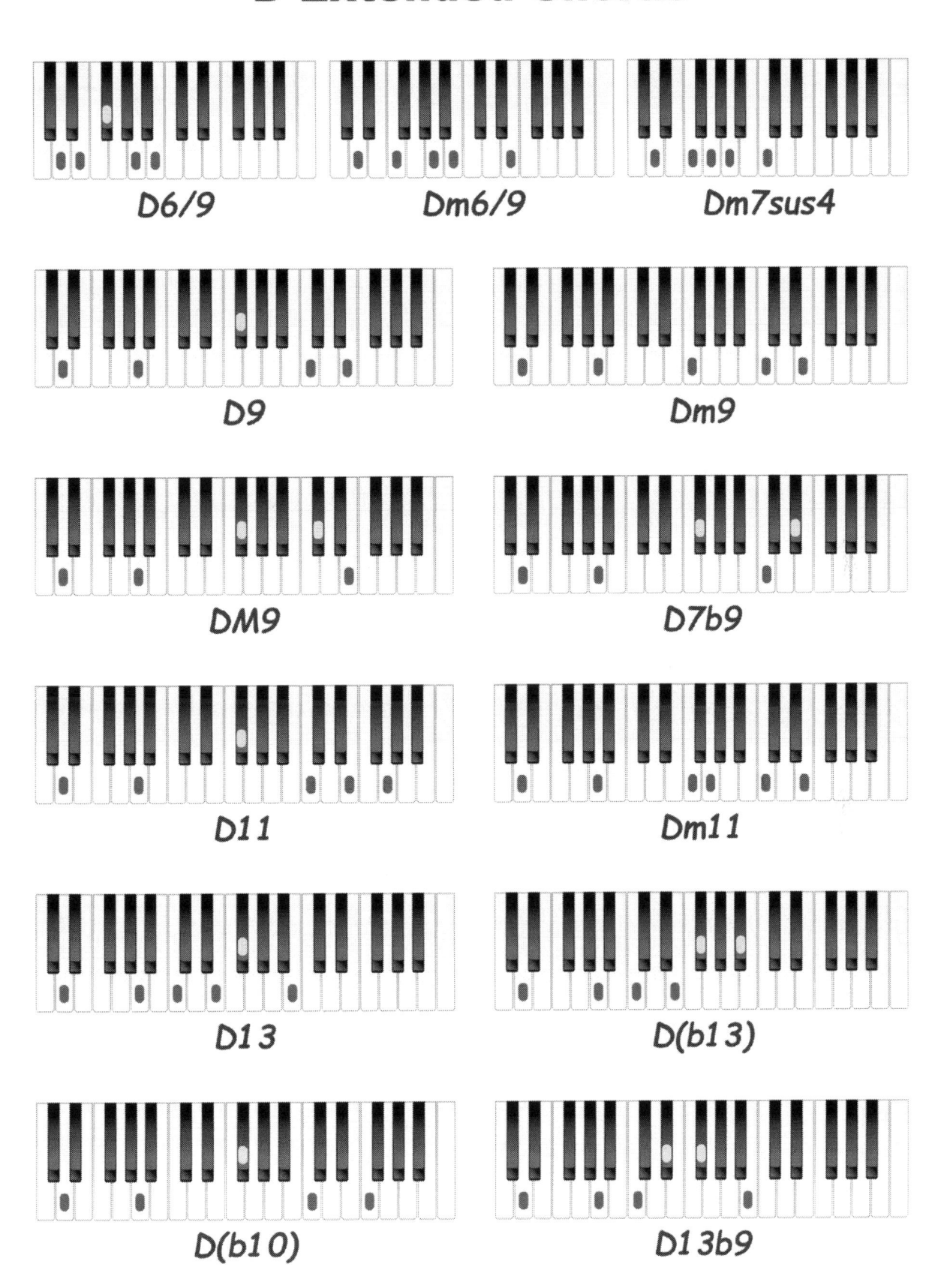

D6/9   Dm6/9   Dm7sus4

D9   Dm9

DM9   D7b9

D11   Dm11

D13   D(b13)

D(b10)   D13b9

E♭ Extended Chords

Eb6/9   Ebm6/9   Ebm7sus4

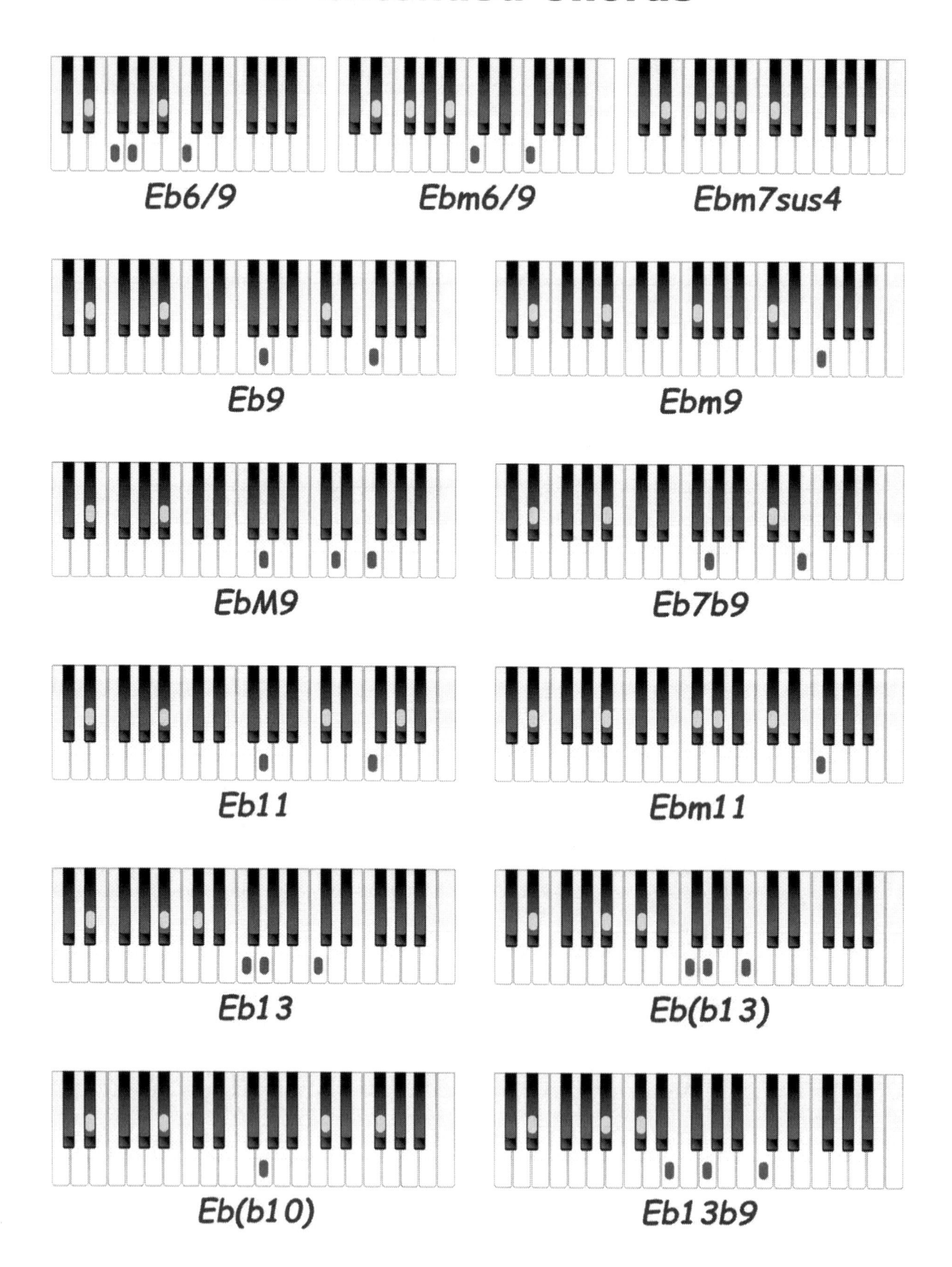

Eb9   Ebm9

EbM9   Eb7b9

Eb11   Ebm11

Eb13   Eb(b13)

Eb(b10)   Eb13b9

E Extended Chords

E6/9   Em6/9   Em7sus4

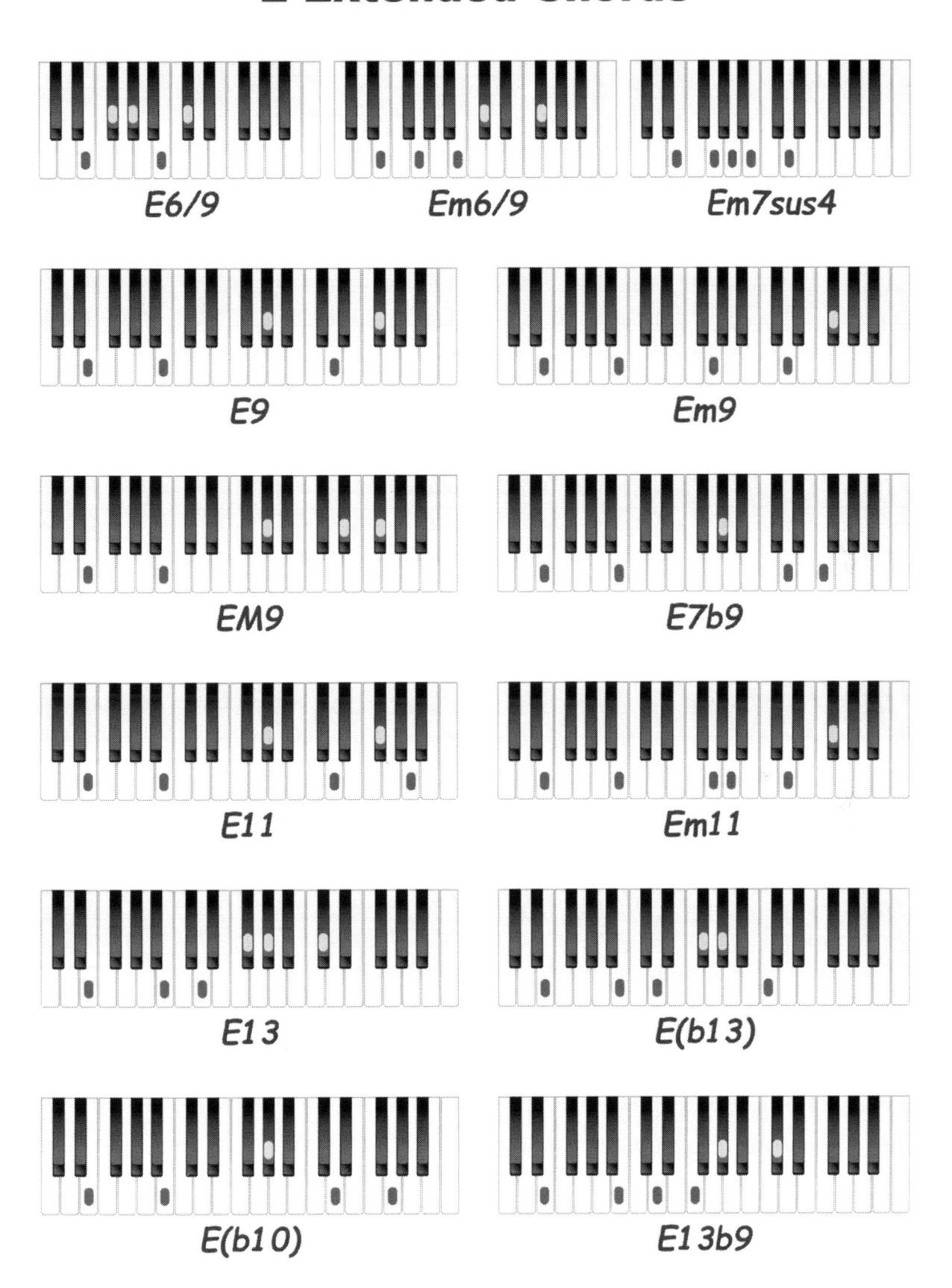

E9   Em9

EM9   E7b9

E11   Em11

E13   E(b13)

E(b10)   E13b9

F Extended Chords

F6/9 Fm6/9 Fm7sus4

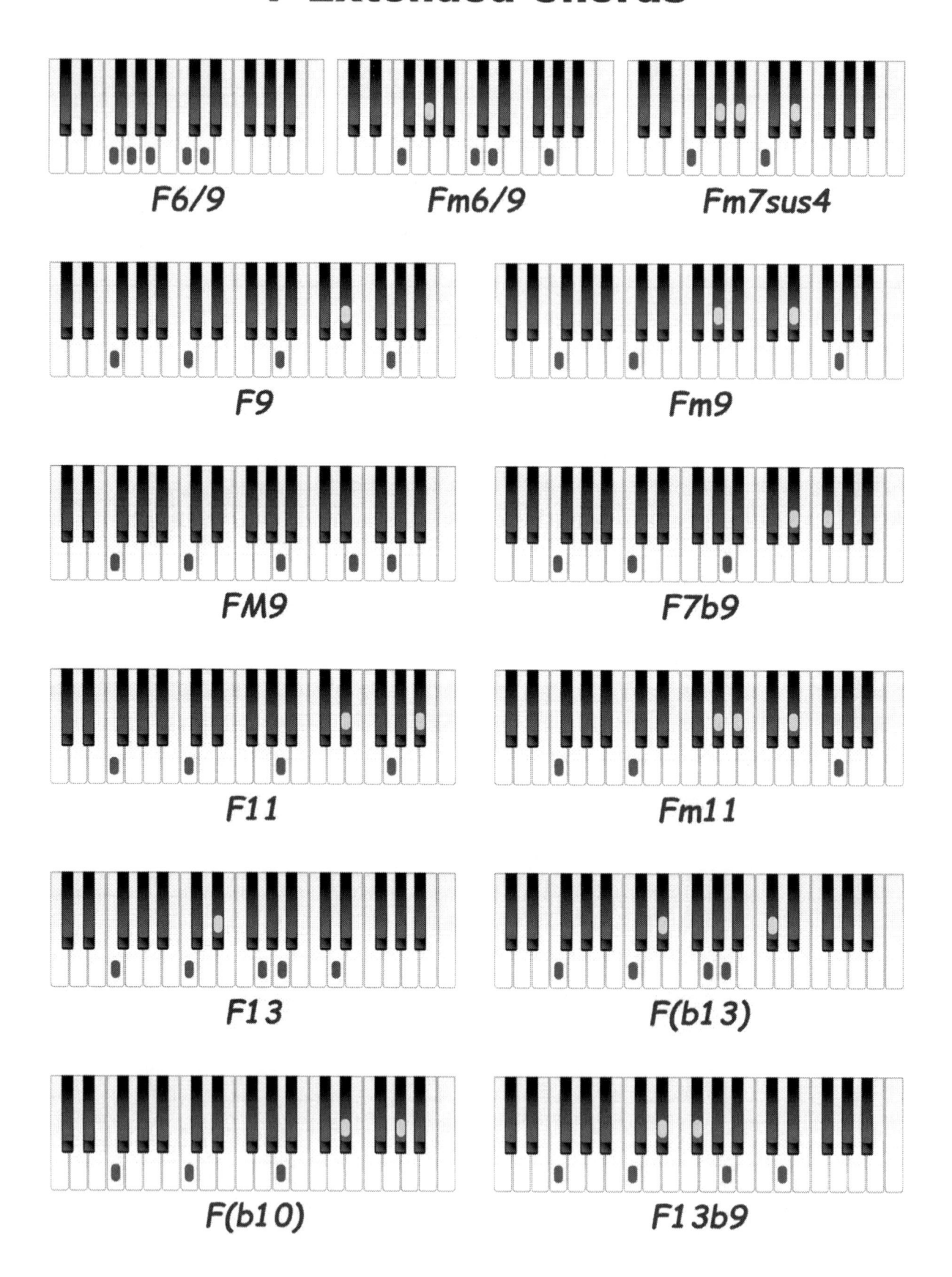

F9 Fm9

FM9 F7b9

F11 Fm11

F13 F(b13)

F(b10) F13b9

F# Extended Chords

F#6/9

F#m6/9

F#m7sus4

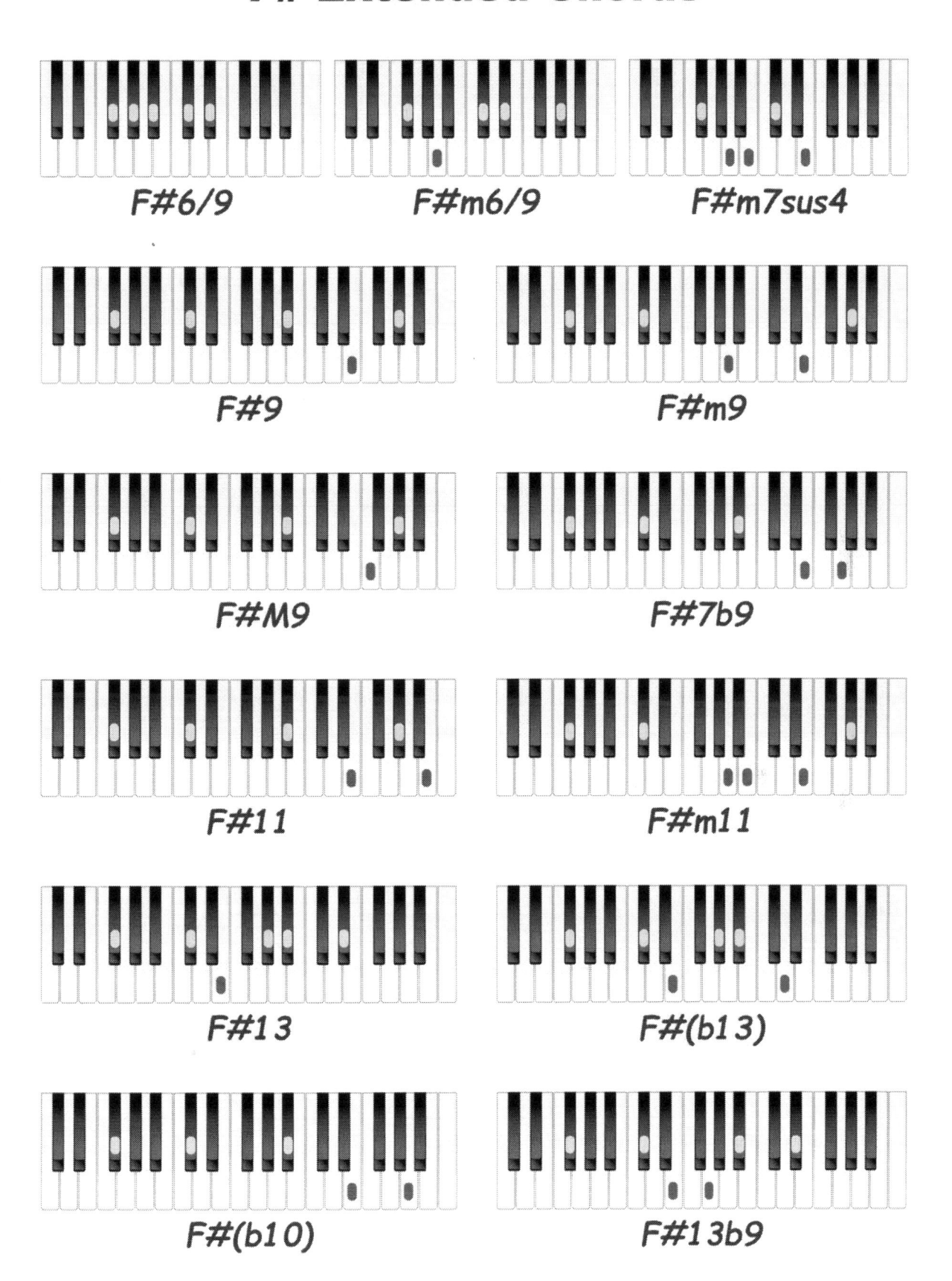

F#9

F#m9

F#M9

F#7b9

F#11

F#m11

F#13

F#(b13)

F#(b10)

F#13b9

G Extended Chords

G6/9 Gm6/9 Gm7sus4

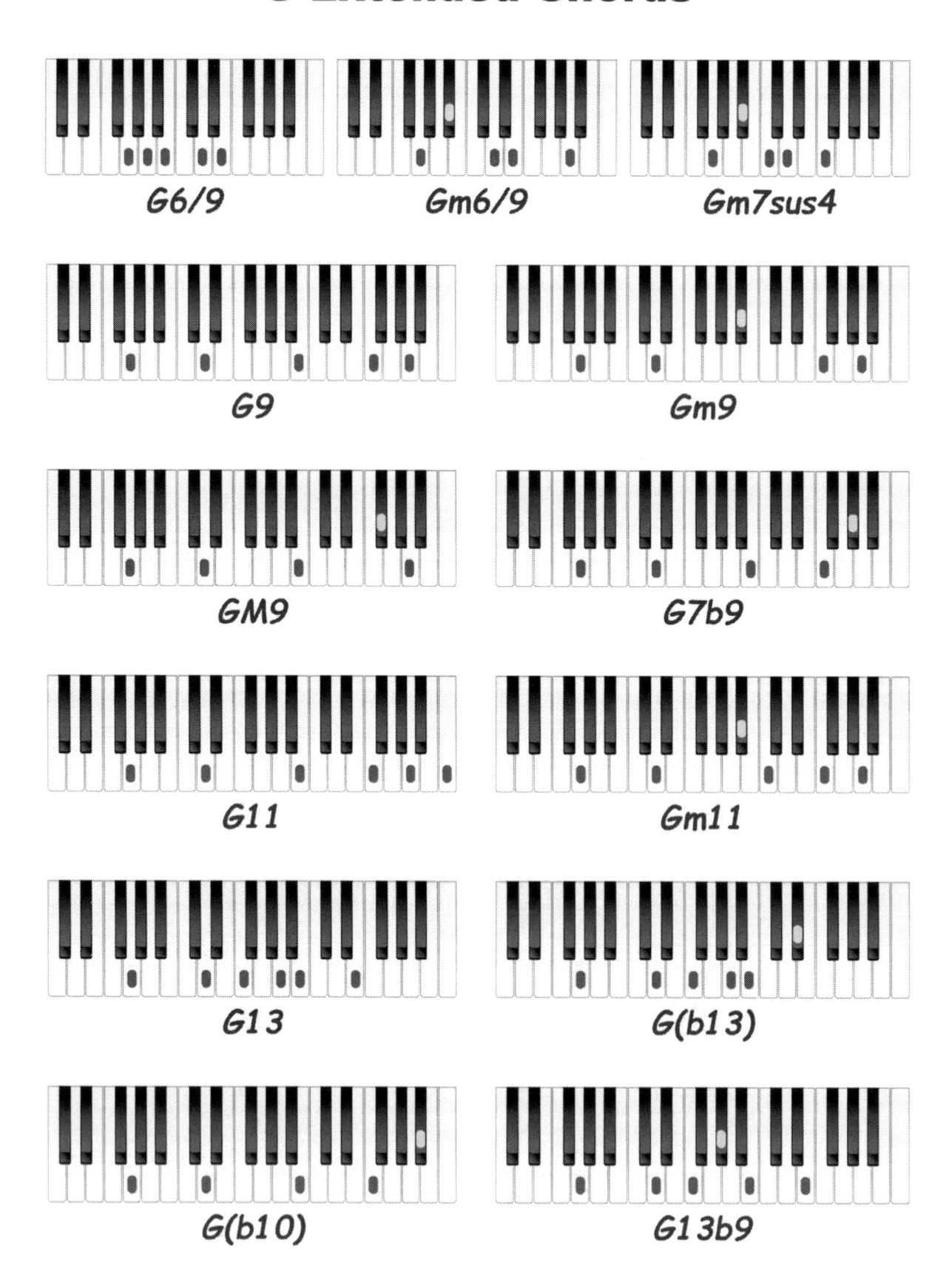

G9 Gm9

GM9 G7b9

G11 Gm11

G13 G(b13)

G(b10) G13b9

A♭ Extended Chords

Ab6/9   Abm6/9   Abm7sus4

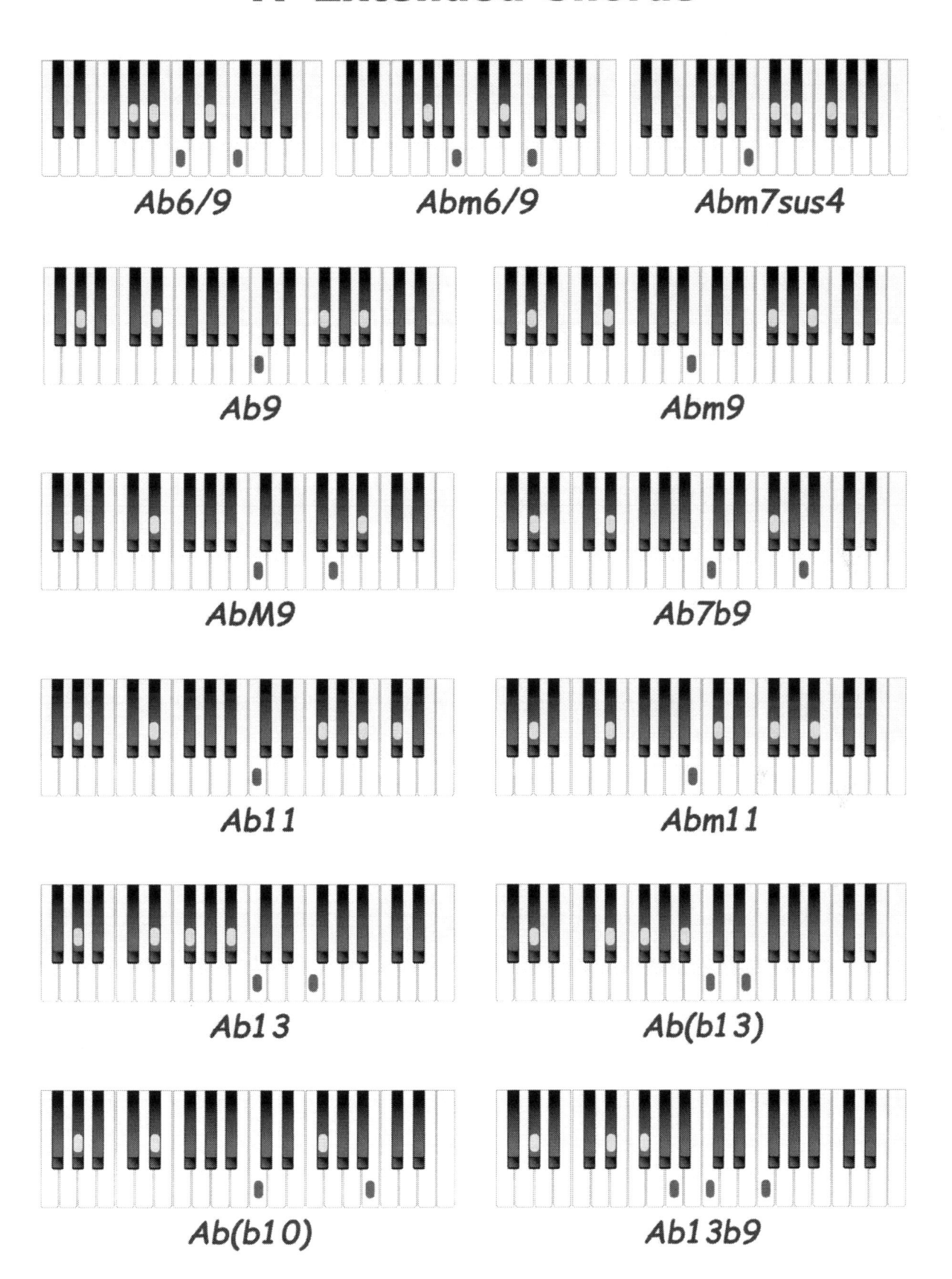

Ab9   Abm9

AbM9   Ab7b9

Ab11   Abm11

Ab13   Ab(b13)

Ab(b10)   Ab13b9

A Extended Chords

A6/9   Am6/9   Am7sus4

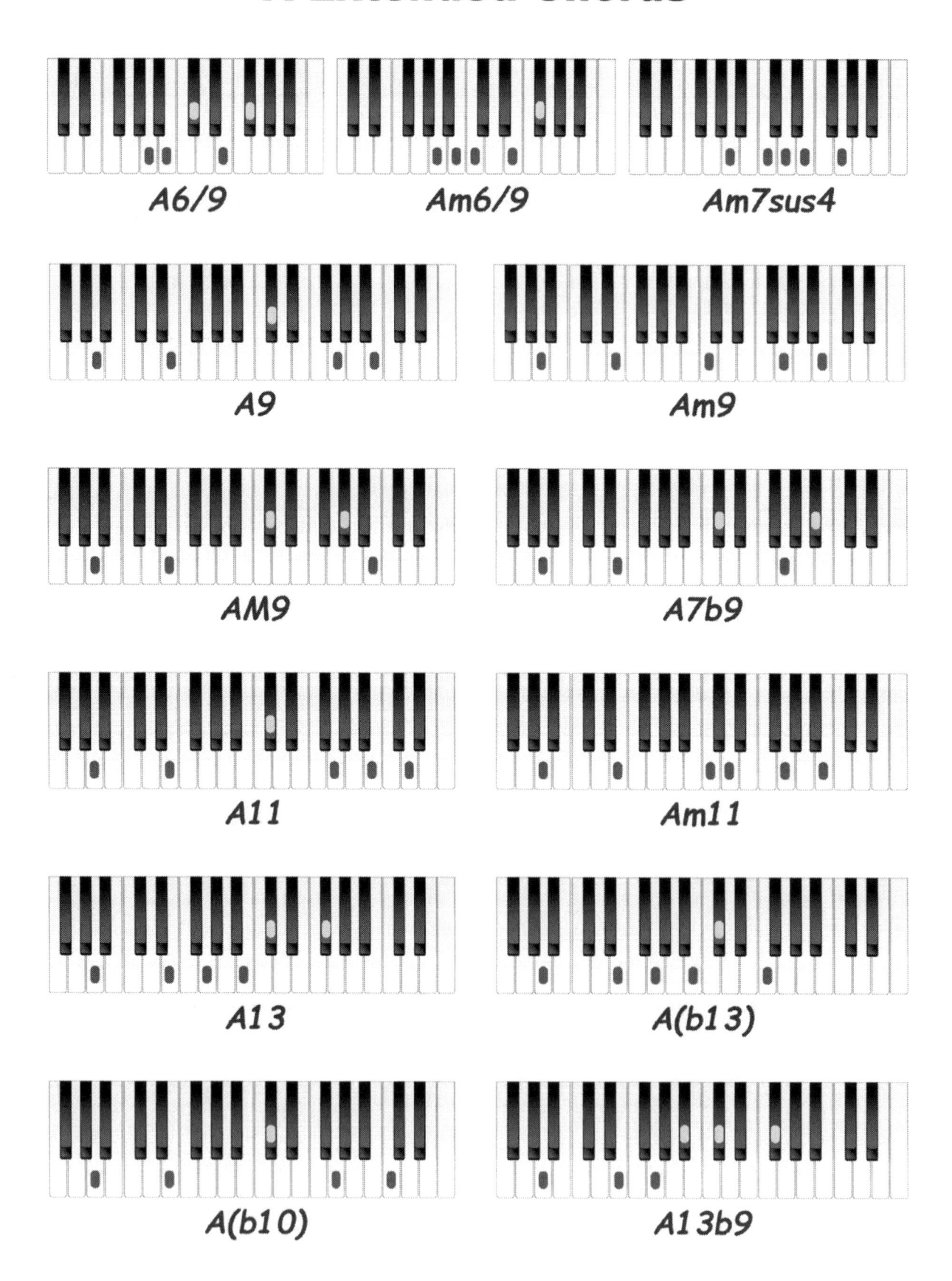

A9   Am9

AM9   A7b9

A11   Am11

A13   A(b13)

A(b10)   A13b9

B♭ Extended Chords

Bb6/9　　　　Bbm6/9　　　　Bbm7sus4

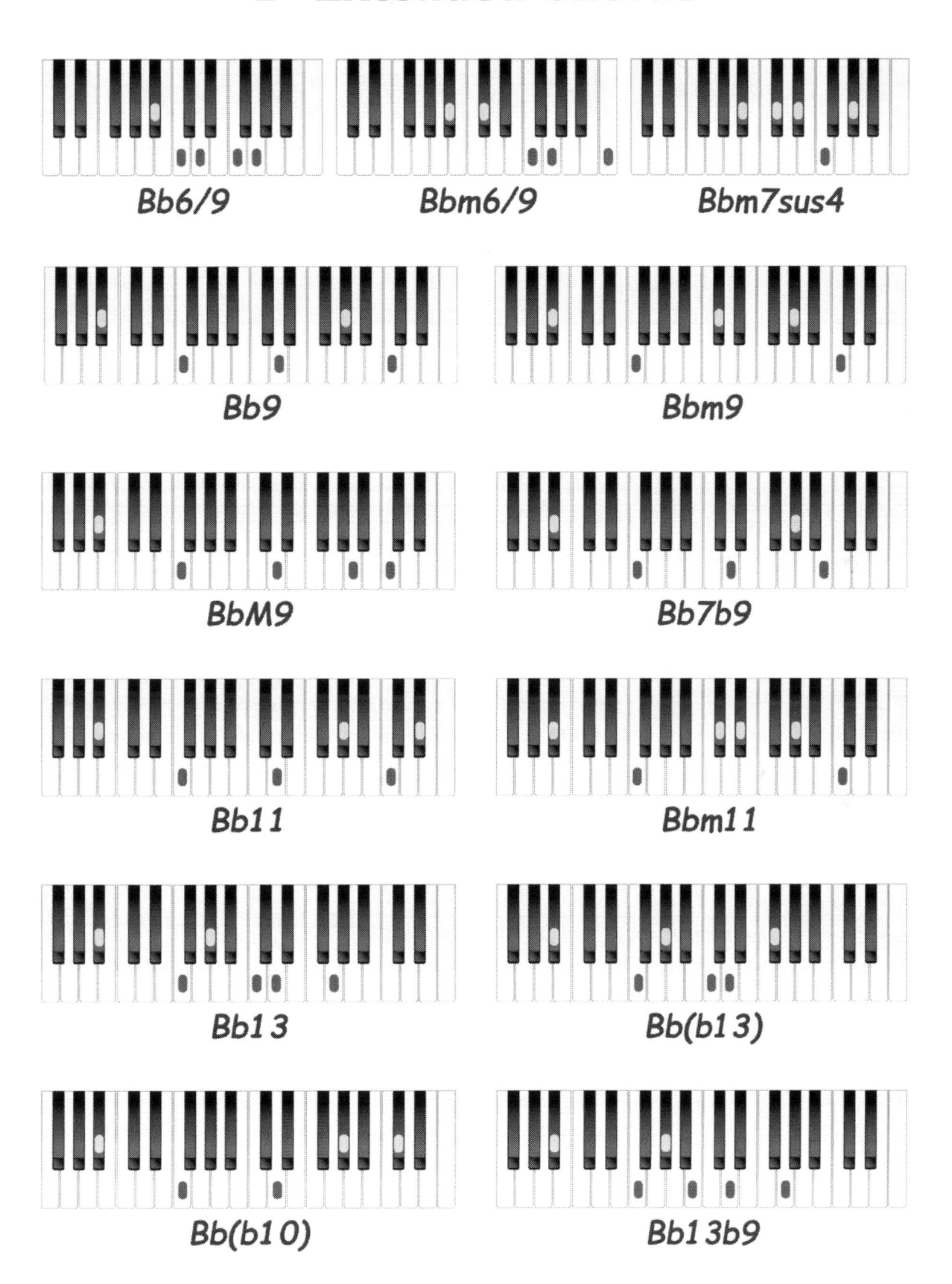

Bb9　　　　　Bbm9

BbM9　　　　Bb7b9

Bb11　　　　Bbm11

Bb13　　　　Bb(b13)

Bb(b10)　　　Bb13b9

B Extended Chords

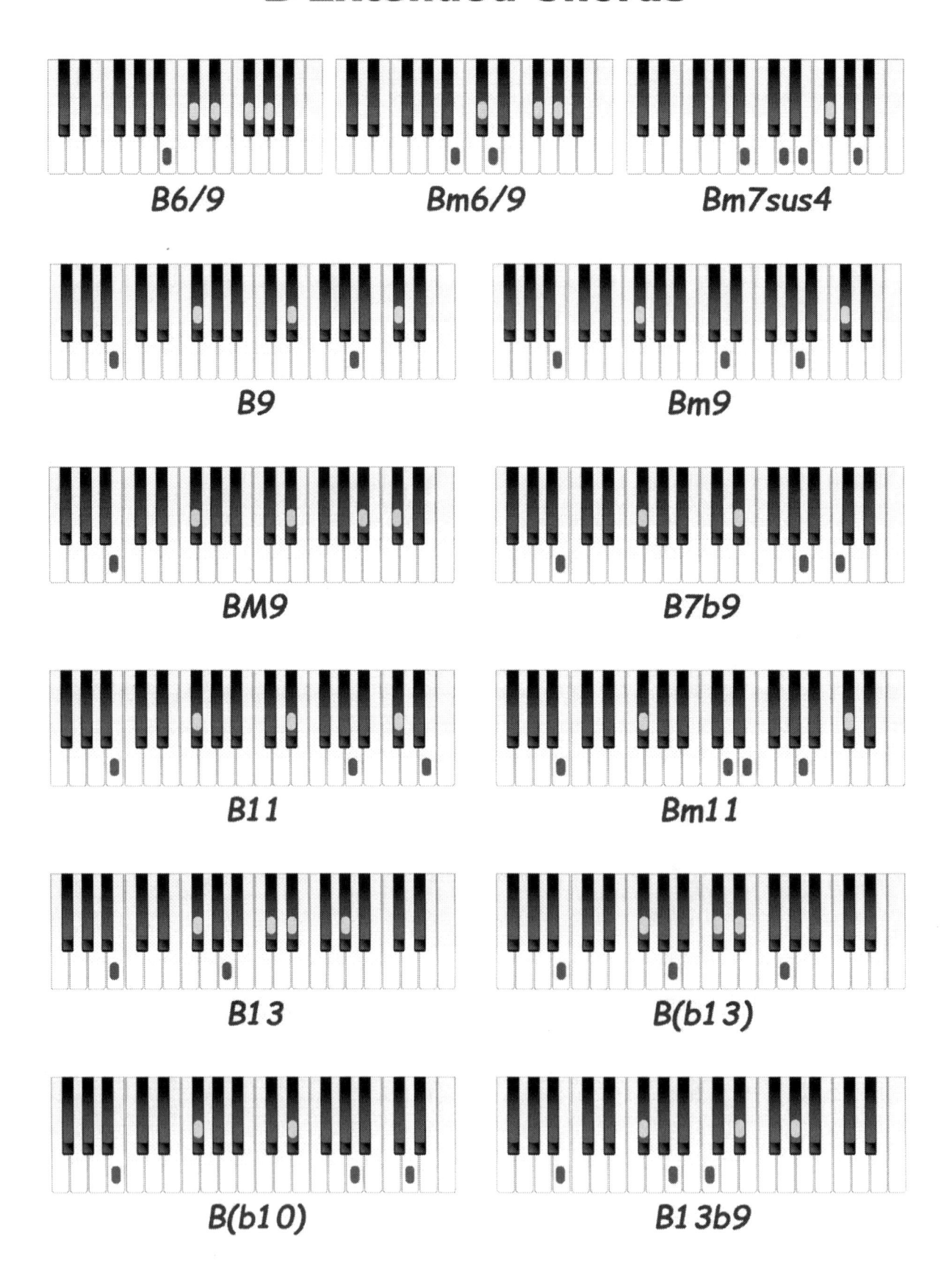

B6/9 Bm6/9 Bm7sus4

B9 Bm9

BM9 B7b9

B11 Bm11

B13 B(b13)

B(b10) B13b9

⬅ Arpeggio Exercises ➡

It's well worth the effort to practice every arpeggio in every key major and minor with both hands together and separately, remembering as always that speed is not important, but accuracy and fluency is! At first the finger crossovers are far more difficult than the scales as they span for much greater intervals. But in all cases, avoid using the sustain pedal when practicing these as doing so will give you a false impression of fluency.

The next few pages show every major and minor arpeggio in every key both in keyboard and notation view with fingering for both hands. Notice that the fingering is identical for every arpeggio starting on a white note, but not so for the ones that start on black notes. Note also that there is no difference between the *harmonic*, *melodic* and *natural* minor arpeggios as the 6th and 7th degrees of the scales are not included.

Broken chords are then shown in the most used keys with left / right hand fingering in notation view only.

You are advised to practice these in the order in which they are listed with each hand separately and then together at comfortable speeds. Remember speed is not an issue but fluency and accuracy is. And remember - no pedal!

When you are familiar with them all, they can be practiced in any order.

You are also advised to practice the **7th**, **M7th** and **m7th** arpeggios in the most used keys as shown in part 1. However, these are not shown here, but the chords from which you can take them have been shown in every key in the last two chapters.

As with the scale exercises, I have only included the hyperlinks on the first major and minor examples on the next page as the others are the same but at different pitches. And again, one example of a broken chord, and the final right-hand exercise.

The audio link for this section is http://learn-keyboard.co.uk/arp_full.html or click on the graphics.

Quick link back to Arpeggios part 1

> *"When the power of love overcomes the love of power the world will know peace!"*
> Jimi Hendrix (1942-1970)
> *Comment: Not only was he one of the world's greatest guitarists, he was also clearly a bit of a philosopher!*

C Major Arpeggio

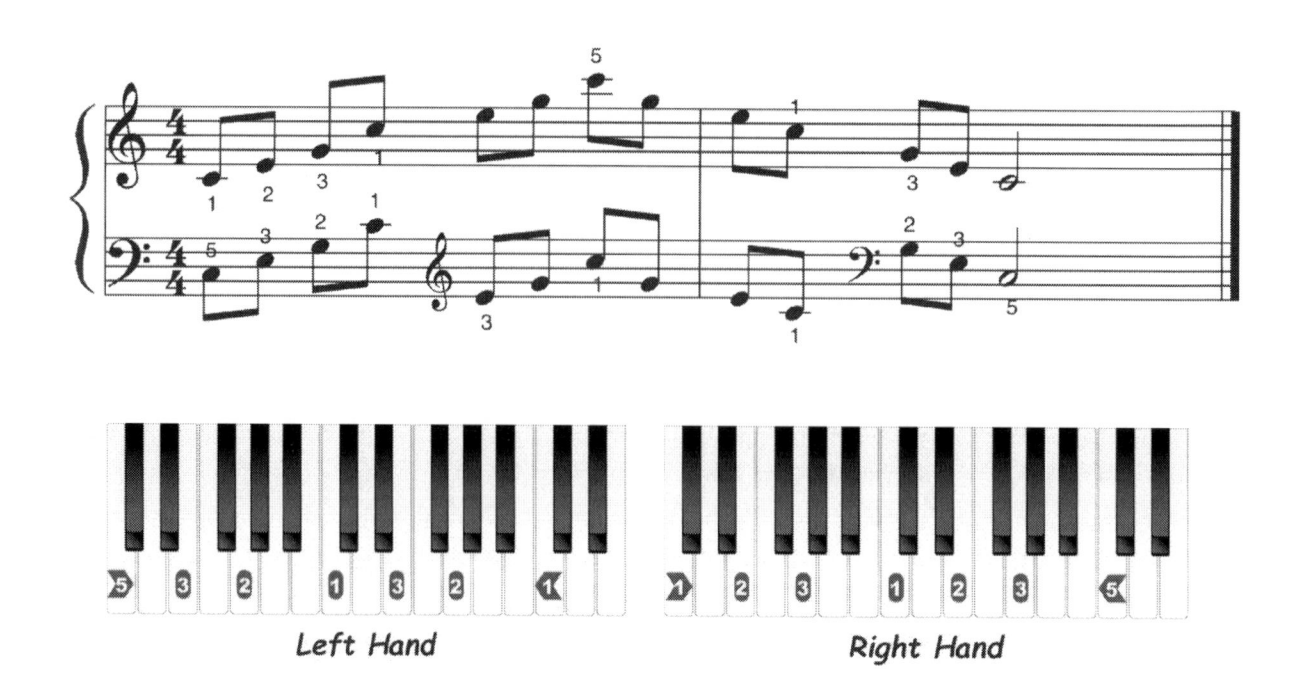

A Minor Arpeggio

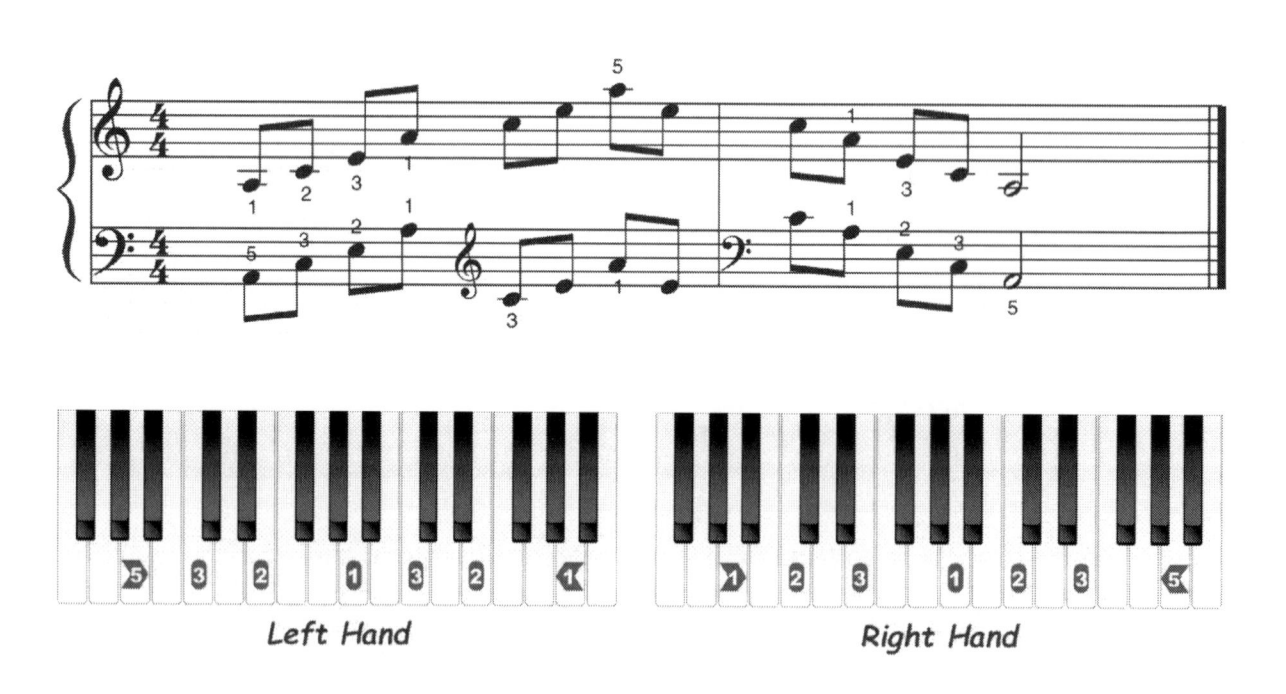

G Major Arpeggio

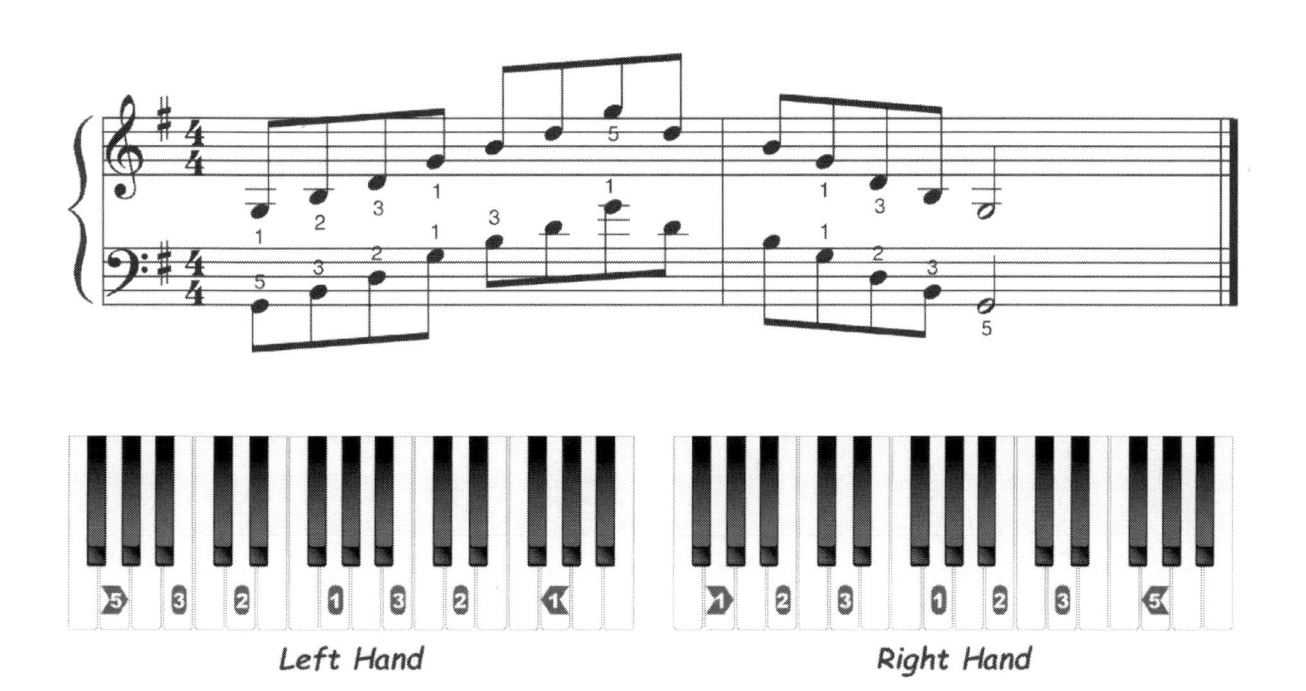

E Minor Arpeggio

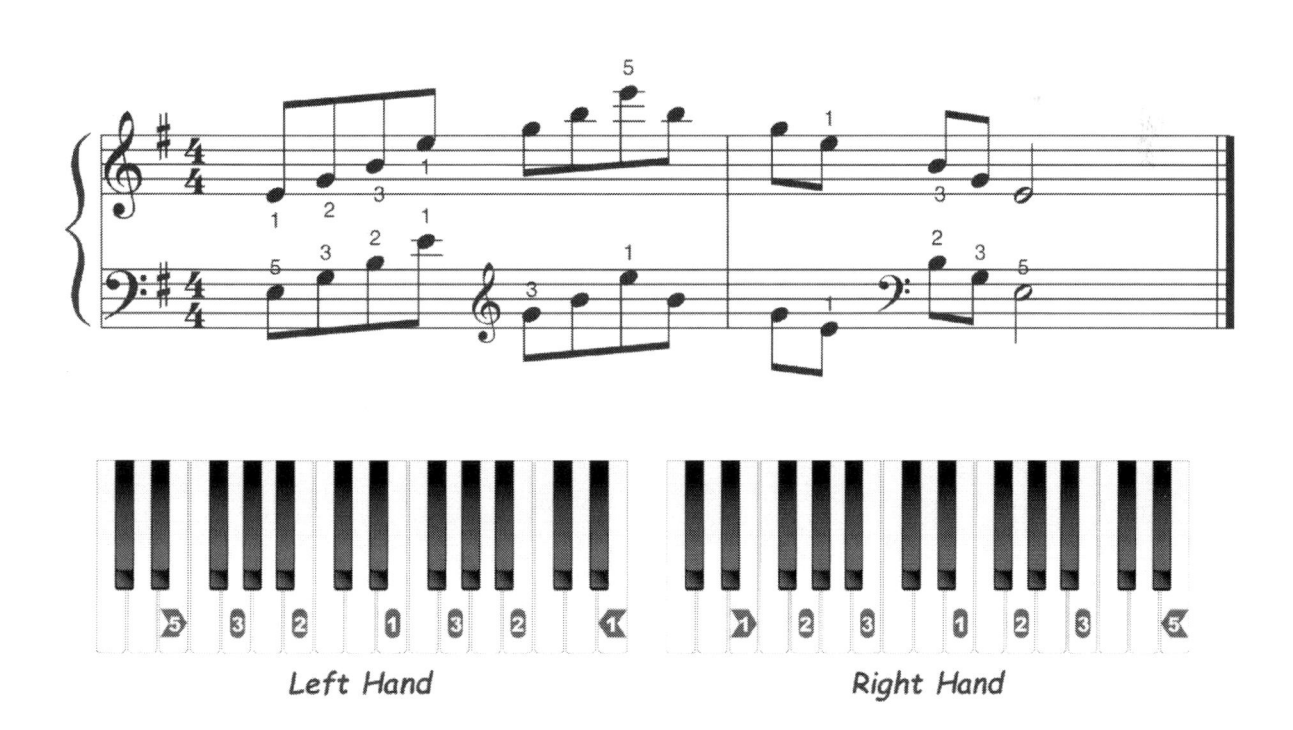

F Major Arpeggio

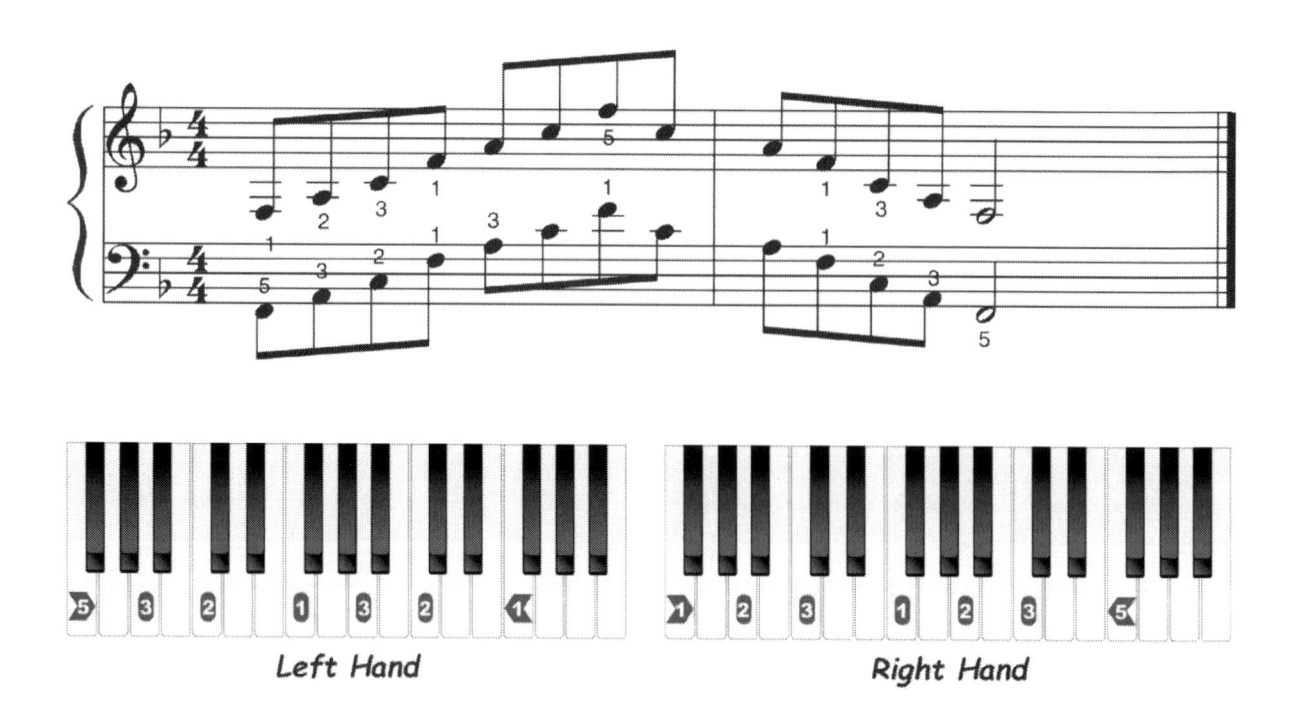

D Minor Arpeggio

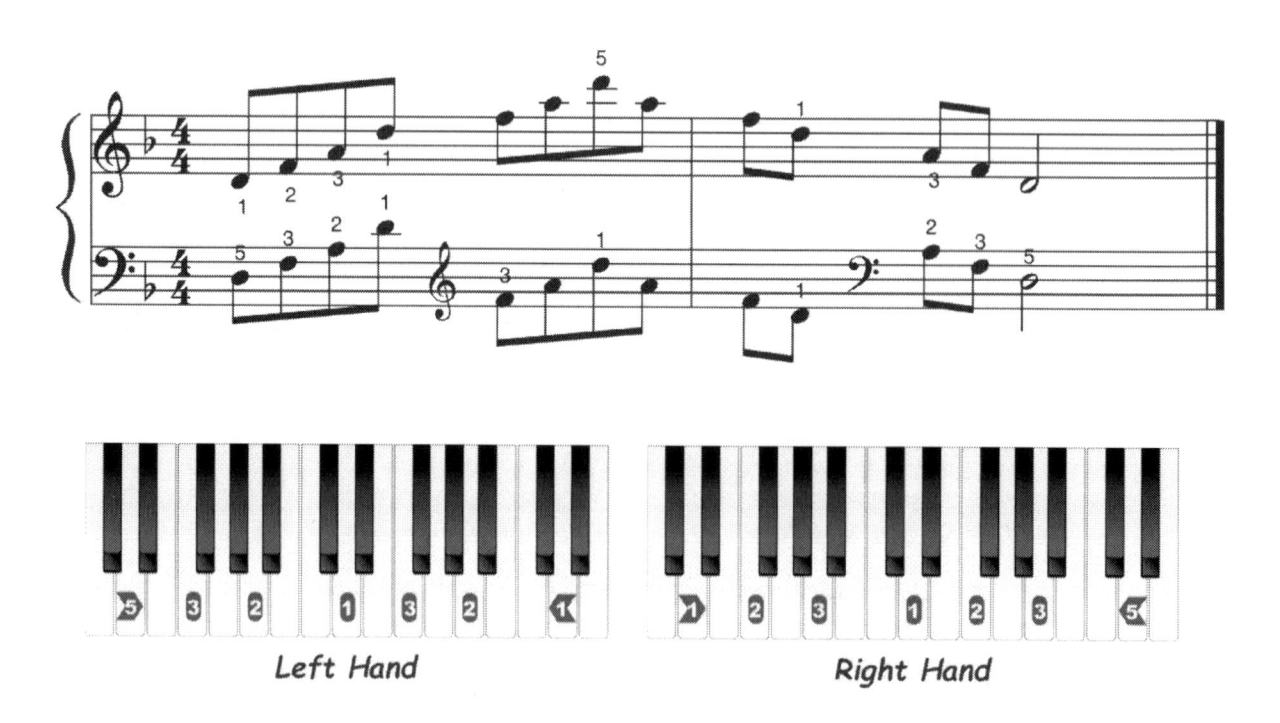

D Major Arpeggio

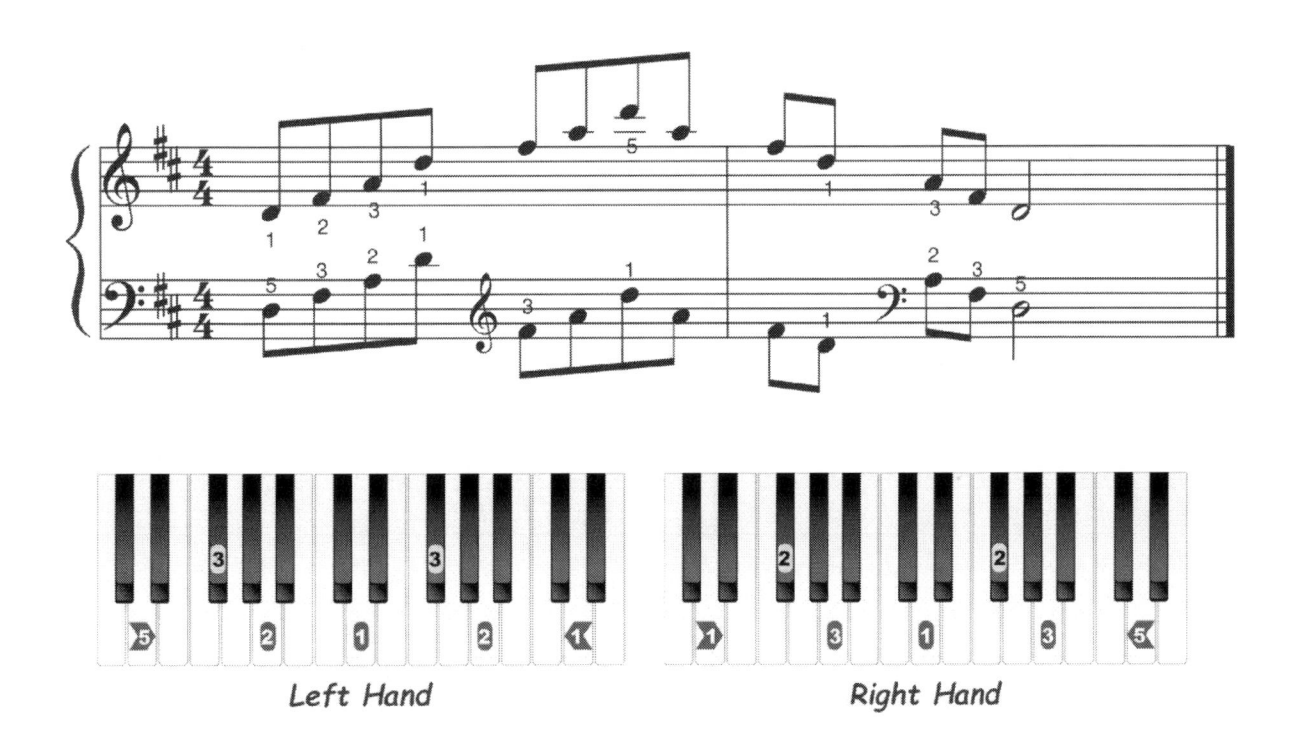

B Minor Arpeggio

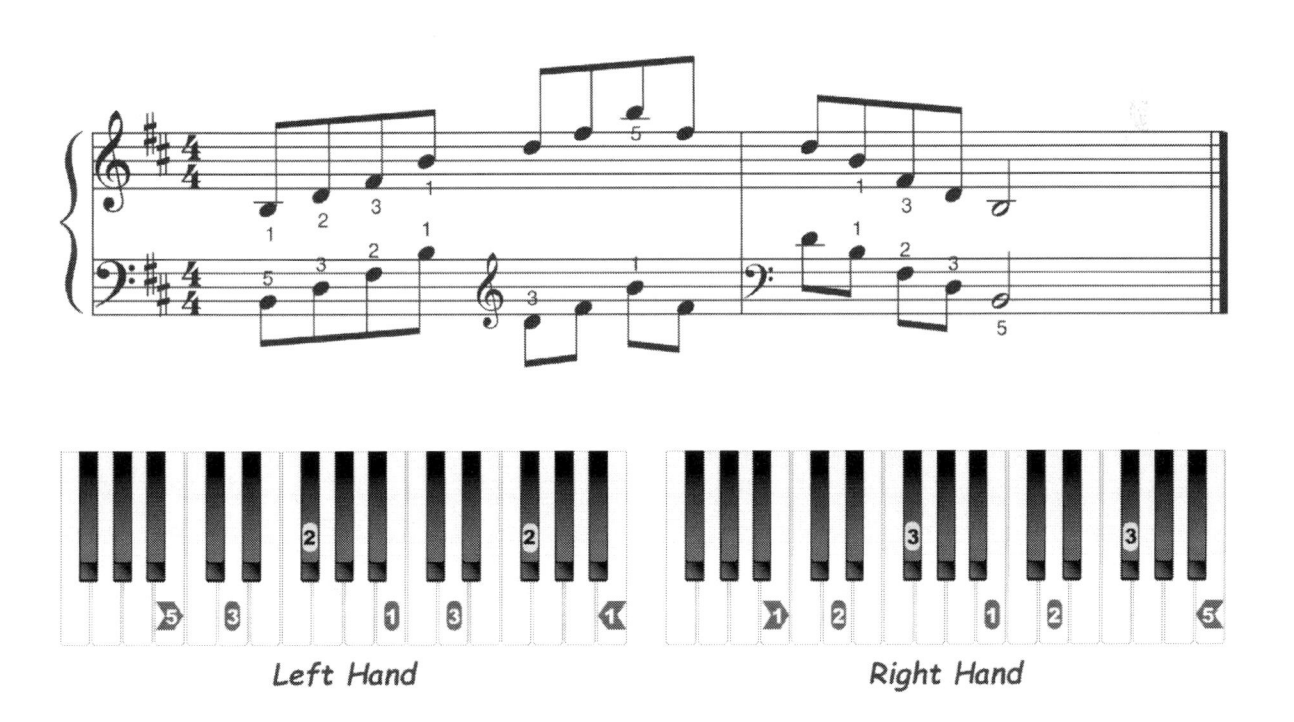

B♭ Major Arpeggio

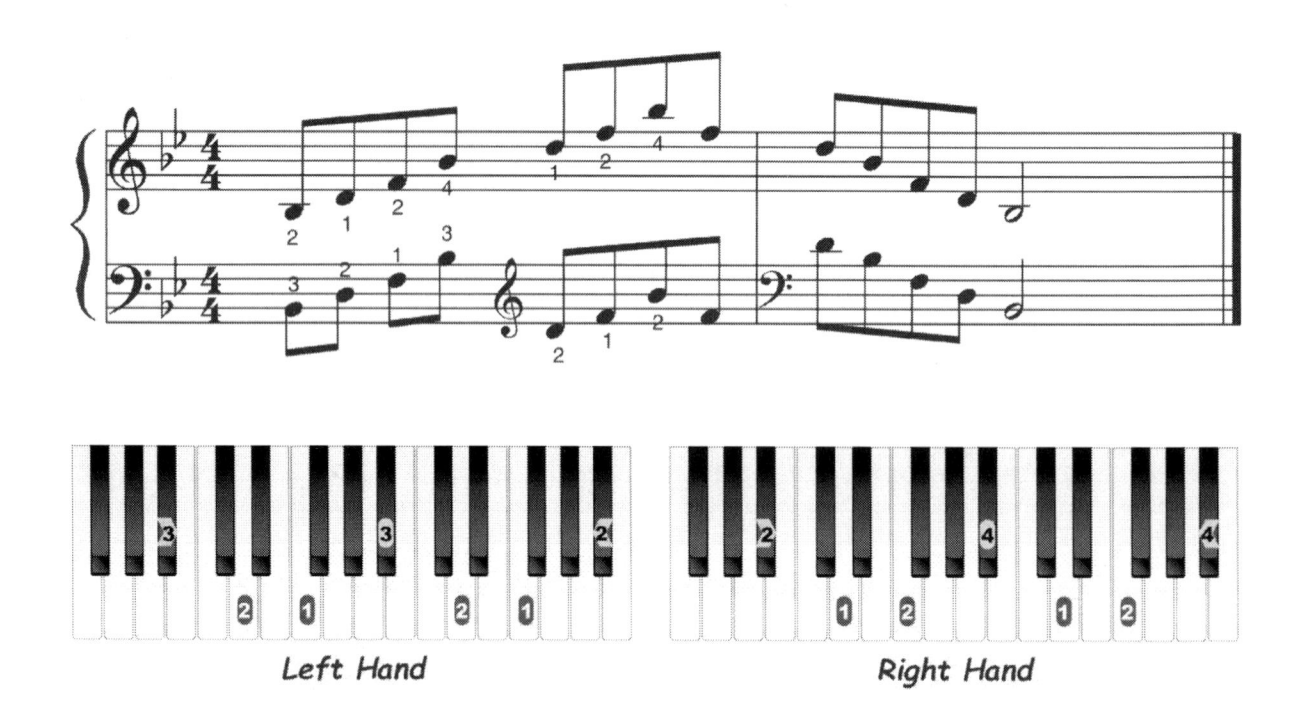

G Minor Arpeggio

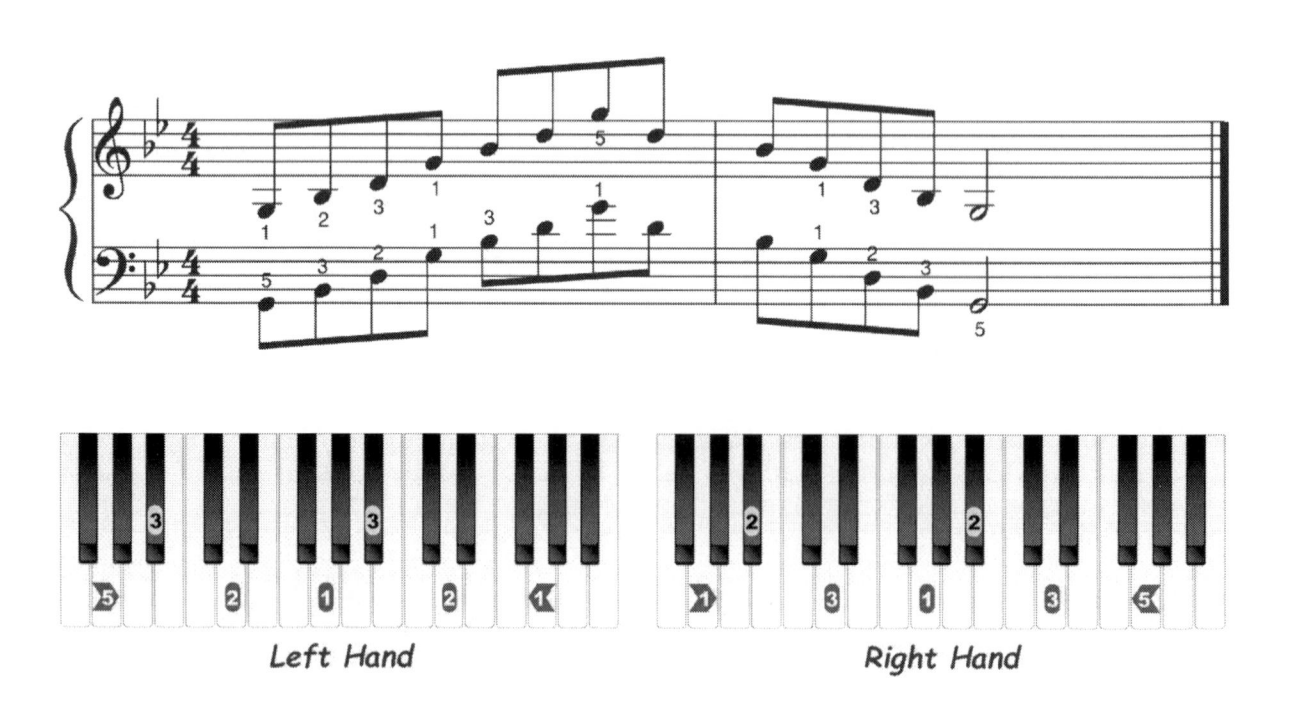

A Major Arpeggio

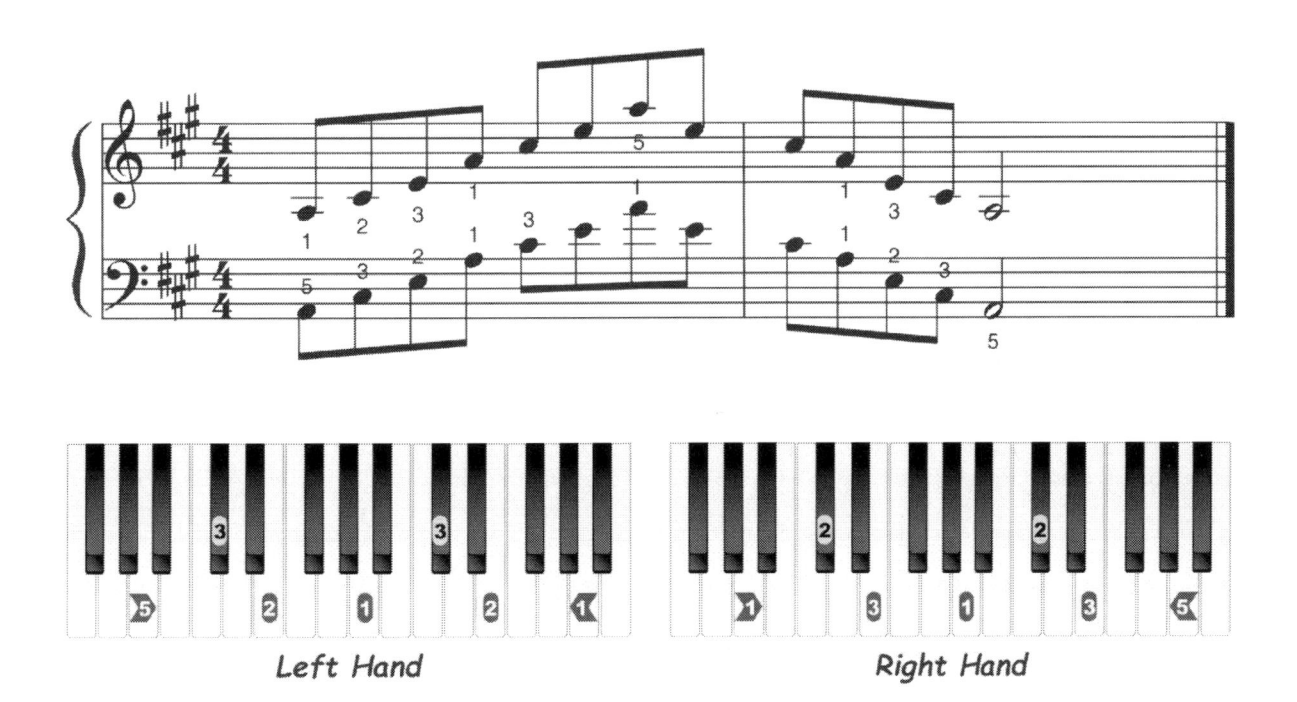

F# Minor Arpeggio

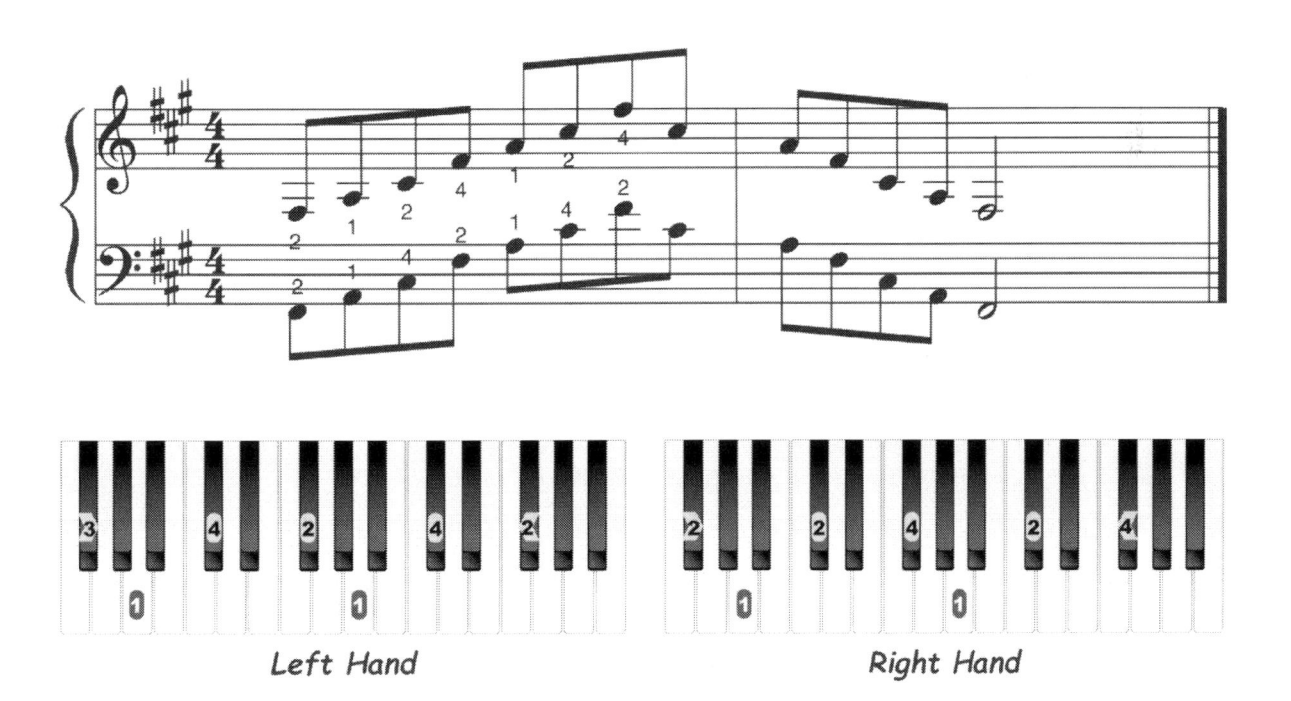

E♭ Major Arpeggio

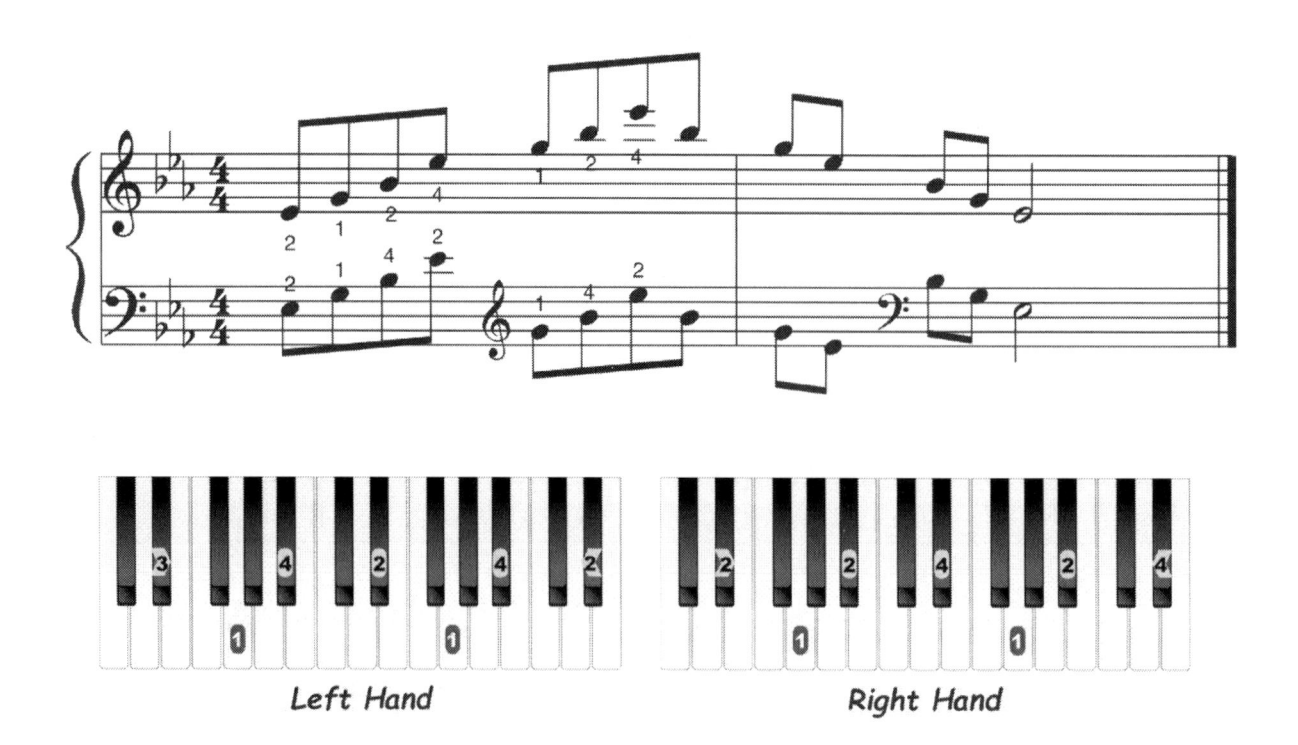

C Minor Arpeggio

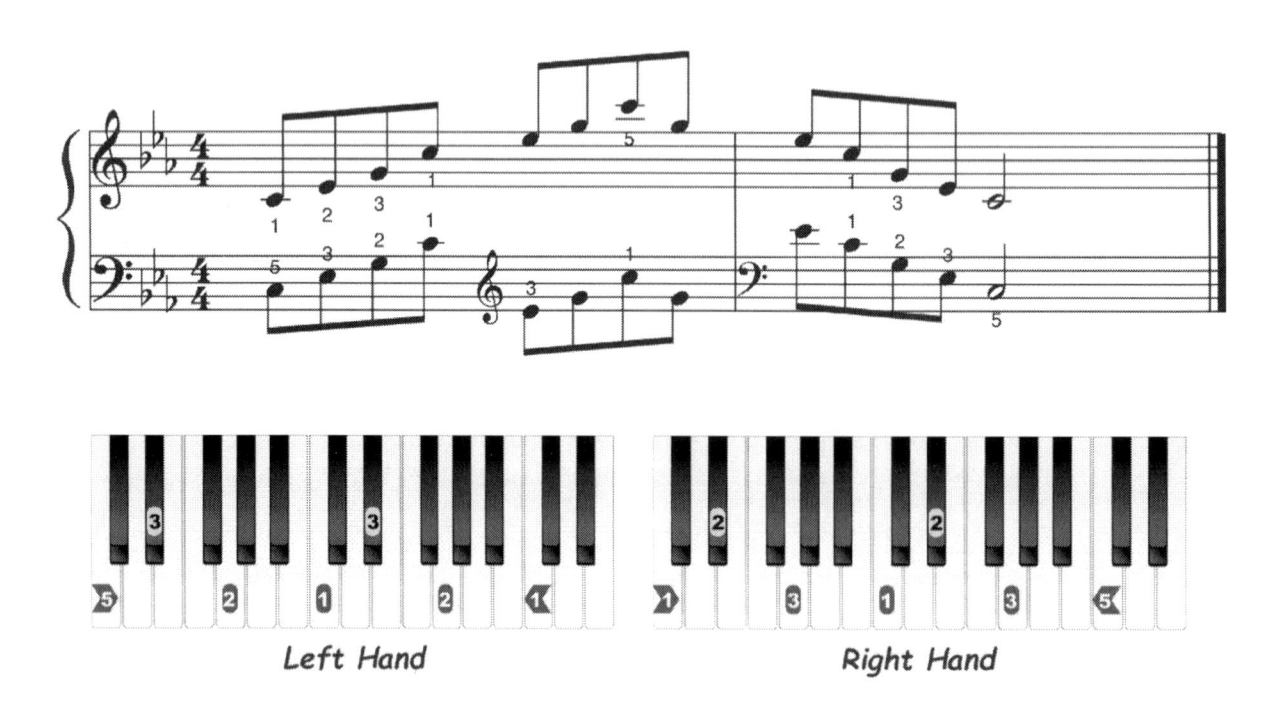

E Major Arpeggio

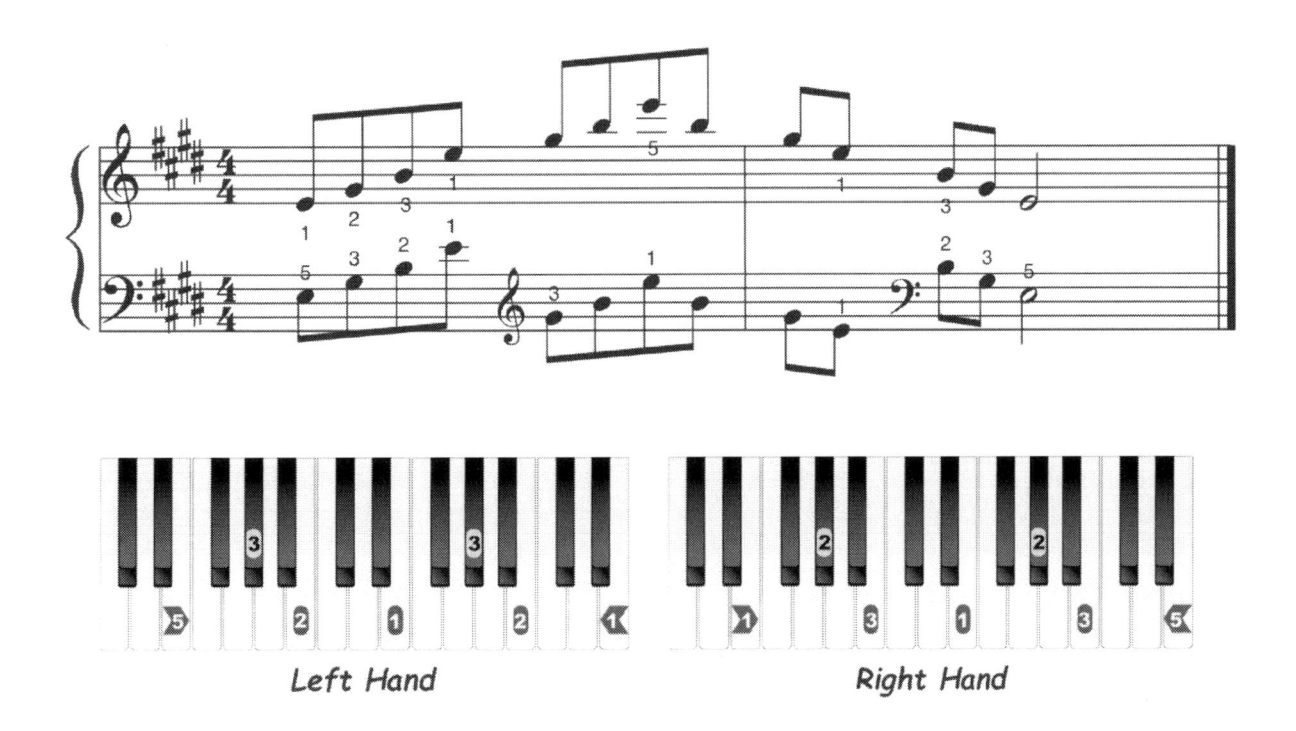

C# Minor Arpeggio

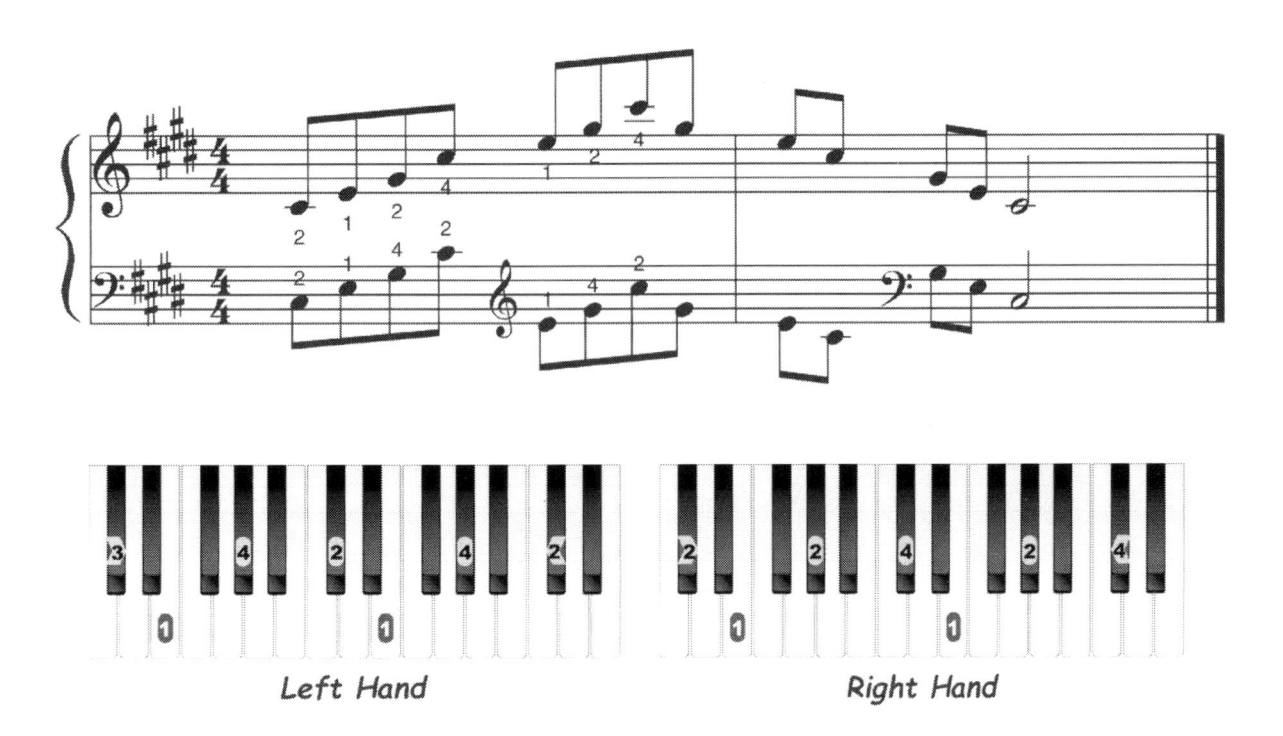

A♭ Major Arpeggio

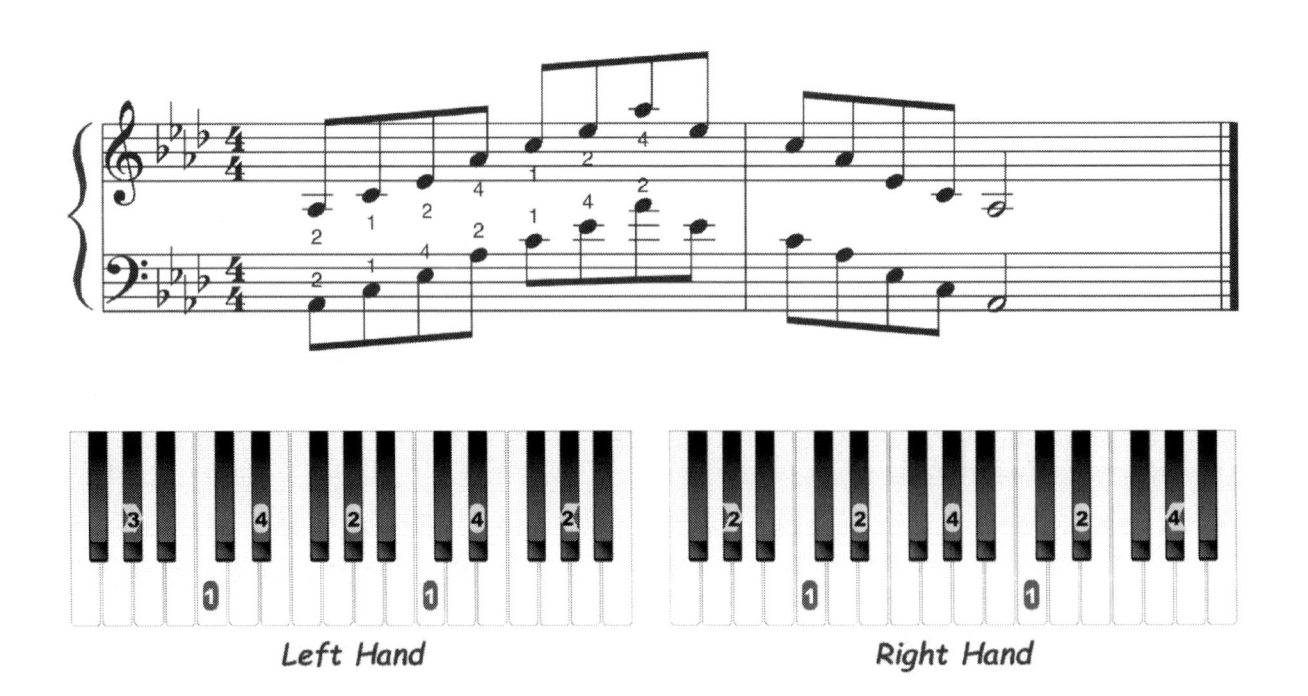

F Minor Arpeggio

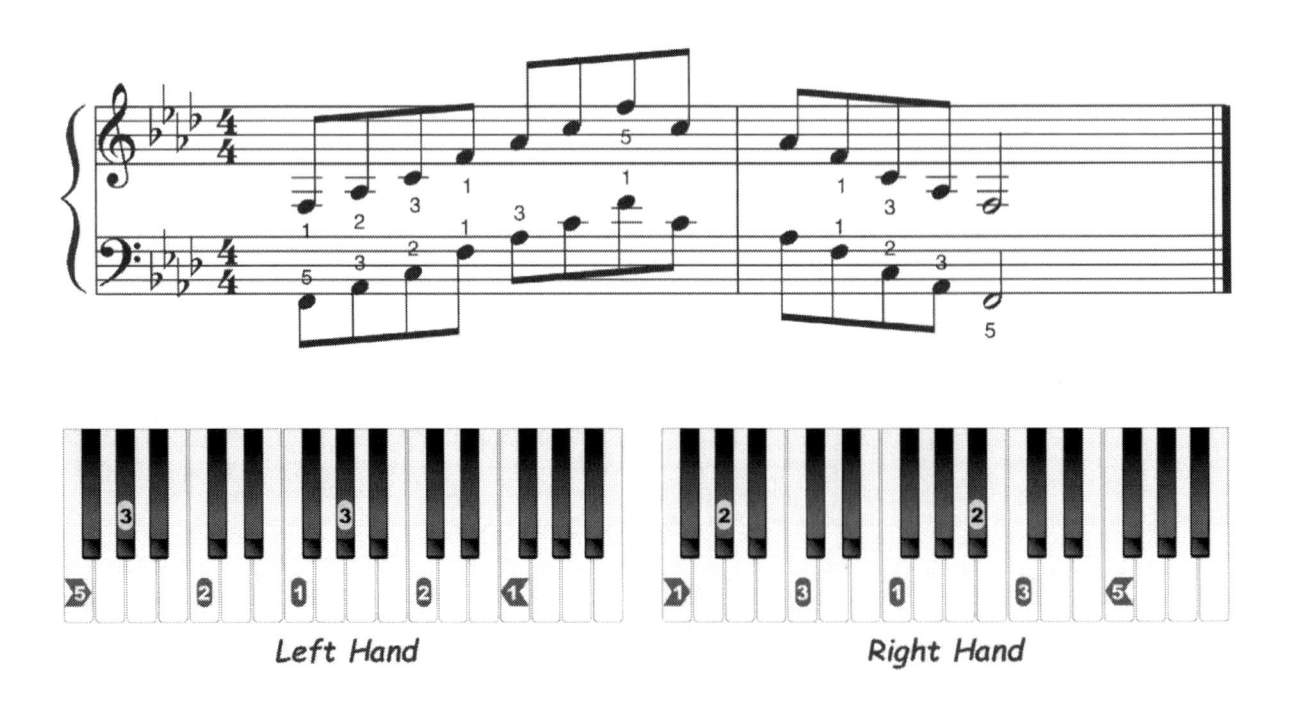

B Major Arpeggio

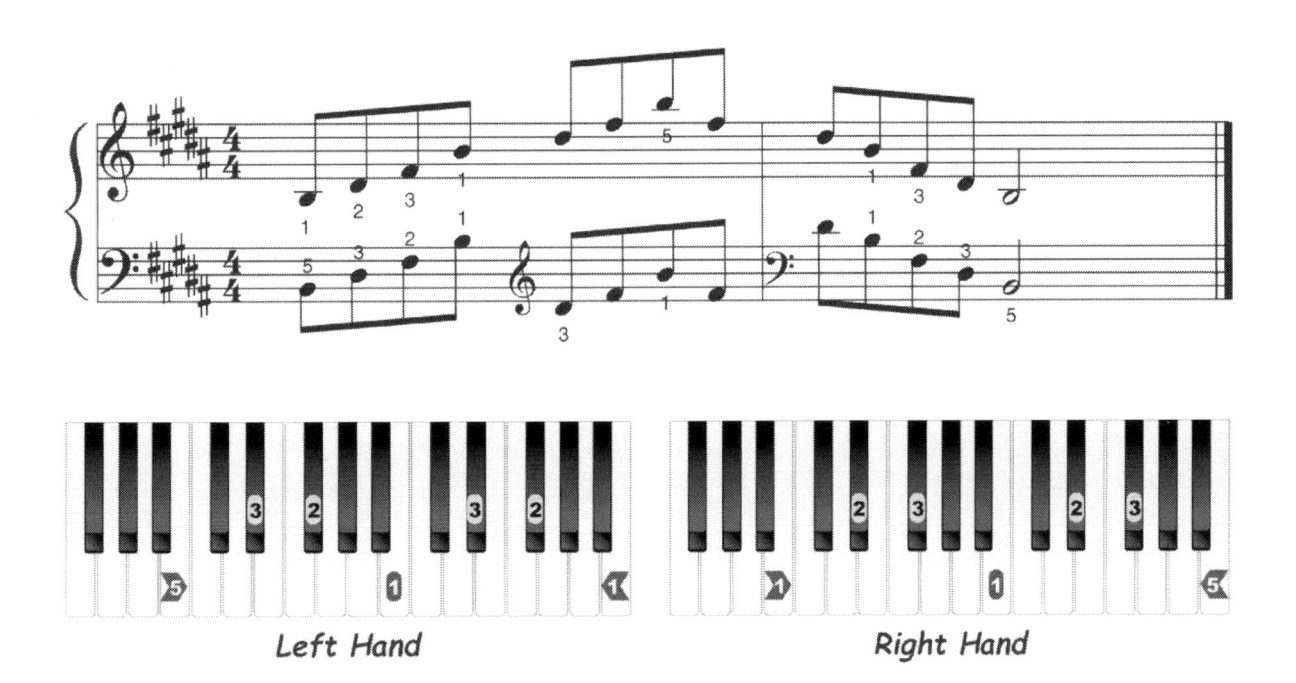

G# Minor Arpeggio

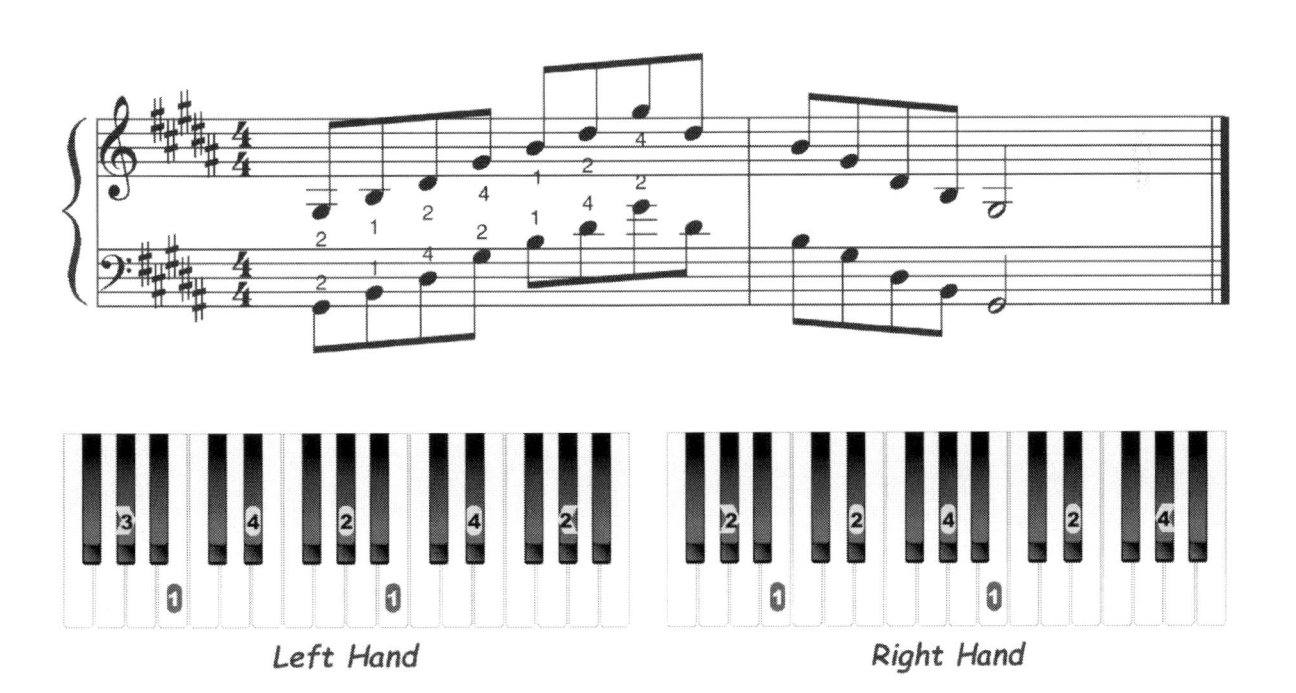

D♭ Major Arpeggio

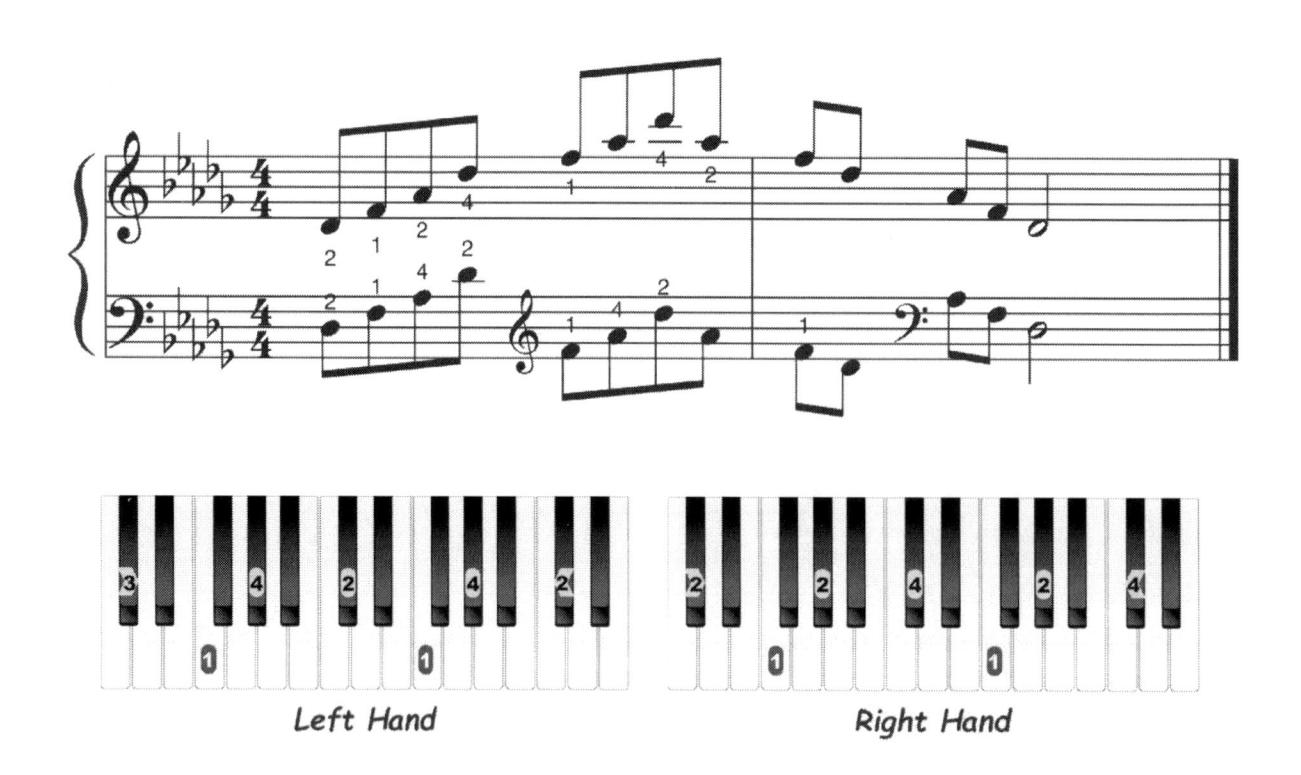

B♭ Minor Arpeggio

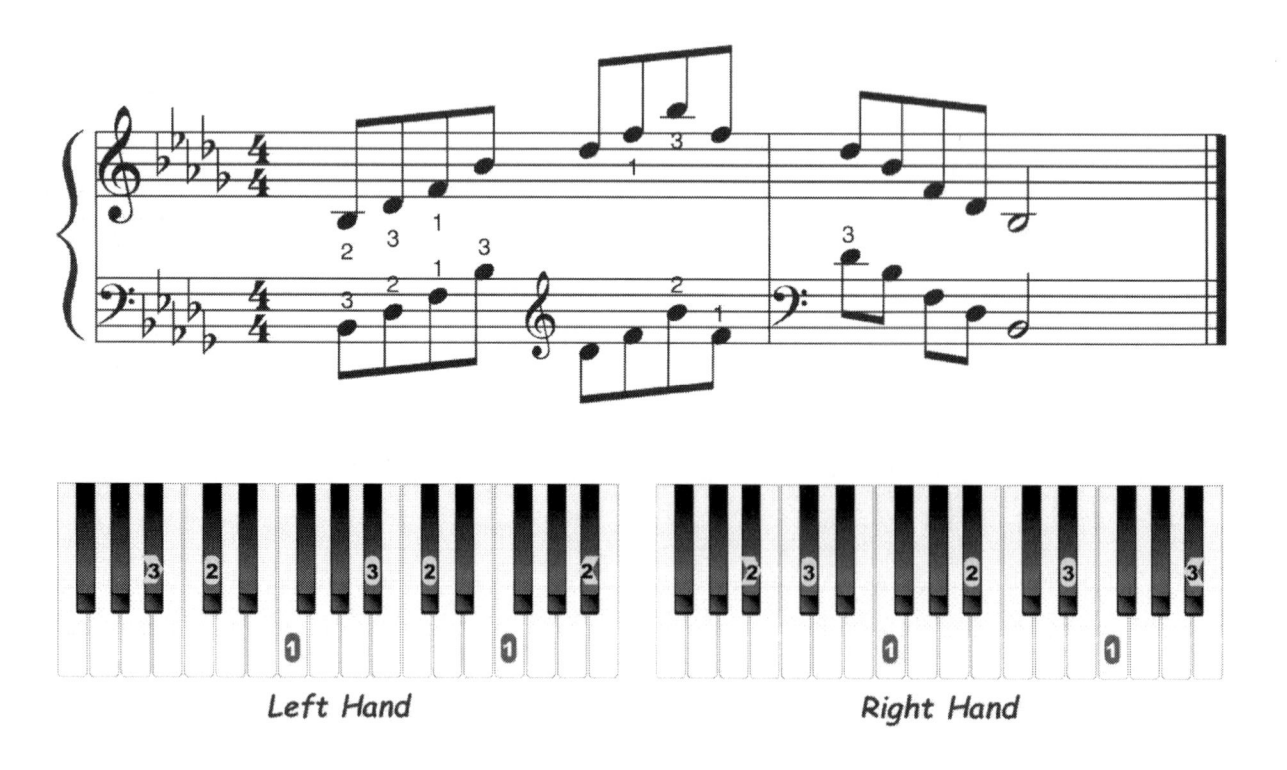

F# Major Arpeggio

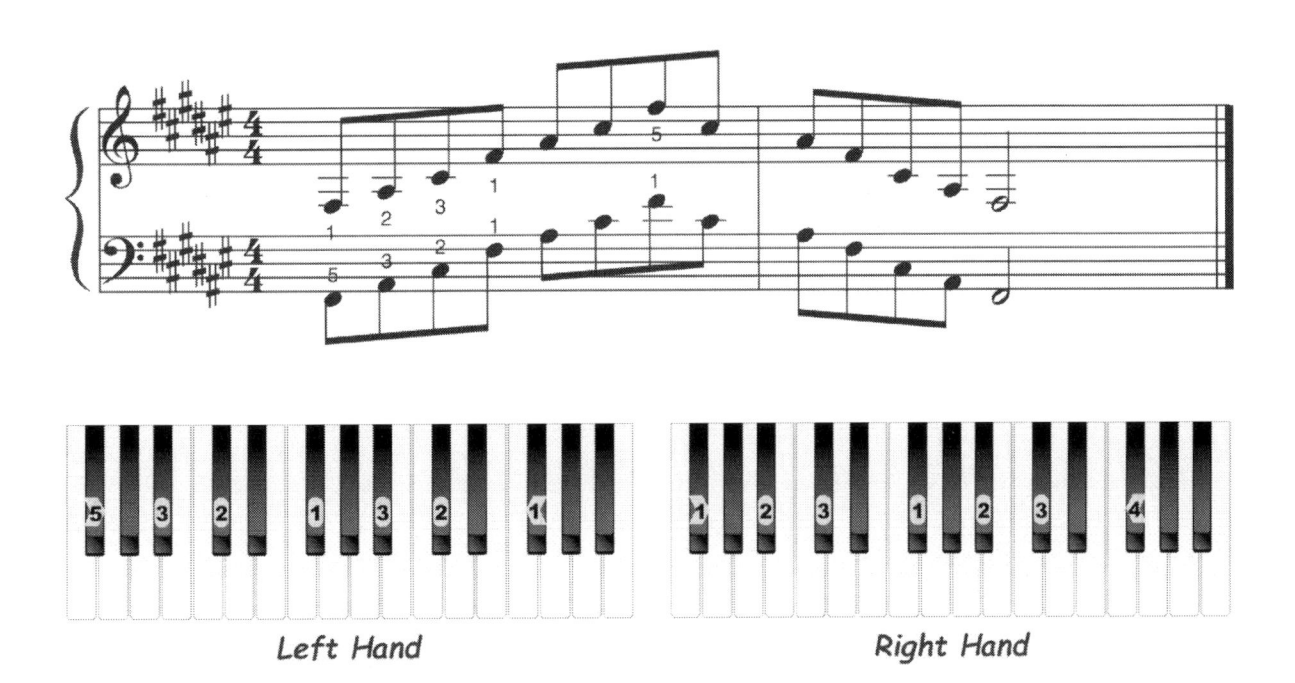

D# Minor Arpeggio

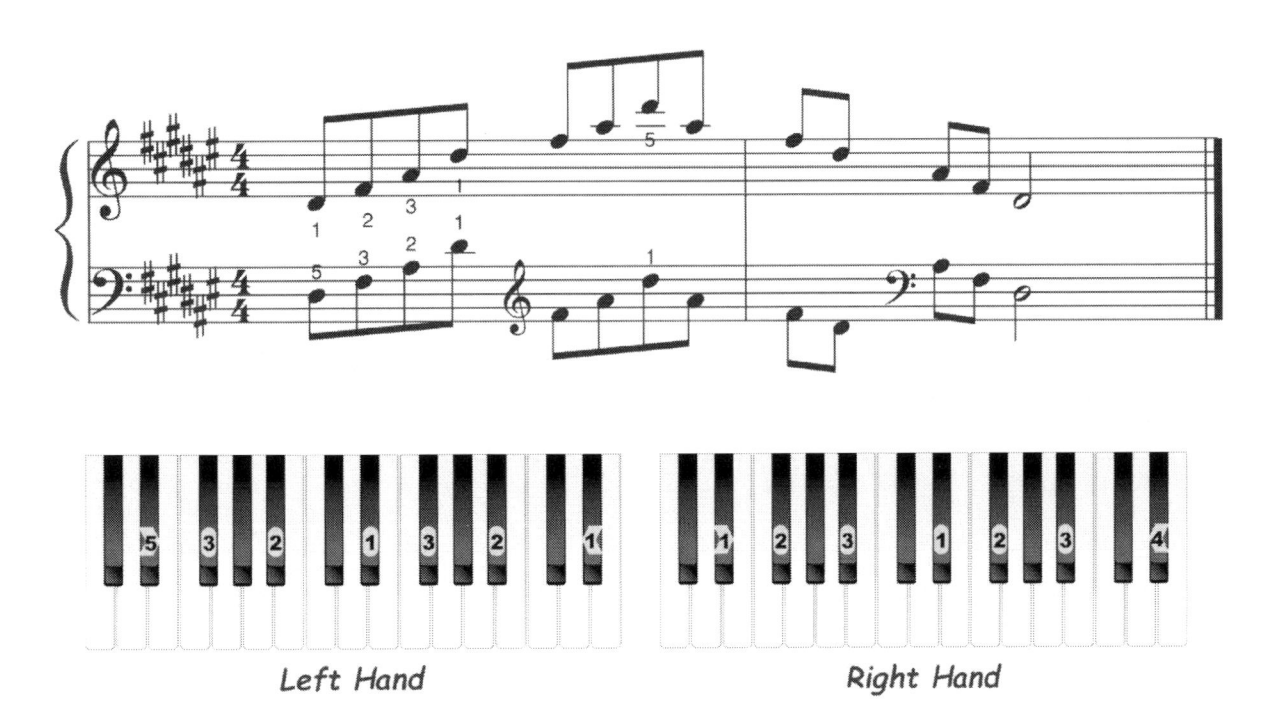

Broken Chords in the most used keys

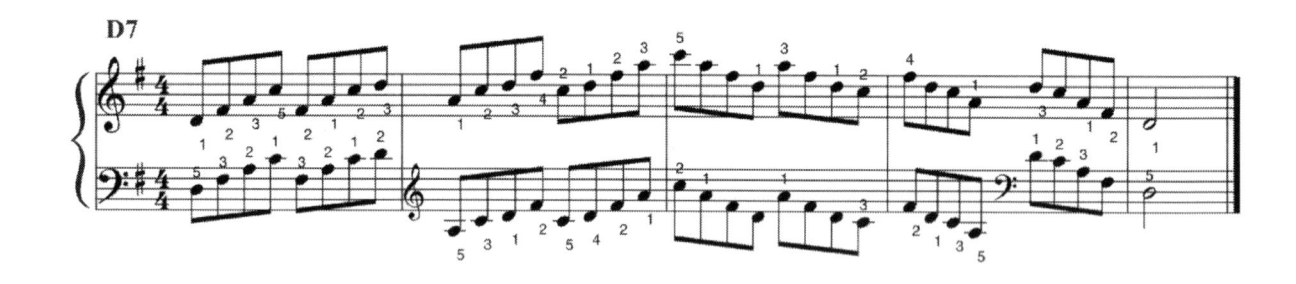

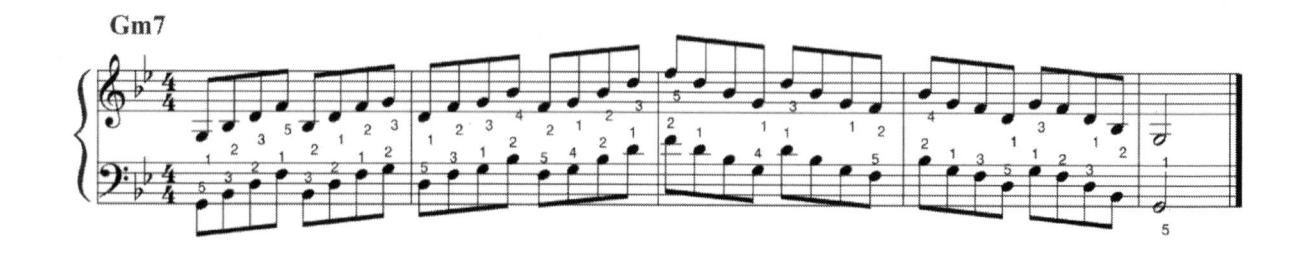

F7

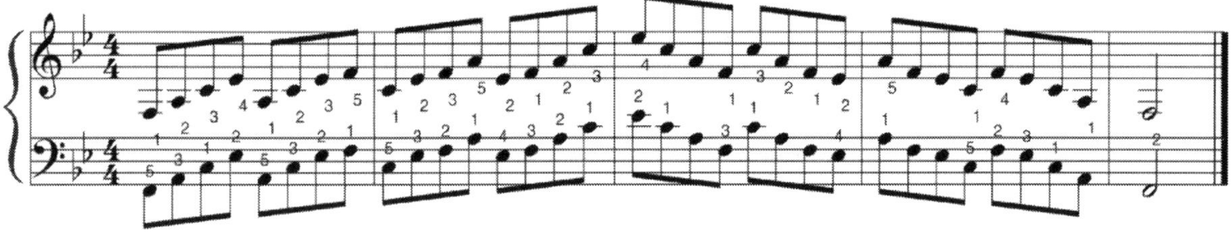

B♭7

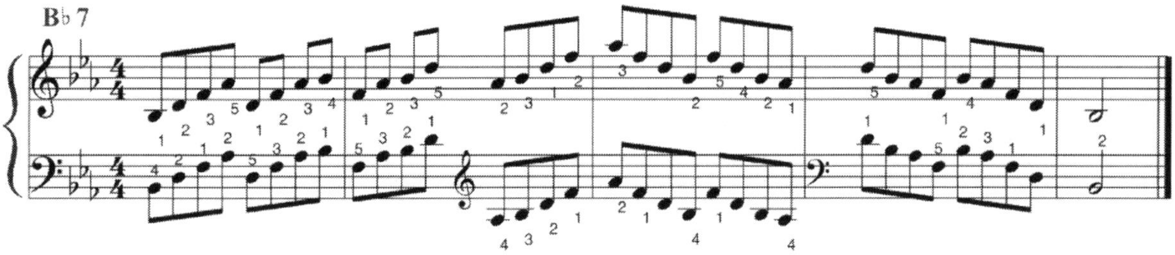

Dm7

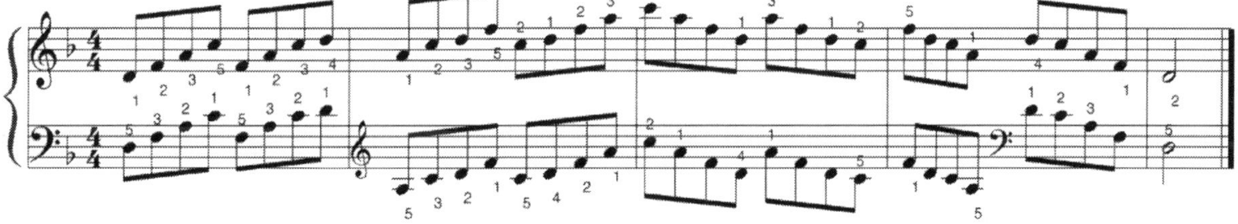

Em7

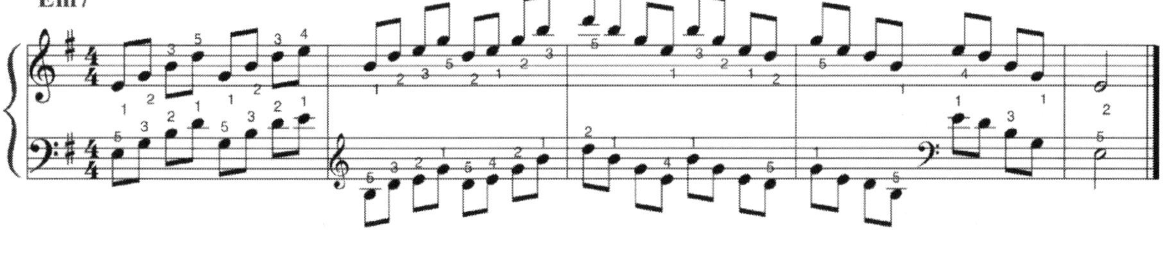

Bm7

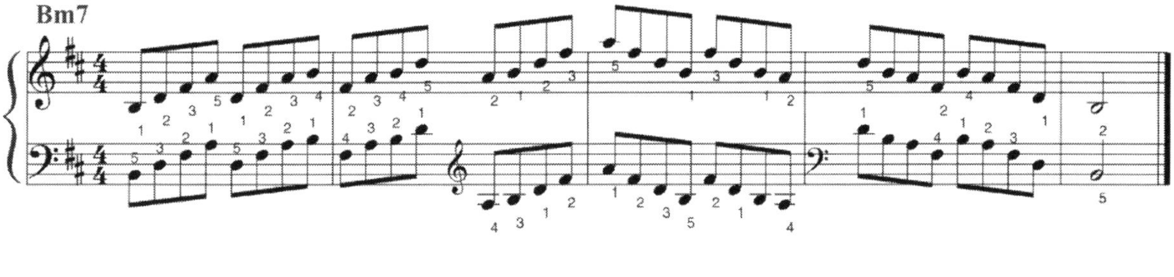

For the Right Hand Only

This exercise takes you through every major 7th and minor 7th arpeggio in 7 keys for two octaves starting on the 3rd. Practice this very slowly at first.

This is a great exercise, for both finger dexterity and theoretical understanding.

← Thank You

Well that's it folks, but finally and most importantly, I'd like to thank you kindly for buying this book. It's been my sincere desire to give excellent value for money with this and all my books. I've worked very long and very hard to achieve this and hope that you think I've succeeded.

If you've enjoyed this, your positive feedback (on Google / Amazon / Lulu etc.) would be very much appreciated.

Please feel free to contact me at http://learn-keyboard.co.uk/contact_us.html if you have any queries. I'd be pleased to hear from you and I will always answer (unless I've snuffed it), but please check your spam box just in case my reply goes amiss.

Download Link

The download link for the pdf printable version of this book is: http://learn-keyboard.co.uk/keyboard_dl.html but please honour my copyright and the hard work I've put into this by using this for your own use only. Thank you!

Quick return link to introduction page

If you have any trouble with the download link, I'll be happy to assist.

What Next?

Well it certainly doesn't end here, this is just the end of the beginning. If you've covered everything herein, you should have a good grounding ready for further advancement in your chosen genre. But keep doing the exercises and keep improving.

If you want to go the classical route, then I strongly recommend that you seek some professional one-to-one tuition.

Further Reading

If you enjoyed the last two pieces herein, I can particularly recommend my *'Original Piano / Keyboard Sheet Music (2nd Edition)'* which includes 16 original great sounding pieces which can be played by mortals. All of the pieces can be heard online before buying at http://learn-keyboard.co.uk/sheet_music.html .

If copying the links be sure to include the underscores between the words (where applicable).

Free Software

I've messed with loads of music notation software, much of which is expensive and very complicated. But *'Melody Assistant'* is neither of these and the basic version is free. Another excellent piece of free software is *'Anvil Studio'* which is good for both recording and music notation. Again, the basic version is free. For recording only and also free is *'Audacity'*.

- Melody Assistant - http://www.myriad-online.com/en/index.htm ;
- Anvil Studio - http://www.anvilstudio.com ;
- Audacity - http://audacity.sourceforge.net/download/windows .

This book was produced using Melody Assistant, Corel Draw, Serif Draw Plus, Microsoft Word, Serif Web Plus X7 and gallons of tea!

Best Regards,

Martin

> *"Anyone who has never made a mistake has never tried anything new!"*
>
> Albert Einstein
>
> *Comment: - I still remember my first gig when we were booed off stage!*

Printed in Great Britain
by Amazon